D0899941

CULTURAL PATTERNS OF ETHIOPIA

QUEEN of SHEBA'S HEIRS

AFRICANA CULTURE AND HISTORY SERIES

CULTURAL PATTERNS OF ETHIOPIA
QUEEN of

 PUBLISHED BY **Acropolis Books** / WASHINGTON, D.C.

SHEBA'S HEIRS

by EDITH LORD

Formerly Adviser on Education to HIM Haile Selassie, Emperor of Ethiopia;
Professor of Psychology, University of Nigeria; Member, U. S. Mission to Ethiopia and
Ghana; and currently Professor of Clinical Psychology, University of Miami, Florida.

AFRICANA CULTURE AND HISTORY SERIES
ACROPOLIS BOOKS, WASHINGTON, D.C.

Volume No. 1
Cultural Patterns of Ethiopia
QUEEN OF SHEBA'S HEIRS
Other Volumes in Preparation
GHANA
NIGERIA

Much of the material in QUEEN OF SHEBA'S HEIRS
is based on CULTURAL PATTERNS IN ETHIOPIA
by Edith Lord, originally printed in East Africa
by Aerad Lithographic Printers, Nairobi, Kenya,
1960, for Limited Controlled Distribution
and the Edition, © Edith Lord, 1963,
Printed in Washington, D.C., U.S.A., for Limited
Controlled Distribution by the U.S. Department of State.

ACROPOLIS BOOKS
Colortone Building, 2400 17th St., N.W.
Washington, D.C. 20009

First Printing, October, 1970
Second Printing, July, 1971

AFRICANA CULTURE AND HISTORY SERIES
VOLUME NO. 1

Printed in the United States of America by
Colortone Press Creative Graphics Inc.
Washington, D.C. 20009

Type set in Compugraphic Bodoni,
Compugraphic Sans, and Pistilli.

Library of Congress Catalog Number 74-75127 *D*
Standard Book No. 87491-011-0

Edith Lord, author and editor of this book, joined the
United States Foreign Aid Agency in 1954 and was
assigned to Ethiopia as an adviser to the
Ministry of Education, a position she held until the
fall of 1959. Dr. Lord, a psychologist, assembled
the material for this book on her own time and
initiative in an effort to contribute to a deeper
understanding of Ethiopians, particularly their beliefs,
attitudes, and values.

103992

His Imperial Majesty Haile Selassie I, in his role as Chancellor of the Haile Selassie I University, gives commencement address. He personally awards diplomas to graduates.

"For too many years, Africa, in the minds of many Americans, has been regarded as a remote and mysterious continent which was the special province of big-game hunters, explorers, and motion picture makers. For such an attitude to exist among the public at large could greatly prejudice the maintenance of our own independence and freedom because the emergence of a free and independent Africa is as important to us in the long run as it is to the people of that continent."

RICHARD M. NIXON, excerpt from his report to President Eisenhower by Vice-President Nixon on his trip to Africa, February 28-March 21, 1957, which included a visit to Ethiopia.

"The American people can make a significant contribution to guaranteeing that a deep and abiding friendship exists between Africa and the United States of America. Learn more about us; learn to understand our backgrounds, our cultures and traditions, our strengths and weaknesses. Learn to appreciate our desires and hopes, our problems, our fears. If we truly know one another, a solid and firm basis will exist for the maintenance of the friendly relations between the African and the American peoples which, we are convinced, both so ardently desire. You may be assured that there will be no failure in the warm and brotherly response from our side."

His Imperial Majesty HAILE SELASSIE I, Emperor of Ethiopia, King of Kings, Elect of God, Conquering Lion of the Tribe of Judah.

Contents

11

Painting on sheepskin depicting meeting of Queen of Sheba and King Solomon.

Foreword

For Americans and others who are intrigued by Ethiopia, for those who plan to visit the ancient empire as tourists . . . advisers, businessmen, industrialists, or diplomats . . . for those who wish better to understand this fascinating country and its peoples, this book is designed.

The volume begins with a quiz and rationale for correct answers emphasizing some of the differences between life in Ethiopia and life in the western world. The next section includes thirty-four essays by Ethiopians on their culture. Within this section lies the heart of this work. Over a period of four-and-a-half years, the author collected about 100 manuscripts from Ethiopians from various parts of the Empire, essays on the ways of life in their villages and cities. The original idea was to abstract facts from these essays and write interpretations for foreigners interested in Ethiopia. Reflection suggested instead that the Ethiopians from many different ethnic groups be permitted to tell the reader about various aspects of their culture directly, without the intrusion of excessive editing. In effect, the author-editor, in this section, is playing the role of the hostess who brings two acquaintances together and says, "Mr. World, may I present Ato* (Mr.) Ethiopia."

There follows a section based on the contributions of many Ethiopians earnestly concerned with helping foreigners to understand them and their country in today's world, the here and now. Then there is the Mosaic of Ethiopia. In this section are some facts about Ethiopia, excerpts from the Penal Code, a list of Ethiopian names and their meanings, an introduction to Amharic, the official language of the country, and a list of books about Ethiopia plus some books generally designed to facilitate the understanding of cultures.

Edith Lord, 1970

---

* Ato, the Amharic equivalent of Mr. is the title of every male on emergence from childhood to manhood. Foreigners jokingly say that the first name of all Ethiopian males is Otto!

Young beauty in "The Switzerland of Africa."

Introduction

. . . Ethiopia, romantic land founded by the son of the Queen of Sheba and King Solomon of Old Testament times.

. . . Ethiopia, oldest continuously Christian country in the world.

. . . Ethiopia, one of the few remaining absolute monarchies.

. . . Ethiopia, a land which annually attracts increasing hundreds of Americans and Europeans as business entrepreneurs, tourists, missionaries, educators, and socio-economic development advisers.

. . . Ethiopia, center of United Nations programs for the continent of Africa.

. . . Ethiopia, recognized world-wide for leadership among the changing nations of Africa.

. . . Ethiopia, whose Emperor, His Imperial Majesty Haile Selassie I, warned the member states of the League of Nations, in 1936, of the dangers of international immorality in words that have haunting relevance today, more than three decades after the demise of the predecessor of the United Nations:

> "I assert that the issue before the Assembly is not merely a question of settlement in the matter of an Italian aggression. It is a question of collective security; of the very existence of the League; of the trust placed by States in international treaties; of the value of

promises made to small States that their integrity and independence shall be respected and assured. It is a choice between the principle of the equality of States and the imposition upon small Powers of the bonds of vassalage. In a word, it is international morality that is at stake. . . . I ask the fifty-two nations who have given the Ethiopian people a promise to help them in their resistance to the aggressor: What are they willing to do for Ethiopia? Representatives of the world, I have come to Geneva to discharge in your midst the most painful of the duties of the head of a State. What answer am I to take back to my people? God and history will remember your verdict."

The man known to the world as Haile Selassie (Holy Trinity) first came to national power in Ethiopia in February, 1917, when Zauditu, daughter of Menelik II, was made Empress with 25-year-old Ras (Chief) Tafari Makonnen, Governor of the Province of Harrar, named as Regent and Heir Apparent. In November, 1930, following the death of Empress Zauditu, Ras Tafari Makonnen, aged 39, was crowned Emperor Haile Selassie I, the 225th Monarch of the Solomonic dynasty established by King Solomon and the Queen of Sheba. The only serious break in the Solomonic line occurred around 1150 A.D. (some sources report exactly 927 to 1260), when the land was ruled by Kings of Zague. These kings traced their descent from Moses and an Ethiopian wife, rather than from Solomon, whose marriage was recorded in Septuagint, Numbers xxii.I, a translation of the Old Testament from Greek originals authorized by Ptolemy II of Egypt ca. 270, in which *Ethiops* and *Ethiopians* are written, as opposed to other translations which write *Cush* and *Cushites*.

In addition to Biblical chronicles of Ethiopia, references to the country and her peoples are found in the writings of many great men, including Homer and Herodotus. One of the oldest nations of the world, Ethiopia can trace its history back a thousand years before Christ. The nation, once one of the greatest empires in the world, adopted Christianity as the official religion in 330 A.D. Ancient relics can be seen today in the well-preserved, eleventh and twelfth-century churches hewn from solid rock in Lalibela, in the ruins of a monolithic church on the outskirts of Addis Ababa, and in the great stone castles near Gondar, built in the early 17th century.

The people of Ethiopia are basically Hamites with a large fusion of Semites from the Arabian Peninsula. In the sixth century A.D., Hebraic influences from Jewish Arabia became fixed on one group of Ethiopians, the Falashas, who, reportedly until the twentieth century, believed that they

16

were the only remaining members of the tribes of Israel, but whose contemporary form of worship differs from that of Israel to the point that each rejects the other as unorthodox. In the seventh century, Ethiopia was land-bound and ringed by the forces of Islam. At present, followers of Islam in Ethiopia are variously estimated at thirty to sixty per cent of the total population, the higher figure representing estimates by predominantly Islamic states such as the Sudan.

During the fourth century, King Ezana converted to Christianity and introduced some modifications in the paganism of his people. By the eighth century, Ethiopia had become "a Christian island in a pagan sea." At that time, Muslim conquests in surrounding areas isolated the land from other Christian countries. From that day to this, Ethiopia has been "a Christian island in a Muslim sea."

The Ethiopian national church, in its history, united with the Roman Catholic Church on several occasions, most recently during a brief period in the first half of the seventeenth century. However, the Ethiopian Orthodox Church at present, and throughout most of its history, has most closely identified with Eastern Orthodox Christianity. A major difference between Western and Eastern doctrine is that the latter is Monophysite (sometimes called *Jacobean* or *Coptic*). This belief ascribes to Christ a single, divine nature as opposed to a belief in the dual nature of Christ as part man and part God.

Ethiopia is a constitutional monarchy with a parliament consisting of the Chamber of Deputies and the Senate. Members of the Chamber of Deputies are elected by universal suffrage, provided for in the Constitution of 1955 which led to the first Empire-wide national elections in 1957. Members of the Senate are appointed by the Emperor.

Ethiopia, in 1935, was the first nation to be occupied by Mussolini's Fascist troops—leading to twelve years of guerilla fighting by Ethiopian resistance groups—and was among the first nations to send troops to Korea in 1951 under the flag of the United Nations.

Prior to 1954, Ethiopia's international stance was clearly pro-western. However, in that year His Imperial Majesty adopted a moderately Yugoslavian type of neutrality and built a palace in Addis Ababa for Marshal Josip Broz Tito; the latter presented the Emperor with a yacht and built a very impressive monument in Addis Ababa honoring those Ethiopians who died during the Italian invasion which sparked World War II. The United States increased its military aid and its economic aid to Ethiopia considerably, plus making an outright gift of a $2 million submarine chaser. By

1957, Ethiopia appeared to be solidly pro-western in foreign affairs. During the summer of 1959, however, His Majesty made a tour of Iron Curtain countries which netted large numbers of economic advisers and technical assistants plus $5 million from Czechoslovakia, $10 million from Yugoslavia, over $7 million from East Germany, and $100 million from Russia. This form of "neutrality" was not well received by large numbers of Ethiopians, leading to the formation of a number of dissident groups representing both conservative and liberal factions. His Majesty delayed considerably utilizing the extensive credits from Communist countries and engaged in some fence-building with western powers, enhancing his stated position as a neutral and dampening dissent among his people.

In December, 1961, there was an attempted coup, while H.I.M. Haile Selassie was on a state visit to Brazil. Crown Prince Asfa Wossen made a radio broadcast in support of the rebels, subsequently stating that captors held a gun to his head while he read the statement agreeing to act as a figurehead monarch of a republican state. If events take their normal course, the Crown Prince will succeed his father as King of Kings, a father who was born in 1892. Reportedly, His Imperial Highness Asfa Wossen is not an ambitious prince; he is a well-educated, liberal, easy-going man who enjoys spending companionable hours with his family and his many friends. Theoretically, he might be quite comfortable as a traditionally respectable figurehead of state after the pattern of England, or, with more militaristic underpinnings, the pattern of Pakistan or Egypt. But what of the peoples of Ethiopia? Do they fit these patterns?

The ruling Christian Amharas, for centuries, have imposed their form of government upon an exceedingly diverse conglomeration of races, tribes, and religious entities. H.I.M. Haile Selassie is truly a King of Kings, but the King of the largest number of Ethiopians is the King of the Gallas, known to his people today as "The Greatest King of Them All." Then there are the Ethiopian Somalis who follow their camels back and forth across the Ethiopian-Somalia borders to the east and the south with little sense of allegiance beyond their extended families. There are the nomadic Arussi, the camel-following Danakils, the Sidama, the Wollos, the Afar-Saho, and the very dark-skinned Ethiopians who live along the western borders of Ethiopia, the borders facing the Sudan (the Land of the Blacks), and whose education is provided by Islamic Malams.

In addition to the Muslims, the Jews, and the very modern young agnostic and atheistic Ethiopians, the rule of the King of Kings must accommodate the beliefs of a large variety of animistic sects, worshipers of

18

trees, stones, snakes, the sun, and other objects.

In the late nineteen-fifties, at the request of the Ethiopian Government, a team of American cartographers using a helicopter to visit relatively inaccessible areas, developed a map of the religions of Ethiopia. The Government directed that publication of the map be delayed for two or three years and then be revised to show compliance with a Royal Decree that neither paganism nor animism was to exist in Ethiopia, and that all persons of such religious bent would be given the interim in which to identify themselves as Christians, Jews, or Muslims.

In addition to the foregoing problems, Ethiopia has the problem of feudal fiefdoms, great land-holders among the aristocracy, regional "princes" with considerable local power. No small power in this landed group is the Ethiopian Orthodox Christian Church which, reportedly, owns from one-third to one-half of all the land in Ethiopia. An estimated twenty-five per cent of Ethiopian Christian males are attached to the Church in one way or another and draw their living, at least in part, from the Church. A large number of females are also Church-bound.

There are the military establishments to be coped with. There is the Regular Army, in part trained by the United States; the Air Force, in part trained by Sweden; the Cavalry, in part trained by Yugoslavia. The navy is not yet a force of much concern. A very important military establishment is the Emperor's Imperial Bodyguard; another is the Secret Police, a ubiquitous and much-feared power in Ethiopia.

H.I.M. Haile Selassie has done more to unify and modernize Ethiopia than all of his imperial predecessors. This grand old man through a variety of roles and techniques—benevolent paternalism, antique autocracy, despotism, enforced democratization, cunning, wisdom, "divine right," traditional prestige, sheer strength of character and an absolutely honest love of humanity—has held together in the twentieth century Africa's oldest independent nation. Is there another Ethiopian in existence who can synchronize into unity a nation with so many varied peoples, powers, special interests, hereditary claims, and new-found "righteous demands"?

Probably the delicate fabric of unity that is Ethiopia will persist without major rents during the life-time of Haile Selassie; thereafter, if not sooner, a measure of chaos can be anticipated as the tenuous cohesion of the empire is damaged by conservative and liberal advocates of essential reforms in land tenure, education, social institutions, political forms, etc. There will be clashes, conflicts of rank, prestige, personality among the princes of the Church, the princes of the state, the princes of the various military establishments, the regional princes, the tribal princes, and a twentieth century phenomenon: the princes of the people, the masses of Ethiopians, ninety per cent illiterate, who tend to see leadership potential in any member of an extended family who is so endowed by God that he can learn to read and write.

The Organization of African Unity, in 1967, was confronted with a situation that challenged its existence: The Civil War between Nigerian federal forces and the breakaway Eastern Region of Nigeria which, on May 30, 1967, declared its independence as the Republic of Biafra. England, Russia, Egypt, and Czechoslovakia joined hands as allies of the Nigerian federal forces. Nigeria refused mediation by other than African nations, proclaiming the conflict an internal affair. The Organization of African Unity appointed a group of African heads of states to mediate the conflict, and named as Chairman H.I.M. Haile Selassie I. The failure was as complete as that which His Majesty experienced with the League of Nations in 1935-1936, when Mussolini declared that annihilation of Ethiopia could be "neither averted nor delayed." The "final solution" of the "Ibo problem" in Nigeria raged on. Czechoslovakia withdrew from the allied force of England-Russia-Egypt-Nigeria, but the damage to the Organization of African Unity and to the prestige of H.I.M. Haile Selassie could not be "withdrawn."

As Ethiopia enters the 1970's, her economic performance is phenomenal. Her accommodations for tourists have increased remarkably, animal husbandry, industry, and mining have modernized by leaps and bounds; transportation by road, rail, and air—both national and international—have experienced amazing growth; finance and banking have shown upward trends; investment opportunities, particularly in agriculture, abound, and the Government has established investors' relief by law for income tax, import duty, and export duty.

But what of the land and the people? And what of the Emperor? And who will, or what will, hold Ethiopia together when He departs? Has America a role to play in keeping Ethiopia, and other African countries viable? If so, what is that role? H.I.M. Haile Selassie has expressed some thoughts relevant to these questions:

"It must be recognized that in Africa today massive forces are at work which will not be denied. It must be recognized, too, that Africa, its people, its present and its future, are of vital concern to

20

everyone, no matter how far removed geographically. In the past, America has too often been content to remain relatively unconcerned about events in Africa, too ready to stand on the sidelines of African history as a disinterested observer. This policy will not serve today, and the attitude which the American people and Government now adopt towards Africa indicates that they, too, realize that a new Africa has emerged on the world scene. As a result, however, Americans have been largely uninformed about us, our peoples, our problems. Among other peoples, more and more is gradually coming to be known, but mainly, we would venture, because the people of Africa have forced the rest of the world to pay heed to them and to harken to the stirrings and reverberations which have resounded throughout this Continent in the last decade. (April 16, 1959)"

President Richard M. Nixon, from a different viewpoint, made similar observations in his 1957 report to President Eisenhower following his trip, as Vice-President, to Ethiopia, Morocco, Ghana, Liberia, Uganda, Sudan, Libya, and Tunisia:

"No one can travel in Africa, even as briefly as I did, without realizing the tremendous potentialities of this great continent. Africa is the most rapidly changing area in the world today. The course of its development, as its people continue to emerge from a colonial status and assume the responsibilities of independence and self-government, could well prove to be the decisive factor in the conflict between the forces of freedom and international communism. . . .

"Africa is emerging as one of the great forces in the world today. In a world in which, because of advances in technology, the influence of ideas and principles is becoming increasingly important in the battle for men's minds, we in the United States must come to know, to understand, and to find common ground with the peoples of this great continent. . . .

"Africa is a priority target for the international communist movement . . . the communists are without question putting their top men in the fields of diplomacy, intrigue, and subversion into the African area to probe for openings which they can exploit for their own selfish and disruptive ends. . . .

21

"The Nile is one of the world's greatest international rivers. Perhaps in no other part of the world are the economies of so many states tied to a particular waterway. The river is so located geographically that whatever projects are undertaken on it within the territorial domains of one state are bound to have their effect on the economies of the other states. (Eighty per cent of the waters of the Nile at flood tide originate from the Blue Nile of Ethiopia. Ed.)

"There must be a corresponding realization throughout the executive branches of the Government, throughout the Congress and throughout the nation, of the growing importance of Africa to the future of the United States and the Free World and the necessity of assigning higher priority to our relations with that area."

THE
QUEEN
OF
SHEBA

The Queen of Sheba

The Emperors of Ethiopia trace their dynasty back to King Solomon. There are many versions of the Solomon-Sheba story extant. Following is a brief summary of the version which appears in the *Kebra Negast,* the version which is considered official in Ethiopia.

Solomon, when building his temple, sent messages to all known governments in the world requesting that they send to him materials of their countries; he promised payment in silver and gold. Makeda, the Queen of Ethiopia,[1] had in her employ a merchant named Tamrin who took to Solomon sapphires, gold, and hard, black wood, impervious to worms.

Tamrin returned to report the glories of Solomon's kingdom and the amazing wisdom of King Solomon. Makeda was intrigued with the tales and determined to visit Solomon in person. Her caravan included 797 camels plus countless asses and mules, all laden with gifts. Arriving in Jerusalem she was received with great honor by Solomon who presented her with clothing sufficient to allow her to appear in seven changes each day; also, he supplied her with excellent foods.

During her six months' visit, she conferred frequently with Solomon and was so impressed with his wisdom that she relinquished her pagan beliefs and adopted the God of Israel. Finally, she indicated her intention to return to her own kingdom. Learning of her intention, Solomon said to him-

---

[1] In ancient times, the territory of Ethiopia included an area near the Red Sea then known as Saba; hence Queen Makeda was also Queen of Saba (Shaba or Sheba); she is mentioned in the Old Testament as the Queen of the South.

Painting on shaved center of sheepskin depicting part of Sheba-Solomon story, from messengers extending Solomon's invitation for a visit to seduction of Sheba by Solomon.

self, "A woman of such splendid beauty has come to me from the ends of the earth. Will God give me seed in her?" For Solomon had a deep desire to father many sons who would rule the cities of the earth and turn them from idolatry to the God of Israel.

Solomon prepared a great farewell feast which included many highly spiced dishes, thirst-provoking dishes, but he served little to quench the thirst. Since the banquet lasted far into the morning, Solomon invited Makeda to sleep in his palace rather than returning to her own. She agreed on the condition that he would not force himself upon her, for she was a virgin. Solomon agreed, asking in return that she give an oath not to take, by force, anything in his palace. Being an honest woman, she readily agreed.

Each retired to separate beds spread on opposite sides of the royal bedchamber. Shortly after falling asleep, Makeda waked with a great thirst. Seeing a jar of water in the middle of the room, she approached and took it. Immediately, Solomon jumped from his bed, seized her, and said, "You have broken your oath not to take by force anything that is in my palace." There ensued an argument wherein Solomon insisted that there is nothing more precious on earth than water. Nevertheless, Makeda drank, for her need was great, and she then slept that night with Solomon.

The next day, Solomon gave Makeda a ring and said to her, "If you have a son, give this ring to him and send him to me." After the queen returned to Ethiopia, she bore a son whom she named Menelik. When Menelik was a man, Makeda gave him the ring and sent him to Solomon in the protection of Tamrin, the merchant. Tamrin was ordered by Makeda to request of Solomon that Menelik be annointed King of Ethiopia and that Solomon issue a decree that only the offspring of Menelik should ever rule Ethiopia.

When Menelik arrived in the land of Judah, the people were confused because his resemblance to Solomon was so great that many thought he was, in fact, Solomon himself. Messengers rushed to Solomon to report, "One has come to our land who resembles you in every feature." So Solomon ordered that the foreigner be brought to him. Menelik offered the ring, but Solomon said, "What need is there of the ring? Without a sign I know that you are my son."

Tamrin gave Solomon the message from Makeda, but so great was Solomon's joy in Menelik that he tried to persuade him, his first-born son, to remain and reign in Israel. Menelik, however, wished to return to Ethiopia, so King Solomon gave him the divine anointment, named him David, and decreed that henceforth only his male issue should reign in Ethiopia.

Zadok, the high priest of Solomon, then taught Menelik the laws of Israel. He told Menelik that he would be blessed if he kept these laws, cursed if he broke them. Following the advice of his mother, Queen Makeda, Menelik then asked of Solomon a piece of the fringe of the covering of the Ark of the Covenant. Solomon honored his request, then he called his principal officers to him and stated, "I am sending my first-born son to rule Ethiopia. I ask of you that you send your first-born sons with him to aid him as counselors and officers."

The next day, Menelik and the first-born sons of the nobles of Israel left the land of Judah for Ethiopia with a great train of wagons bearing many gifts. They had a miraculously easy trip back to Ethiopia. Arriving in that land, Menelik ruled well, with his counselors and officers from Israel; and since that time, the sons of Menelik have ruled Ethiopia and the sons of the nobles of Israel have been counselors and officers of the Emperors of Ethiopia.

His Imperial Majesty Haile Selassie I, 1956, on a visit, in his capacity as Minister of Education, with members of the Ethiopian-United States cooperative education program. Dr. Edith Lord is standing between His Imperial Majesty and Vice Minister Ato Akelewerk.

I
Cross-Cultural
Confusion

An American Adviser in Education being driven to a school some distance from Addis Ababa in company with an official of the Ministry of Education, had the following experience: When a flat tire stopped the car, the driver caught a ride to the nearest village for help. While waiting at the side of the road, the American and Ethiopian were greeted by a passing shepherd. Introductions were made. The shepherd, with side-glances at the American, made his plea to the Ethiopian official: Americans were invading his village, cutting the hair from sheep who needed their coats to survive cold weather, putting medicine into sheep which changed the color of their hair, and killing some sheep for no reason at all. The shepherd begged the Ethiopian official to do something about this invasion of destructive Americans. He confided that the people of the area feared that the Americans planned to inject Ethiopians, too, changing their skin color as the color of the sheep had been changed.

A subsequent inquiry revealed that American agricultural technicians had, in fact, been operating in the area. They had directed the killing of inferior rams in order to increase the quality of the herds. They had inoculated sheep to cure disease or prevent disease. They had sheared sheep to demonstrate improved wool-gathering techniques; they had, by selective breeding and other processes, introduced pure-breeding, with attendant elimination of off-color and off-breed lambs.

WHAT IS YOUR CROSS-CULTURAL I.Q.?

Most people enjoy taking quizzes, especially if there is no penalty for a low score and if the subject matter covers an area about which they are dubious of their knowledge. There is no fun in taking a quiz on a subject about which one knows either everything or nothing. Some readers may prefer to delay checking their cross-cultural I.Q. until they have finished reading this book. The more adventurous and fun-loving will probably enjoy taking the quiz before reading the book. Whether or not you take the quiz, it is recommended that you read the rationale for the best answers immediately following the quiz-questions, because the discussion presents an abecedarian introduction to some major differences between American and Ethiopian cultures.

Following are 25 incomplete statements, each with a choice of three possible endings. Some of the items are "universals" in that they are true anywhere in the world; others are "specifics" for the Ethiopian culture. Read each incomplete statement; choose the best ending, "best" in terms of Ethiopian values or beliefs, as you understand them, and put an X in the space before that ending.

1. An Ethiopian Orthodox Christian does not .
   a) drink alcoholic beverages.
   b) eat pork.
   c) sanction divorce.

2. A courteous person, invited for dinner, will arrive
   a) earlier than the hour specified.
   b) exactly on time.
   c) somewhat later than the hour specified.

3. If a host over-pours a drink to the point of spilling some of the liquid, it means that he
   a) is showing special courtesy.
   b) is nervous or anxious about his guest.
   c) has poor neuro-muscular control.

4. To call an Ethiopian by his second name (his father's name) is
   a) a courtesy.
   b) an intimacy.
   c) an offense.

5. To address a casual friend without the prefix Weizerit, Weizero, or Ato (Miss, Mrs., or Mr.) is
   a) rude.
   b) friendly.
   c) humorous.

6. Ethiopians and white Americans can safely give one another blood transfusions
   a) under no circumstances.
   b) if the pigment (color factor) is first removed by laboratory techniques.
   c) if they are of the same blood type.

7. Personal cleanliness is
    a) next to Godliness.
    b) a cultural value, unrelated to morals.
    c) primarily a mark of intelligence.
8. If a hostess offers additional servings of a food, courtesy demands that the guest
    a) accept at least a small portion.
    b) state frankly whether or not he cares for more.
    c) refuse at least the first offer, even if he is hungry.
9. Basic intelligence, throughout the world, is
    a) distributed similarly, regardless of race or nationality.
    b) highest among pure racial strains, lowest among persons with mixed racial backgrounds.
    c) related to skin color, the darker races being less intelligent, the lighter races more intelligent.
10. If an Ethiopian gentleman enters the office or home of an American woman, Ethiopian etiquette would require that she
    a) rise, greet him, and sit down.
    b) rise and remain standing until he accepts a seat or leaves.
    c) remain seated and offer him a chair.
11. The average Ethiopian's contempt for manual labor is a
    a) widespread attitude which Americans should repeatedly disparage until it is eliminated.
    b) traditional attitude which Americans should attempt to understand.
    c) fixed attitude which Americans must accept and adjust to without modification.
12. An Ethiopian who speaks in a voice so soft that one must strain to hear him is usually showing
    a) very little consideration for his listener.
    b) good family background and training.
    c) excessive timidity, shyness, or fear.
13. An Ethiopian is likely to feel annoyed if a new American acquaintance
    a) insists on addressing him with full titles.
    b) sits beside him without talking.
    c) asks questions about his family or his work.
14. The majority of Ethiopians are, from the anthropological viewpoint, racially
    a) Negroid.
    b) mixed Negroid and Caucasian.
    c) Caucasian Hamites or Semites.
15. Ethiopian cultural arts—music, literature, painting—are
    a) much older than American cultural arts.
    b) about the same age as American cultural arts.
    c) a relatively recent development.
16. If a new Ethiopian acquaintance in your home picks up and examines various articles such as books, art-objects, etc., he is
    a) conveying a complimentary sense of appreciation.
    b) merely showing a normal, natural sense of curiosity.
    c) being deliberately rude.

17. The Ethiopian calendar, with the New Year beginning on September 11, and with its seven-year lag behind the Gregorian calendar used in the United States, is
    a) evidence of Ethiopia's lack of culture.
    b) considered by some Western theologians to be more nearly accurate than the Gregorian calendar.
    c) a result of Ethiopia's isolation and failure to learn of the needed corrections.
18. Young Ethiopian trainees are slow to ask questions of their teachers or advisers because they
    a) do not understand enough to know what questions to ask.
    b) have been taught that it is rude to question older or wiser persons.
    c) are born naturally shy.
19. There are many languages and dialects spoken in Ethiopia, but most Ethiopians speak
    a) some Amharic, the official language.
    b) some English, the second official language.
    c) only the language of their own ethnic group (tribe).
20. Muslims in Ethiopia are
    a) by far the most numerous religious group.
    b) about as numerous as Christians.
    c) numerically far fewer than Christians, but more numerous than pagans.
21. Among Ethiopians, lowest status is given to
    a) soldiers.
    b) farmers.
    c) tradesmen (shop keepers).
22. The *least* common form of marriage in Ethiopia is
    a) church marriage.
    b) civil marriage.
    c) "common law" marriage.
23. His Imperial Majesty's lineal descent from the Queen of Sheba is officially recognized by Ethiopians as
    a) a myth.
    b) a legend possibly based on fact.
    c) an historical fact.
24. The annual number of religious fast days in Ethiopia is approximately
    a) 200.
    b) 100.
    c) 50.
25. A foreigner in Ethiopia is expected to
    a) urge Ethiopians to accept American and European cultural values.
    b) attempt to understand and appreciate the Ethiopian culture.
    c) avoid cultural matters and concern himself with enjoying his visit if he is a tourist, or with the technical aspects of his job if employed.

Go to the next page for the "right" answers, and a discussion of the rationale for scoring each item.

RATIONALE FOR KEYED ANSWERS TO CROSS-CULTURAL QUIZ

KEY TO "RIGHT" ANSWERS: 1-b, 2-c, 3-a, 4-c, 5-a, 6-c, 7-b, 8-c, 9-a, 10-b, 11-b, 12-b, 13-c, 14-c, 15-a, 16-c, 17-b, 18-b, 19-c, 20-b, 21-c, 22-a, 23-c, 24-a, 25-b.

More than one of the alternative answers to an item may have some merit. However, there is a "best" answer in every case; "best" as determined by research, history, fact, or local customs and values. Following is a discussion of the rationale for the keyed answers:

1. The key is *b*: An Ethiopian Orthodox Christian does not eat pork. The attitude of Ethiopian Orthodox Christians toward eating pork is identical to that usually associated in America with the attitude of Orthodox Jews. Among Ethiopian Christians, there is no (or very little) distinction drawn between behavioral edicts from the Old or the New Testaments. Mosiac law is considered to be the foundation of Christian law; the Old Testament is considered to be the foundation of the New Testament. Both books are the Bible of Ethiopian Orthodox Christians.

Many beliefs, superstitions, and practices are associated with pigs and the eating of pork. The pig is considered to be akin to the Devil; hence, only his children on earth will eat pork. On the other hand, if an infant is fed a bite of bacon, this minor infraction by adults on the innocence of a babe not only does not damn the child, but actually fools the Devil, and thereby gives the child protection from the Evil Eye.

2. The key is *c*: A courteous person, invited for dinner, will arrive somewhat later than the hour specified. There is a saying in Ethiopia, "Only poor people eat dinner before 10:00 o'clock in the evening." Much importance is placed on food in Ethiopia, and feasting accompanies all important occasions. In fact, one can scarcely distinguish between a marriage feast and a funeral feast except by the lack of music, dancing, and heightened gaiety at the latter ceremony; the feasts are equivalent.

"Big" persons are expected to provide periodic feasts not only for their family and friends but also for "little" persons of their acquaintance. Reciprocity, a sort of social requirement in America, is practically unknown, and certainly unvalued, in Ethiopia. In fact, it would be considered presumptious for many of the guests at a feast to attempt to reciprocate by returning the invitation.

Let us say that a dinner invitation requests guests to arrive at 8:00 P.M. Those "poor people" who usually eat before 10 o'clock, and the hungry people who accept the invitation primarily for the food, may arrive at the scheduled time (but *never* earlier). However, courteous guests who have no special need of mere food but who welcome the opportunity to spend a pleasant evening with the host will arrive anywhere between 9:00 and 11:00, and will enjoy feasting with him around ten or thereafter. Incidentally, a guest in an Ethiopian home, whether invited or not, is always offered food and drink, and is expected to partake thereof. Of course, the host will eat and drink with the guest at any time of the day or night.[1]

3. The key is *a:* If a host over-pours a drink to the point of spilling some of the liquid, it means that he is showing special courtesy. To fill a glass less than to the brim is considered meanly parsimonious, or may indicate that the poverty-stricken host is out of provisions, or the partially filled glass may be an intentional insult reflecting the host's reluctance to accept the recipient as a guest. Good manners, pride, and self-esteem, plus a demonstration of courtesy and welcome demand that a guest's glass be filled to overflowing. Incidentally, there is no such thing as "a *little* more" or "only another *half* a glass." If a guest accepts a second drink, it will be a glass full to the brim or over-flowing. This practice is disappearing in the urban centers of Ethiopia, but it persists in the rural areas.

4. The key is *c:* To call an Ethiopian by his second name (his father's name) is an offense, or at least embarrassing. An Ethiopian's name, his own name, is his first name, his given name. The second name is not his name; it is his father's name—his father's first, or given, name. To call a person by the second name is almost to deny his existence and to refer exclusively, or primarily, to his father; this is an offense.

5. The key is *a:* To address a casual friend without the prefix Weizerit, Weizero, or Ato is rude. Only a child or a servant is spoken to by his name without a titular prefix. An exception to this practice is found among close friends in informal or private groups. Even the closest friends, however, will address one another by title and name in formal or public situations. Many Ethiopians, especially men, have military, civil, honorary, or family titles; Dejazmatch Mamo is never called Ato (Mr.) Mamo, and Ato Mamo is never

---

[1] One evening the author, as house guest in an Ethiopian home, ate dinner four times in three hours as four successive guests dropped in to bid the host a holiday greeting.

called merely Mamo, except in intimate circumstances, unless one intends to be deliberately rude or discourteous.[2]

6. The key is *c*: Ethiopians and white Americans can safely give one another blood transfusions if they are of the same blood type. This is a scientific fact. All human beings of the same blood type can give one another transfusions. All known types exist among all the races of man. This also is a scientific fact.

7. The key is *b*: Personal cleanliness is a cultural value, unrelated to morals. There is no evidence that personal cleanliness is correlated with spirituality; however, some religions, for example Islam, prescribe certain washing-rites as a preliminary to prayer. Likewise, there is no evidence that a positive correlation exists between intelligence and personal cleanliness. The world is full of clean morons and unwashed geniuses. Cleanliness per se, then, is neither right nor wrong, Godly or un-Godly, a mark of brilliance or of stupidity. Cleanliness is a value which probably varies as much within a culture as between cultures.

8. The key is *c*: If a hostess offers additional servings of a food, courtesy demands that the guest refuse at least the first offer, even if he is hungry. Ethiopia, in common with many other countries, for example Japan, has a number of cultural patterns related to eating that are almost rituals. The courteous guest will refuse additional food or drink at least twice. The courteous host will insist on repeating the offer at least through the third time. Without appearing greedy or overly hungry, a guest may accept the third offer. Without appearing inattentive or stingy, a host may desist in his offers after the third insistence. The host who particularly wishes to honor a guest will put food into his mouth; three such hand-administered servings are considered the minimum courtesy.

Most Americans, especially those familiar with Mexican-American food, quickly learn to like the highly spiced Ethiopian dishes. Over-eating at feasts is almost an occupational hazard for Americans in Ethiopia. No matter how much one eats, however, the host is quite likely to say, "You spoiled my feast; you did not eat a thing! Let me give you something to eat." Thus is the guest made to feel truly welcome to anything and everything the host can put at his disposal.

---

[2] Persons with high titles are occasionally addressed by title alone without mention of the name; e.g., "Thank you, Dejazmatch." An even briefer, but courteous, address is exemplified by the following statement once made to the author by an Ethiopian friend: "You must forgive me for leaving early, but I have an appointment with His Excellency, my father."

9. The key is *a*: Basic intelligence, throughout the world, is distributed similarly, regardless of race or nationality. This is a scientific fact. Persons unfamiliar with research in the area of intelligence are often misled by their observations of the way in which intelligence is used, not used, or misused by various ethnic or national groups. The way in which a person uses his intelligence is greatly determined by his cultural environment within the family group, the neighborhood, or the nation.

10. The key is *b*: If an Ethiopian gentleman enters the office or home of an American woman, Ethiopian etiquette would require that she rise and remain standing until he accepts a seat or leaves. Although Ethiopian women enjoy more legal benefits (e.g., inheritance and property rights) than do their American sisters in some states of the United States, the social nicety of "ladies first" is not a part of the Ethiopian culture pattern. Men are "first," are "more important," and, in general, are more respected by both men and women. This cultural fact may be one reason why both men and women are expected to rise and remain standing while a gentleman is on his feet. However, the gesture of courtesy goes even further: Everybody rises when *anyone* of importance, male or female, enters an office or a parlor.[3]

11. The key is *b*: The average Ethiopian's contempt for manual labor is a traditional attitude which Americans should attempt to understand. When this item was pre-tested, prior to publication, twenty percent of the Ethiopians queried chose answer *a*, suggesting that Americans should ridicule the Ethiopians' contemptuous attitude toward manual labor; ten percent chose *c*, suggesting that Americans should accept and adjust to the attitude. The author agrees with the seventy percent of the Ethiopians who feel that Americans should attempt to understand the attitude.

Contempt for manual labor in the Eastern Hemisphere is centuries older than the United States of America. The whole complex of caste, class, dynasty, divine rights, and slavery is related to this traditional, ingrained attitude. Ridicule provokes resentment even among those many Ethiopians who recognize the attitude as a deterrent to economic development. Help is wanted and needed in the modification of the attitude toward eventual development of a concept of the dignity of labor. No one would attempt to modify the design of a combustion engine until he understood the existing design perfectly. The design of human attitudes is infinitely more complex.

---

[3] Informed Ethiopians easily forgive American women for failing to rise; in fact, a high-ranking Ethiopian minister has begged the author not to rise for him, saying, "I know it is not the custom in your country."

12. The key is *b:* An Ethiopian who speaks in a voice so soft that one must strain to hear him is usually showing good family background and training. Shakespeare caused King Lear to observe that his daughter's voice "was ever soft, gentle, and low, an excellent thing in woman." Ethiopians go further in giving high value to the soft voice for all human beings; in fact this country has frequently been referred to as having "a whispering culture." Mothers feed butter to infants to soften their voices; parents punish children for speaking loudly or raucously. Adults, reared under this value-system, find it difficult physically as well as psychologically to speak privately or publicly in a loud voice.

13. The key is *c:* An Ethiopian is likely to feel annoyed if a new American acquaintance asks questions about his family or his work. In general, Ethiopians do not mind sitting quietly, without conversation, throughout a social evening. In fact, they prefer no conversation to inquisitive questions. Questions about family and work are considered inquisitive coming from new acquaintances.[4]

14. The key is *c:* The majority of Ethiopians are, from the anthropological viewpoint, racially *not* Negroid. The majority of Ethiopians are Hamites or Semites. "The Hamites are Caucasians, characterized by tall stature, dark, or even black skin, wavy hair and oval face."[5] Semites are a Caucasian race. That part of Africa which is now Ethiopia is believed to have been peopled by a Negro race some ten centuries before the birth of Christ. However, by approximately the year A.D. 1, the Hamites and Semites had driven these people into the south and southwestern parts of Ethiopia, where they are found to this day, a minority Negro group called Shankillas.

15. The key is *a:* Ethiopian cultural arts—music, literature, painting— are much older than American cultural arts. The Ethiopian Orthodox Church, until 1948 administratively associated with the Egyptian Church of Alexandria, has been the traditional preserver and perpetuator of painting, music, and literature which date back to the Ethiopian Christian Kingdom of Aksum in the fourth century, A.D., 1,100 years before Americus Vespucius left Italy to navigate unknown seas and to become the eponym for the American continent.

----

[4]One is cautioned to avoid the direct question, "Who is your father?" This wording happens to be the literal translation of an Amharic vulgar curse, implying, "Have you a father?"

[5]Webster's *Dictionary.*

16. The key is *c:* If a new Ethiopian acquaintance in your home picks up and examines various articles such as books, art-objects, etc., he is probably being deliberately rude. While a close friend, or even an acquaintance of some time, may indulge curiosity or appreciation by handling your possessions, such behavior is unheard of on the part of a *new* acquaintance of good breeding. Americans in Ethiopian homes will probably be forgiven for violating this rule of behavior since Ethiopians are becoming more and more accustomed to the "peculiar" behavior of Americans.

17. The key is *b:* The Ethiopian calendar, with the New Year beginning on September 11, and with its seven-year lag behind the Gregorian calendar used in the United States, is considered by some Western theologians to be more nearly accurate than the Gregorian calendar. Inquiry has revealed that at least some theological seminaries in the United States recognize the Ethiopian calendar as probably more nearly accurate than the Julian-Gregorian calendar, as a result of recent scholarly studies of Church history. The extent of this conviction is not known to the present author.

18. The key is *b:* Young Ethiopian trainees are slow to ask questions of their teachers or advisers because they have been taught that it is rude to question older or wiser persons. Grey hair and wisdom are thought to be synonymous by the majority of Ethiopians. "The Elders" in a family or a community merit great respect merely as a consequence of having lived longer. Coupled with this value, there are some rather rigid attitudes toward children and child-rearing which are, no doubt, familiar to any American past the age of fifty. Children should be seen and not heard. Children should speak only when they are spoken to.

While such a developmental environment is likely to produce youths who are slow to ask questions because of seeming shyness, such shyness is not a natural, inborn trait, it is a result of cultural conditioning. No amount of impatience on the part of an American product of progressive, self-expression schools of education will modify this Ethiopian characteristic, but sympathetic understanding may, in time, inspire young Ethiopians with confidence and courage sufficient to permit them to break with tradition and enter into a free, questioning relationship with an American adviser or teacher.

Incidentally, failure on the part of an American to respect an Elder—regardless of his capacities or accomplishments—does not endear the foreigner to Ethiopians.

19. The key is *c:* There are many languages and dialects spoken in Ethiopia, but most Ethiopians speak only the language of their own ethnic

group (tribe). There are two official languages in Ethiopia: (1) Amharic; (2) English. In the Government schools, Amharic is the medium of instruction during the first four to six years; English is the medium of instruction from the fifth or seventh grade through college. Within several generations, it is possible that one or both of these languages will be understood and spoken throughout the Empire. At present, however, the vast majority of Ethiopians, not having had the advantage of schooling, speak and understand only the language of their own ethnic group. In addition to numerous distinctly different languages with different language-family-roots (e.g., Hamitic and Semitic), there are many dialects which have grown so far apart that communication is not possible between groups of common origin which have become geographically and dialectically separated; the Galla groups are a striking example of this phenomenon.

20. The key is *b*: Muslims in Ethiopia are about as numerous as Christians. Ethiopia has been called "A Christian island in a Muslim sea." No one knows the exact numerical distribution of Christians, Muslims, and Pagans. The Muslim population is variously estimated at roughly one-third to one-half of the population. The Pagan population is, at least nominally, gradually beginning to be counted as either Muslim or Christian or Falasha (Jewish).

Christianity is the state religion of Ethiopia, and has been since the fourth century. However, the 1955 Constitution guarantees freedom of religion, and the 1957 *Penal Code of the Empire of Ethiopia* recognizes religious law of non-Christian groups. [6]

21. The key is *c*: Among Ethiopians, lowest status is given to tradesmen (shopkeepers). Occupations of traditional respect among Ethiopians are those of the warrior, the priest, and the farmer. Manual labor bears the stigma of slave labor.[7] Commerce, trading, keeping shop are considered lowly, undignified occupations. In fact, the majority of tradesmen in Ethiopia are Arabs, Greeks, Armenians, Italians.

22. The key is *a*: The *least* common form of marriage in Ethiopia is church marriage. Church marriage among Christians is particularly rare among the Amharas, is probably more frequent among the Tigrians, espe-

---

[6] For example, Article 616 outlaws bigamy, but Article 617 provides the following exception: "The preceding Article shall not apply in cases where polygamy is recognized under civil law in conformity with tradition or moral usage."
[7] The 1957 Penal Code, Article 565, sets the following penalty for Enslavement: "Rigorous imprisonment from five to twenty years, and a fine not exceeding twenty thousand dollars."

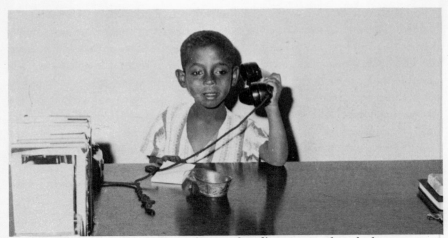

A young Ethiopian, for the first time, hears a friend's voice on the telephone.

cially the Eritrean Tigrians. However, a popular form of marriage is a civil ceremony which has the blessing or the sanction of the church. One reason put forth by Ethiopians to explain the reluctance of a church marriage is the fact that there is no provision for divorce following the church wedding. Traditionally, Ethiopian marriages are family-arranged, and neither the bride nor the groom is, in terms of choice in marriage, a "free-agent" until after the family-arranged marriage has taken place. Either party may then, rather easily, divorce the spouse and marry a mate of personal choice. Divorce is quite common in Ethiopia and carries little, or no, social stigma. Common law marriage is quite prevalent, especially among pagans and Gallas. Also there is a sort of "trial marriage" arrangement, found at almost all levels of society, which occasionally precedes an actual contractual marriage.

23. The key is *c*: Makeda, Queen of Saba (Sheba)—identified in the Old Testament as The Queen of the South—is believed to have visited Solomon in the tenth century B.C. She conceived a child by him, Menelik I, who was subsequently annointed King of Ethiopia by Solomon. This story was written into the Ge'ez canons of the Ethiopian Orthodox Church during the thirteenth century, thus making it a religious "fact." The most recent official document to state the circumstances as facts is the 1955 revision of the Constitution of Ethiopia. The liaison between Makeda, Queen of Saba, and Solomon, and the relationship of H.I.M. Haile Selassie I to the progeny of that union are officially recognized in Ethiopia.

24. The key is *a*: The annual number of religious fast days in Ethiopia is approximately two hundred. Fasting in Ethiopia is both more frequent

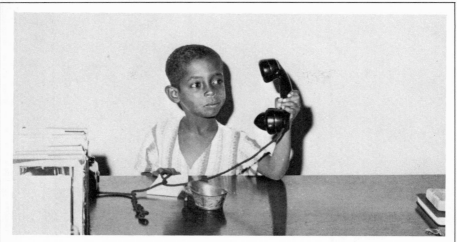
Then he looks into the telephone to "see" his friend! "What hath God wrought?"

and more rigorous than fasting in most other Christian countries. The forty-day Lenten fast, with which western Christians are familiar, is extended to fifty-six days in Ethiopia; the weekly Friday fast, familiar to Roman Catholic Christians, is doubled in Ethiopia to include Wednesday as well as Friday as fast days. In addition, there are numerous one-day to one-week fast periods throughout the year in observance of various religious rites. All together, the religious fast days in Ethiopia total something over two hundred per year.

25. The key is *b*: Foreigners in Ethiopia are, generally, expected to attempt to understand and appreciate the Ethiopian culture. In the pre-testing of this item, really a judgmental item, not a single Ethiopian or American chose response *a*. A third of the Ethiopians, and twelve per cent of the Americans chose response *c*. The author concurs with the majority of Ethiopians and Americans in concluding that foreigners in Ethiopia should attempt to understand and appreciate the Ethiopian culture.

If you originally obtained a score of 15 or above on the foregoing test, you are probably immediately ready to thoroughly enjoy a visit to Ethiopia or to do constructive work in that country. If your score was between 10 and 14, you probably would enjoy your trip more if you did some additional study prior to departure for Ethiopia, or perhaps a bit of soul-searching would help. If your score was below ten, perhaps you had better stay home; for, to obtain such a low score, you must be poorly informed on universally known facts plus having beaten the laws of chance on this multiple-choice quiz. A bit of homework is in order. Reading this book might help.

A GALLA WOMAN

ETHIOPIAN CULTURE

Ethiopian Priests in ritual song and dance to accompaniment of rattles and drums.

II
Ethiopian
Customs

ETHIOPIAN PROVERBS

If one person talks, everyone can hear; if everyone talks, no one can hear.

Family habits go to the market place.

Think about what you hear before you speak, chew before you swallow.

To lie about a far country is easy.

When you eat a crow, call it a pigeon.

One stone is enough against fifty clay pots.

You cannot build a house for last winter.

A good man earns more than his wages.

To get good results it is necessary to use good means.

Eat fish with care.

Do not bite unless you are prepared to swallow.

After the hyena has passed, the dog barks.

You cannot instruct a wise man, you cannot strike a lion.

One goes and goes and returns with himself.

If cooperation and love are not ours, we cannot buy a cloak nor a shroud.

If the heart will not see, the eye cannot see.

A child cries the same whether his mother goes to the well or dies.

ETHIOPIAN CULTURE: ⸻
Essays by Ethiopians

The following essays by Ethiopians on culturally-related topics were acquired over a period of four-and-a-half years from a variety of sources. Most of them were classroom exercises submitted by students of the author and her colleagues at the University College of Addis Ababa or by students at the Haile Selassie I Public Health College and Training Center in Gondar. In every case, permission to reproduce the essays was obtained from the student directly or through his instructor. Many of the essays are excerpts and adaptations of materials produced by the Ethnological Society of the University College of Addis Ababa; permission to reproduce the materials was obtained, in writing, from the officers of the Society who also serve as editors of the Ethnological Society Bulletin. A few of the essays were written as a result of special request by the present author to friends and Ethiopian colleagues in order to obtain data not included in essays from other sources. In every case, the writer submitted his essay with the understanding that it was to be reproduced for public consumption. The fact that so many writers of essays requested that their names be withheld is possibly a reflection of the general state of fear and insecurity which prevails in Ethiopia among masses of people who are newly emerging from a state of peasant anonymity to positions of responsibility and productivity in a somewhat modern constitutional monarchy. *

The author receives a continental "thank you" for a sugar candy from a rural lad. Hand-kissing is common among Ethiopian Muslims.

*Special appreciation is here extended for cooperation from Dr. Herbert Walther, of the University College of Addis Ababa, and from Dr. Herbert Moller and Mr. Don Johnson of the Haile Selassi I Public Health College and Training Center in Gondar.

FORMS OF GREETINGS AND OTHER SIGNS OF RESPECT IN ETHIOPIA[1]
Tilahoun Paulos

In Ethiopia the different tribes have developed their individual forms of greeting and signs of respect; among the most interesting are those of the Amharas and Tigreans, with which I am most familiar as I was brought up to observe them. I shall discuss these signs and respects as they are carried out between equals, and towards elders and superiors.

Among commoners as well as noble people the signs of respect of a child towards his father (also true of a minor towards his elder) can be divided into three sections corresponding to the age of the son. A child, generally up to the age of fifteen, kisses the feet of his father. He does not do so every time the father comes into the house, but only when the father has been away from home for some days. If love and longing are mingled with respect towards his father, the child presses his lips against the foot of his father, who then picks up his child from his feet by the chin and kisses him or her on both cheeks. Among the Amharas, where the rule is reciprocity of kisses, both kiss each other at a turn.

From age fifteen up to the age of marriage, the son kisses the knees of his father. After marriage, in the case of the Amharas, the son bows down and then proceeds to kiss and be kissed on the cheeks. In the case of the Tigreans, it is a general rule that only the elder must kiss the younger, while either of two equals may kiss. Among the Amharas, both must offer their cheeks in turn, if they are considered equals. The gradual promotion of the son from the feet to the knees and then to offering cheeks is in itself a sign of respect on the part of the father towards his growing child. Kisses are a sign of respect.

In dealing with the signs of respect practised particularly by the common people, we may classify them in two groups: those practised outside the house and those practised inside the house. The signs of respect performed outside the house are both simple and few. When two people who know one another meet on the way, both must uncover their heads; in the case of men, they raise their hats; in the case of women, they pull back the shemma, or shawl, which they wear over their heads. The two people then

[1] Abridged and reproduced with permission of the Ethnological Society of the University College of Addis Ababa from Bulletin No. 7 of the Society, December, 1957.

bow to one another with a smile, say to one another, "Good morning," or, "How are you?" and then continue their way.

Most of the signs of respect practised by the common people, however, are to be seen within the house. To illustrate the various signs of respect practised within the house, we may suppose an incident. Let us say that someone is invited to dinner by his friends. When the guest reaches the gate of the house where he is to have dinner, he sends someone, as he usually has someone, whether son or servant, to accompany his invitation, to the house of his host to announce his arrival.

The host then goes out of the house and takes his guest in. If there are other people in the house, they must all stand as the guest comes in. To their standing, the guest responds with a bow and then tells them to sit. When he is offered water to wash his hands, both before and after dinner, he must rise from his seat in respect for the one who pours water for him. When food is placed on the thatched table, the husband or the host must break the *injera* (bread) first and then offer it to his wife. Then every one, ready to do justice to the food, begins to help himself or herself. It is taboo for women to break the *injera* first. The husband, if the woman of the house has one, or her son, if he is quite grown up (at least aged fifteen), breaks the *injera* and then offers it to her. After that she can bring the soup or the meat to the table. The woman with no husband or son does, of course, everything herself. During the meal, if one drops a piece of bread, one must pick it up, kiss it, and put it on the edge of the table. Children, especially those below the age of fourteen or fifteen, do not eat with their parents. If their parents are not so strict, they allow them to eat at the same moment as themselves, but at a different table. If the parents are very strict, the children are forced to wait until their parents have had their fill before they may eat. When dinner is over, and the guest goes out of the house, the husband, or the son if the husband is not present, or the wife, if neither is present, must accompany him up to the gate.

In describing the signs of respect towards superiors, the third division of my topic, I shall deal first with the signs of respect practised inside the house, and then those practised outside.

When someone, let us say a man of lower social rank, wishes to enter the house of a superior to greet him or to make some private appeal, he must first of all take off his shoes and then give them to his servant, if he has one with him. If not, he leaves them outside in a safe place. Then he must twist his shemma round his waist and, holding the end in one hand, enter the hall and, crossing both arms at the lower chest, bow very low to the ground before his host. Having done that, he throws that end of his shemma which he is holding over the back of his shoulder, and then remains standing near the wall until he is told to sit. When given permission to sit, he must choose a lower place. He does not sit in a position he likes, but must cross his legs, straighten himself, and bow his head a bit, looking most of the time at the floor.

The superior, in his turn, when greeted by his inferior, bows his head a little. He himself does not say such words as, "Good Morning," or "How are you?" It is the courtiers who stand near him who speak for him. I asked an elderly gentleman why the lord himself does not speak, and he told me the lord says, "How are you?" only to those people who are just below him in rank, or to those who are his special favourites.

We may suppose it is now the time for the banquet. When the food is brought into the hall, the vassal must stand up. He must also remain standing when the lord washes his hands, both before and after the meal.

When the lord washes his hands, one of the courtiers must remove the end of his shemma from his shoulder and form a sort of curtain between the standing vassals and the lord. I asked old people the reason for this. Some told me that it is to protect the lord from an evil eye, and others told me that it is to protect him from criticism by his inferiors as to the way he washes in case he does not follow the correct manner of washing practised by the nobility.

After the lord has washed his hands, if the towel is late in being fetched or a little bit dirty, one of the standing courtiers must offer his white garment to the lord to dry his hands on.

During the evening meal, someone (usually a servant) must stand holding a torch, but he must not look at the food. He must turn a little to one side, away from the table, and look at the wall in front of him, or the roof, or at some other object.

No vassal can eat at the same table as the lord unless he is next in social position or receives a special favour. All the vassals in the hall sit around a thatched table, usually less decorated than that of the lord. Also, the food offered to the vassals is usually of a different quality from that offered to the lord.

When the lord sneezes, all the vassals must raise themselves from their seats slightly and bow down saying, "God bless you." If one of the vassals has something to say to the lord, he must approach him with a bow and, putting his hands over his mouth, must whisper in his ear.

If the lord wants to speak to someone, and he calls a name, the one called must quickly stand up and say, "Yes, my lord." If he is ordered to do something, he must bow down promising that he will do so. Even if it is impossible for him to execute the orders, in public he must still promise to do so and then in private, some other time, explain to the lord that it is impossible for him to carry them out.

In the house where the lord is present, no loud voices should be heard. The noblemen who are in the same hall with the lord must whisper to one another when speaking. If two want to say something to each other, and yet are not close enough so as to be able to whisper, one of them may signal one of the servants standing by and tell him to carry the message.

Sometimes (especially among the more coarse country squires) when the lord wishes to spit and is obviously searching for some suitable spot to dispose of his accumulated saliva, it is the custom for an attendant who observes his lord's distress to offer the end of his shemma outstretched so that the lord may spit on it. Such a case is, however, rare as it is considered a sign of the lord's bad upbringing.

A servant, after finishing washing the feet of his lord, must kiss them as a sign of love and subjugation. When a vassal enters the compound of his lord and sees no attendant to inform the lord of his presence, he must never call, but he may clap his hands.

The signs of respect towards a superior which are practised outside the house are as many and varied as those performed within the house. A nobleman, when on a journey with someone of superior rank, cannot mount his mule unless he is given permission to do so. Till then he must walk on foot, at the side of his superior, carrying his gun, as he normally would have one, on his shoulder. When the superior mounts his mule, the inferior who happens to be near must hold the stirrup for him.

If the courtier is given permission to ride his mule and, after a while, the lord speaks to him, he cannot give any answer until he dismounts his mule. Having given the answer, he cannot remount his mule without a second permission.

When a commoner, riding his mule, meets on the way a nobleman whom he knows, coming from the opposite direction, he must quickly dismount his mule and then bow down low to the ground. Having done so, he must, on foot, accompany the lord until given permission to return; whereupon he must first go ahead of the nobleman a few paces and bow in the direction in which the nobleman is going before he can mount his own mule and go on his way.

If two noblemen of equal social rank meet on the way and both are on mules (as they should be), both must dismount, and, having bowed to one another, remount and separate. If one is younger, he waits till the elder has seated himself on his mule before he himself mounts.

At a cross-road, the nobleman who is younger, or is inferior in social rank, must let the superior or the elder one pass first. It is absolutely forbidden for a servant to ride the mule of his master.

These then are the signs of respect that have been practised by the Amharas and Tigreans through the flow of centuries. Nowadays, with the modernization of the country, many of the signs of respect I have described are being considered as things of the past.

RECREATIONAL ACTIVITIES[1]

Nature provides us with many mental and physical gifts for enjoying entertainment. So recreation has always been, and still is, one of the basic needs that help to accelerate the advancement of normal wellbeing in life. Some of the recreational activities in Ethiopia are the following:

A. Children 2-8 years of age.

The marvelous use of soil by children: Groups of children come together. Soil is collected and piled. A stone which has a flat surface and another one of global structure are taken. Soil is put on the flat stone and the tiny hands of the child grind the soil with the round stone; after that, the soil "flour" can be used for many purposes.

1. It is mixed with water and then cooked. Then a sumptuous meal is theoretically assumed to be served.
2. Saucepans, dishes, cups, etc., are made by the wonderful technical fingers of the little kids.
3. Mud-people, mud-horses, mud-camels, mud-cows, etc., are created by the little ones.

[1] The two authors' names withheld by request.

Ethiopian children playing a friendly game of marbles.

Ashangulit: This is an interesting and instructive plaything of children. It is similar to a doll. It is made of different colours and qualities of cloths. A number of ashangulitoch are produced by the children themselves or by their parents, relatives, or friends.

The ashangulitoch are gathered together. They are divided into groups according to idea principles to symbolize marital, familial, and social life.

Emboay Lamie: Emboay is a round, wild fruit. Many emboayoch are taken and put in a circle of stones. The big emboayoch are assumed as cows and oxen and the little emboayoch are calves. Thereby the children play the game of milking and looking after cattle.

Yeketel Bate: The children cut leaves and collect them. They make the leaves into houses.

Yenahet Feres: Branches of trees are cut down. The children play riding horses by dragging the branches between their thighs and running forward.

Yeaheka Teyet: Mud is made into the shape of a saucepan. Its base is thinly moulded. The mud-saucepan is turned upside down, and it is thrown with force onto the ground. This makes an explosive sound. The children enjoy hearing the explosion.

52

B. 8-12 Years of Age

Gena Chewata: This game is very similar to hockey. The group divides into two teams. The game is played with a wooden ball and sticks. A flat, grassy playground with a central starting point is taken. The captains of the teams meet at the starting point. The ball is placed between their sticks. By touching the ground and crossing each other's sticks three times, they start the game. Scores are counted when the ball passes either end of the field. Usually this game is played at Christmas time. It is a very exciting and fascinating game.

Feres Gelbiya: This is horse riding. At festivals and on other occasions, the skillful horse riders decorate their beautiful horses according to fashion. They choose a grassy plain and gallop with terrific speed along the plain till they become contented.

Eskesta: For festivals and very important events, such as marriage, people sing and dance. Eskesta is an enchanting dance performed by remarkable rhythmic movements of the neck and shoulders in accordance with very de- lightful singing and rhythmic clapping of hands.

Weha Wana: This is swimming.

Debebkosh. This is a game which is exactly the same as hide-and-seek. A group of children call a meeting. One child is elected as the chief of the group. He seats himself at a convenient central spot. Another child is ap- pointed as the seeker. The seeker covers his face with his hands and puts his head on the lap of the chief. The chief must make sure that the seeker is not seeing while the other children hide. The seeker says "Kukulu," and the chief replies "Alnegam" until all other children of the concerned group in the game are hidden. The chief sees that the children have hidden themselves properly. The seeker says "Kukulu," and the chief answers "Nega." The chief then releases the seeker. The seeker goes and tries hard to find any one of the hidden children. All the hidden children attempt skillfully to reach the chief without being caught by the seeker. Therefore, anybody who reaches the chief and touches him is saved from being caught by the seeker. One or more children may be caught by the seeker. Nevertheless, the child who is caught first replaces the seeker and the game starts all over again. If the

Two Ethiopian boys enjoy painting with water colors.

seeker is unfortunate or so unskilled as to catch nobody, he has to take his position again as a seeker to commence the second round of the game. The game is played until the children are exhausted. This game is one of the exciting games of childhood. But it does a lot of good things for the child. Some of these are the following:

1. It trains the child to be skillful, to tackle and find out short-cuts for the solution of problems.

2. It adds more running ability to the child.

3. It helps the child to be active and practical in his duty.

Kelebosh: Two or three children gather together. Five pebbles are collected. Any one of the children can start the game. The game is played by holding one pebble in one hand and resting the rest on the ground and picking them up one by one, then two by two; after that, all four at once. All the time, one pebble is tossed while the rest are being picked up and held together with the tossed one. Thereafter, all five are put on the dorsum of the hand, tossed, and caught. The game has got many tricks to it. The winner is the one who accomplishes the game by performing the greatest skill in all the tricks.

C. 21-75 Years of Age

Gebeta: A flat piece of wooden board, stone, or ground is chosen. Twelve symmetrical holes are made in it. Four pebbles or marbles or iron or coral are put in each hole. Usually the game is played between two persons. Each hole is assumed as a house. At the beginning of the game, each person takes one row of holes; that means six holes. Before commencing the game, the players use lots in order to determine which one of them begins first. The winner is the one who possesses twelve houses (holes) by collecting the pebbles or marbles to his zone.

Tarik: This is a story related by the aged men about the good old days and their past noble deeds. They tell of their experiences and adventures in childhood. They talk about the wars they fought and victories they won, the leaderships they gained and the exciting features of human activities. They speak of great kings, rulers, leaders, brave warriors, and nations of the past. They discuss the advantages and disadvantages of the past and the present in all respects of life.

Begena: Begena is the harp. It is played by an old man who is experienced in singing a tune which is suitable for the strings of the harp. Usually, the old man plays the harp to set forth songs for the glory and goodness of God.

Weste-Ze-Getem: This is an ironical or idiomatic poem composed by a witty and learned man. This clever and amusing poet presents his poem to kings or to distinguished and highly educated people on occasions such as festivals and or formal ceremonies. The preparation takes quite a time. It requires tranquility, absolute concentration, and meditation, accompanied by a beautiful natural environment.

Adew: This is hunting. Courageous and devil-may-care adventurers travel for months to dense forests inhabited by unruly, wild animals. The hunters use their utmost skill to shoot down or stab to death the wild animals such as lions, tigers, elephants, etc. As a matter of fact they do kill the animals. When they come back home they bring with them the skins of their victims. They feast, sing, and dance in memory of their deadly and/or terrifying adventures. They boast of their unsurpassable bravery. They are presented with earrings to put on their penises in commemoration of their fearless deeds.

BUHE[1]
Akalou Wolde Michael

Buhe is a holiday celebrated about the 21st of August. The origin of this term, *Buhe* is uncertain. Some say that it may have come from the word *buho* which means dough. This derivation seems quite reasonable because one would find dough in nearly every Ethiopian home the day before *Buhe*. This is due to the necessity of baking bread for the morrow.

In earlier times the holiday was celebrated on a mountain. There children built very crude all-grass huts. The clergy say that they built huts because Peter in the Seventeenth Chapter of the *Gospel of St. Matthew* said: "Lord, it is good for us to be here; if Thou wilt, let us make here three tabernacles, one for Thee, one for Moses, and one for Elijah." Near these huts there was usually a bonfire around which gathered people from many villages, bringing with them very dry loaves of bread. As soon as the bonfire began to blaze, the loaves were thrown up into the air three times and each time allowed to fall on the ground. The loaves which were not broken were put on one side in a basket, those which were broken were placed on the other side in a basket. Then the unbroken loaves of bread were eaten while the broken were thrown away.

As time went on, the manner of celebration changed. It is impossible to say when the change took place; for it was very gradual. *Buhe*, unlike any other Ethiopian holiday, comes during the fifteen fasting-days of the month of *Nahase*. Therefore, great feasts as those of Easter and Christmas are not held. As a result the people cannot stuff themselves with all sorts of food. Because no good dish is served, and moreover because it is rainy (for Nahase is the month of the heaviest rain), it seems that the older people began to neglect the custom. So the holiday was left to children.

Beginning from the evening of the twelfth Nahase, boys group themselves roughly according to their ages and villages. Each group consists of a minimum of 10 boys to a maximum of 40 boys. Then a leader who has a good voice and knows a lot of *Buhe* songs is chosen. The duty of this boy is to lead the group in singing. Others who may have as good a voice as the leader may help in leading the group, and they usually do so. Then two treasurers are chosen. In the early days there was only one treasurer, for people then gave only loaves of bread to the singing boys; no money was given. But as time went on, people began to give money; for it was easier to give money

---

[1] Abridged and reproduced with permission of the Ethnological Society of the University College, from Bulletin No. 7, December, 1957.

than to bake bread. Moreover, the young boys, being heedless of the importance of this traditional custom, prefer jingling coins to the cumbersome bread. Some people, however, still continue to give bread, and hence it is necessary to have one treasurer for the money and another for the bread. Finally, the strongest boy is given a thick bat, and this boy remains at the rear to ensure the safety of the group, for it is customary for one group to loot what the other has accumulated.

After everything is organized the leader takes over; they start off at about six p.m., going from house to house singing. The songs are tiresome, monotonous repetitions of words and phrases usually in the form of a poem in the sense that they are rhyming couplets. The leader sings a line or two, the group repeats them, and finally they all shout together signifying the end of a particular stanza by the crude chorus. They go on singing half of the night and the whole of the next day and sometimes the whole night and the whole day after that.

As they come near the gate or the door of a particular house, they sing a special kind of song directed to the people in the house, so that they will prepare the money or bread promptly. One of these is as follows:

"The mistress should rise and light the lamp, and the master
should rise and look into the money purse."

When they get either the bread or money, or both, they bless the givers as follows:

"He who insults my mistress, let him have the odour of a bedbug,
and he who insults my master, let him itch."

Finally, they sing the following: "May He keep us together," or in other words: "May He not separate us"; then they leave the house. If they are not given either the bread or money they tend to be very rough. Hence instead of blessing the house they curse it.

Now it must be clear that this is in no way a form of begging. It is done only because it is a custom; it is never done out of necessity. Unfortunately, however, some city rogues in towns have begun to use this occasion for collecting money. That is why the gathering of boys on this day is not allowed in Addis Ababa. Another possible reason for this is that the shouting and singing of the boys became unbearable to the inhabitants of the bigger towns.

At the end of the final day, that is, on the thirteenth *Nahase*, the boys share the bread and money equally, with a little extra for the leader and the treasurers.

Ethiopian Christian priests with traditional instruments.

To a foreigner, the most striking part of *Buhe* is the practice of torchlight on the evening of this day, especially if the foreigner takes a bird's eye of a particular village or town. He may think that particular place is on fire. Sometimes one or two houses may burn as a result of this practice, but this is rare and happens from sheer carelessness.

The torch is made from bundles of dry sticks tied together. In the countryside torches are homemade, but in the towns they are bought. Some people, therefore, make quite a bit of money every year by selling torches. Every house provides torches for every male member. On the evening of the thirteenth *Nahase*, beginning from sundown, the torches are lit (it is a custom to light them from the main house, not from the kitchen or any other place), and they are taken outside the gate, if there is one, or in front of the house, if there is no gate, and are collected to form a bonfire. The females do not take part in this event unless a particular home consists only of a husband and a wife, in which case the wife is allowed to accompany her husband. Small children, regardless of their sex, are allowed to go near the bonfire. Nowadays, however, women may be seen around the bonfire, but the idea is still frowned upon by elderly persons.

As the bonfire burns, the people around it sing songs such as those sung by the boys during the day. Along with this is another practice— the use of the lash, made of strands of fibre, twisted or braided together and fastened to a short stock or a long, pliant handle. On this occasion, it serves for two purposes. First, the boys during the day use it to produce noise; secondly, the adult people at night use it to flog each other.

During the torchlight ceremony, daring young men enlist themselves for a duel, and they fight with the lashes. There is no ill intention in the fight. They just lash each other's legs (not because they want to win the favour of any woman, but to display their courage and endurance, for indeed it shows great endurance) until one of the parties cries out defeat. The contest is not arranged and conducted according to rules; hence, one of the parties may use it with the intention of harming a rival. However, most times, the duel ends peacefully. Finally, when the fire dies out, usually around nine p.m., everyone goes back to his home and this marks the end of *Buhe*.

COMMUNITY LEADERSHIP[1]

Individuals choose as their associates those who will satisfy one or another of the following criteria: Similar personality, occupation, economic standards, religion, other characteristics. The associates of an individual are not restricted within the groups we have mentioned above. It is not uncommon for farmers to associate with doctors, merchants, or government officials. Christian priests sometimes have some Muslim friends.

In certain villages, the elders form an association. Such a group can give advice to numbers of young persons in the village whenever needed. If certain problems arise or are introduced to the village, these elders gather and discuss the matter, then hand their recommendations to the local governor.

Since human beings depend upon social interaction for many of their adjustments, a society consists of all the members of the same group who adjust together. For example, nowadays we have many relations with the world around us through communications media. We have constant, regular, and dependable Ethiopian Air Lines Service, routes over the sea, and roads, plus rails on land. Interior communication has already shown its benefits by accelerating the spread of knowledge throughout the country and enabling one part of the country to exchange ideas, products, etc., with other parts of the country. For example, honey, teff, and butter are much cheaper in Gojjam province than in Addis Ababa, and modern equipment is cheaper in Addis; therefore, goods such as honey, butter, teff, etc., are sent to Addis Ababa from all parts of Ethiopia to be sold. We can exchange ideas with the remote countries as well as with neighbouring countries.

Ethiopia's social strata do not have well defined borders; however, they may be classed as high, medium, or low. Status is based on the following criteria: Wealth, education, occupation, bravery, personality, etc. A married woman enjoys the social standing of her husband's class: e.g., the wife of His Excellency the General-Governor is called Her Excellency. Children are respected among their contemporaries according to their family status. Anyone can shift from low to upper class and from high to lower class. If a man in a low stratum gains, by some way or another, in one of the above-mentioned criteria, there is no barrier at all which obstructs him from going to a higher class; for the man who was in a high class, the reverse is true. Heredity is not supposed to be of much concern here. H.I.M. Haile Selassie I has already de-

[1] Three authors' names withheld by request.

clared that it is not important to be born from high or low families, but it is very desirable to achieve for oneself an important place; e.g., the sons of common people, such as farmers, priests, and guards, have occupied the highest available positions in the government.

Leadership may vary with the culture of different communities; however, since there are persons who tend to be leaders and others who tend to be followers, natural leadership by one's own personality is very common. For instance, if a man is clever, brave, and has done good deeds for his country, people respect him, accept his ideas, and will be led by him. Leadership may be based on age. Old persons are respected, and their advice may lead quite a number of people because they have experience of social life acquired by age.

Persons are elected by their own community to settle many problems concerning the community. For example, they can make agreements between quarreling persons before the case reaches the court; they establish new markets or modify old ones, and specify the dates of the market which are suitable for the community (mostly Saturday); they establish or repair churches, mosques, etc., in the village; they try to discover criminal or dishonest people in the community, and give such information to the available authorities; they give advice to the community on building bridges and pathways.

Hereditary leadership is very common in Ethiopia. In principle, this type of community leadership is the same throughout the country, but details vary in each region. Following are the most frequently found titles:

1. *Balabat (Korro, Gult-Gaiz,* and *Debre-Shoom).* This is one who inherited leadership from an ancestor. His area of control consists of one or more Chicka-Shooms. His main job is to transfer orders and messages from local governors to Chicka-Shooms or to the community, or communities.

2. *Chicka-Shoom.* This is almost the same as Balabat or Debre-Shoom, but the title is lower and sometimes is not inherited; some Chicka-Shooms are merely appointed.

3. *Gebet.* This is a kind of leadership in the church which is hereditary.

When a father dies, the older son takes over the hereditary leadership. Heredity is less important, especially in government offices, than to be appointed to leadership.

61

Leadership through education entitles a man to the following distinctions:

1. *Alleka* (Chief of the Parish) is appointed leadership in certain churches according to the knowledge he possess; 2. *Marigetta* (Director of church songs) is awarded on the basis of education; 3. Nowadays, any position in a government office may be held by an educated young man, regardless of his hereditary background.

Leadership by election occurs as follows:

1. Representatives for Parliament are elected; 2. Representatives of the municipality are elected; 3. Councils are elected by the people of their own area to discuss and settle problems.

Every Ethiopian, male or female, who is above twenty years of age, who thoroughly understands the purpose of election, has been given the right to participate in elections, provided that she or he (electors) meet the following requirements. He or she:

1. Must be a citizen; 2. Must be a resident of the village for at least a year; 3. Must be free from any mental disorder; 4. Must not be a prisoner or notorious criminal.

Any person who is elected by the people in the required manner, and who is accepted by the government, can represent the community which he belongs to. Requirements are as follows:

1. Age: Not less than 25 years; 2. Wealth: He must have one-thousand dollars or movable property estimated at a value of one-thousand dollars or immovable property estimated at a value of two-thousand dollars in the province for which he is being elected; 3. He must be a citizen and be well known in the same province for which he is elected. He must be free from crimes and not previously punished for a crime. He must have a certificate describing that he is free from crime, even though he was not punished. He should not be a person who has committed a crime punishable with a fine of five-thousand dollars or imprisonment of 6 months (exterior or interior). He must not be bankrupt and must be free from known debts.

Any person who has the following characteristics, wholly or partially, is respected and admired among his contemporaries and within his community.

1. *Family Background:* This includes families who are or were wealthy, have had a hero, or have had high standards in occupation for centuries; such families are respected and admired by the people even though they are poor for the time being.

2. *Occupation:* People appointed by the central government or the local government are respected because of the authority they have. Moreover, the community believes that they also have high mental capacity and are clever enough to solve any problem which might arise.

3. *Education and Training:* People who are educated in various fields are respected and admired according to the extent of their knowledge. For example, popes, bishops, priests, and other personnel of the church are respected and admired. Local midwives and wogeshas are respected and admired highly, and they are asked to aid in cultural diffusion.

4. *Wealth:* Persons who are wealthy are honourably regarded. There is a proverb saying that, if there is money, there is a path in the air.

5. *Age:* Aged persons are respected by younger people since they came to this world before them and have seen many things and have had many experiences. They are so respected that if they curse somebody, it is believed he will meet evil things in his future.

6. *Personality:* This includes behavior, loyalty, honesty, intelligence, sympathy, confidence, etc. People are respected because of a good personality. If they have in combination the basic traits described above, they are admired highly and occupy the highest available positions in the community, regardless of their social stratum.

7. *Brave and Feared:* A few years ago this requirement referred especially to hunters who killed lions, elephants, buffalo, etc. But nowadays the title "Brave and Feared" is given to one who benefits the community as a whole.

FAMILY ROLES[1]

The main role of the family is to raise children and transfer culture to the next generation. In addition, the family may provide economic services for its members; it may help to educate them, give them religious guidance, furnish recreation, protect them against dangers of various sorts, and try to fulfill any desire or wish of the family. In addition, one of the best roles of the Ethiopian family is to advise and to punish those under control. For example, if a boy in a family becomes disobedient or does mischief, he is advised once or twice; if he repeats what he was told not to do, he will receive severe punishment. Adolescents are deeply advised.

The actual Ethiopian family consists of the husband, wife, children, servants and maids. In some parts of the country, the family may include the parents of the husband and wife as well as the servants and others who live under their support.

Family organization ususally starts with marriage. Mates choose each other due to love or are chosen by the families. In some parts of Ethiopia, marriage is proposed only through the authority of the parents. After they marry, the couple spend some days in the house of the husband's parents, usually a fortnight. But if the parents of the bridegroom are rich and anxious to have them for a longer time, the couple may stay for some more days. After this, the parents of the bridegroom and all his intimate friends contribute some amount of money, furniture, or utensils and other things which make up a proper household. From this day onward the couple are responsible for their own life.

The father of the bridegroom as well as the mother will keep an eye on them until they are fully organized. If they fail, the parents will try to help them in any way to overcome their failure. If the couple are lucky, they get children; also, some of their parents and kinship families may come to live with them, and thus the family is extended. The members of the family have affection, love, loyalty, and respect for each other. The secrets of the family remain confined among them. This is the main way in which the Ethiopian family is organized.

There are few variations in Ethiopian family organization. Variation of marriage due to religion is an outstanding taboo. However, youngsters of the opposite sex living in the same vicinity may fall in love with each other. In this case the boy or the girl changes or takes the religion of the other, and

[1] Author's name withheld by request.

A square house built of straw and sticks.

they are married. The parents of the one who changed his religion do not agree or accept this matter, and they will say, "You are not my son (or daughter) any more." Polygyny is common among Muslims. In some parts of Ethiopia, the male can marry as many wives as he wishes, if he has enough money; in other parts, the number of wives is limited. The main object of having many wives is to produce many children. There is no *polyandry* in any religion or any part of Ethiopia.

The husband has full authority. The wife obeys any order given by the husband. She has no right to accept anything or to do something which has been demanded by anybody. When she is asked something, she says, "First I must tell my husband, and if he agrees I will accept what you say."

Homes are broken mainly for the following reasons:

Quarrels: After marriage the couple may live for a long time happily and affectionately, but a time may come when the love from one or both sides declines. This status leads them to quarrel now and then. The quarrels may be due to jealousy; e.g., the wife may hear or suspect that her husband has a woman friend or proposes to marry another woman. His first wife, by this true or false information, is upset and wants to quarrel and to leave his house. On the other hand, the neighbours may not like the woman, and they may tell her husband false or true information that his wife has a lover and spends most of her time with him, whenever he is not at home. If the husband is clever enough, he will secretly investigate to prove the accuracy of this information. He will keep or divorce her according to the truth of the information. If the man is nervous or foolish, he will accept the information and, without any proof, he will dismiss the woman.

Death: Everybody knows that death is the chief cause for breaking the home of a family, and this often brings poverty. Usually the parents prepare a written will and keep it with them. When someone, especially the husband, dies, the rest of the family share according to the will. Usually the children get a larger share than the other members of the family.

If the woman does not give birth to a child after a long period of marriage: When an individual proposes to marry, he will ask whether the family of the girl has a family history of being fertile, with many children. Hoping to get children, he marries a girl from such a family. The man lives with her for a long period of time. If they do not get a child, the husband thinks that his wife is sterile, and he wishes to divorce her and marry another woman. So the home is broken.

If the husband (or wife) is a drunkard: In every part of the world there are drunkards, no matter how literate they are. Even though they are drunkards, they need wives. During or before marriage, the wife may not know that the man is a drunkard. But after living together for sometime, she studies his behavior. She may be troubled that the husband comes back home very late. Besides this, he may try to fight with her every night without reason and torture her. If this continues for some time, she will be fed up and want to get away from him. In this way the home may be broken. Very rarely some women may have the habit of drink, and eventually they may be drunkards too. Such women may not have time to take care of their homes, and they may not notice the children or the husband. In turn, the husband

66

Two rural Ethiopians stand before house thatched with straw and sticks. Note large hand-made water jars.

may divorce such a wife. Younger children who are under breast feeding remain with the mother. The bigger ones may live with the father or the mother. If they are supposed to live with the mother, the husband has to give a certain amount of money monthly. This is done by his free will or by legal means.

Disease: One of the family, either the husband or wife, may get a certain type of contagious, chronic disease, such as leprosy, or tuberculosis. When the healthy ones realize that there is no chance of recovery, they may ask kindly to separate from each other, or some may escape without informing the diseased one. Some may remain, helping the patient up to the end of his life. But the average mate, in some way or another, separates from the patient and thus the home is broken.

Poverty: There are many causes of poverty. One cause is drunkenness, another is an inability to work, or accidental loss of money. No matter how poor they are, married couples try to help themselves; but if they fail, they part and try their chances separately. Therefore, the home is broken.

Dissatisfaction in sex (either the man or the woman): The man may not be able to satisfy the woman or the woman does not satisfy the man in sexual intercourse, so they try to find a way to divorce. This occurs rarely, and does not apply to church marriages.

Other factors: No matter how much in love the partners were before marriage, they may come to hate each other very much and even think of killing one another. The husband may intend to kill his wife by some kind of instrument, and the wife may propose to kill her husband by poison. Such hatred may lead to divorce or separation.

The following points may prevent the failure of the marriage: proper mating, enough money, good health, good personality; in addition, the husband should have enough knowledge to solve any problem which he encounters. The wife also must have ability to some extent. If two or more of these points are lacking the divorce rate will rise.

The chief difference in the roles of men and women is, especially in the country side, occupation. The women mostly do the house work and take care of children, also, they help their husband by doing simple things on the farm, bringing in food, and preparing the things which are needed on the farm. When the crop is harvested, they take it to the market to sell. Herds of cattle may be taken care of by the women. The man ploughs, harvests, collects, and threshes. Other than farming, men may work as teachers, house builders, carpenters, mechanics such as in a local mill, clerks, cooks, soldiers, guards, and office workers.

Women can be teachers, tailors, clerks, spinners, guardian tutors, or midwives. When a woman is old enough, she holds the highest status in the community and takes part in reconciliations of married couples, and she is believed able to give good blessings. She is accepted as an observer at any ceremony or party.

All that has been stated above depends upon and varies with the cultures and ritual customs of different provinces.

THE GALLA WOMEN AT JARA
Yeshi Teferri[1]

The little village we have been visiting is about one kilometer from Jara Centre. It is at the junction of the road to Majite. The name of this village, too, is Jara. At present the number of its population is sixty-one inhabitants. They are all Moslem Gallas.

The main occupation of these people is cattle keeping, and when the grass is not sufficient for their cattle, they move to other places in quest of better pastures. Then after about four months of wandering about, they come back to Jara village and settle again for the rest of the year, till the grass is once more finished. Their second occupation is farming. Around their village they own some land where they grow crops. Because of the first occupation they may be called nomads, and because of the second one, sedentary. Hence they can be called semi-nomads.

During our first visit to this little village, we asked all the women and girls to gather in an open space near their huts. The first time, some of them were a little shy and so did not come to us. But others were brave enough to come to greet us and shake hands. When we got quite a large number of them, we started showing them some simple knitting and samples of sewing. We asked them if they were willing to learn how to do such things. Most of them answered that they would be glad to learn.

After staying with us about an hour, they started going. They told us they were busy. Since we could not keep them longer for the first visit, we did not try to start anything. So we made an appointment for the following week, said goodbye to them, and left the village.

For the next week's visit, we took some materials and needles to teach them some knitting. We brought some tables made out of reeds and placed them under a big tree very near to the village. Unfortunately we could not get hold of many girls and women. It was the busiest period of the day. We found only three girls. The rest were busy, some milking their cows, others cooking food for their lunch. We decided to wait for more girls to come. In the meantime, we were talking to these few girls and to some men from the village. The men told us that since the women are busy the whole day, doing almost all the work for the family, they couldn't come to learn. We asked them to tell us about the work the women do. The following is the answer we got.

[1] The author is a teacher in the UNESCO Community Development Workers' Training Center at Majite.

Early in the morning the women fetch water from the river and then cook breakfast for their families. As soon as this is done they clean the cattle pens, then grind or pound some grain for their lunch. About twelve noon some start milking their cows while others cook, mostly some pancakes for lunch. When all this is done, they eat their lunch, and most of the girls go with their cattle to the grazing ground. The rest stay in their huts. They cook for supper and look after their babies and children. Some women spin and do basketry too. When the men build houses, the girls help them in ways such as bringing thatch for the roofing. Briefly, the women and girls work very hard, even harder than any one could expect.

Having learned that at the present stage, because of the lack of leisure time, women and girls could not learn, we stopped our first programme, which was to teach, and started to learn more about them. Hence, during the last visits we have been making, we won more confidence and friendship, and at the same time we learned some of their most urgent needs.

The huts in this village are built from wood and thatch only. Most of them are very small, and their doors are so small that one has almost to crouch while passing through. Inside, most of the huts are divided into two rooms by wooden walls. The room farther away from the door is raised a little above the floor level. This serves as a bed for sleeping. The other room is for cooking and doing other things, too.

We have visited all the huts, and in all of them I noticed that there is not enough household equipment. Most of the things they have are gourds. Here I think that the lack of sufficient equipment is one of the main reasons why women and girls are kept busy all the time. As an example, let us take the water pots they use. Because these pots are too small, the women have to go to the river to fetch water twice a day. But if this pot was bigger, one journey a day would be enough and would mean saving both time and labour. Since they don't have bigger things to store food in, they do their grinding, pounding and cooking only for their immediate needs.

Because of the above facts, I believe it would be very valuable to have a model house in their area. This should be equipped with inexpensive and local, yet useful, things. Here, to start with, they can be introduced to a quicker and more efficient way of doing things, specially of cooking. Besides this, they could be taught to plan a day's work. This would leave them with enough leisure time to learn other things such as health, literacy, diet, child and baby care, sewing, and knitting. There is a great need both for practical medical work and health education. Diseases caused or aggravated by dirt are especially common.

The total number of the population is sixty-one. Out of these there are eleven boys between the ages of four and fifteen years and four adults between twenty and twenty-two years who attend the literacy class. This means about twenty-five per cent are learning, which shows that these people are very keen for education. Furthermore, many people from the surrounding villages say that they will move nearer to the Jara Centre to settle there. At present one of the chiefs, Kanyasmatch Mama, is building his house close to Jara Centre. There is no doubt that we can do a great deal in this area to expand the work, if the Government is in favour of our so doing.

THE PEOPLE OF RAYA-AZABO LAND
Seyoum Ayele and Ghion Hagos[1]

The Ethiopian-United States Cooperative Education Program was eager to grasp better understanding of the peoples who inhabit the land of the Rayas and the Azabos. These peoples had no relationship with the Ministry of Education; no teachers were assigned to the area; no children of the Azabos or the Rayas entered the annual competition for subsidized education beyond the eighth grade. Furthermore, some rather frightening stories about these people circulated in Addis Ababa. We volunteered to visit Raya-Azabo land to try to discover some truths about these Ethiopian people, to attempt to learn something of their history and their way of life, and to explore their attitudes toward modern education of their children.

Accompanied by a native of Azabo land who had somehow acquired some modern education and who wanted help for his people, we left Addis Ababa for a visit to these rather isolated people in Wollo and Tigre Provinces. The Ministry of Education gave us a letter of introduction to the Governor, which we delivered directly we arrived at Korbata. He immediately sent messages to the chiefs and village elders asking them to assemble to meet us. That same evening, we made our first direct contact with the Raya people. While explaining the purpose of our visit, we mentioned that we were very much interested in learning their attitude toward education for their children. That set them off, and immediately we were friends and not

---

[1] Condensed and slightly revised.

Hunting party. The two with side-arms, trainees of Dr. Edith Lord, are on a provincial tour hunting stories for school journal, "Time to Read." In foreground, largest spear point, is Ghion Hagos, co-author of the report, "The People of Raya-Azabo Land."

strangers. One by one they rose to speak warmly in favour of education. All of them ascertained that the introduction of education in their communities would change the course of their lives, and they assured us that they would cooperate with us willingly on all occasions.

We were reserved and watchful at first because the Rayas are notoriously known as testicle-gatherers. Traditionally a man is not the head of his house until he has presented his betrothed or his wife with another male's testicles. But as we met and talked with the Rayas from the various communities, as we came to know them better, sharing the same food and lodgings with them, we were surprised to find them a normal, decent people, and we never once witnessed any sign of hostility during our stay with them. And contrary to popular belief, the Rayas are not nomads but a group of peaceful farmers. They have no separate language. Tigrinia is their first language, but a large number of them also speak Amharic. Some still speak Galigna, the language of their ancestors, the first settlers in Raya soil.

Long ago, they tell, at about the time of Mohammed the Left-Handed,[1] a Galla woman crouched on the banks of the Awash River to drink some water. While cupping her hands for the drink, she saw a mirage of a distant land with cattle roaming wild in the open fields. She gathered her people and told them to follow her to a land far away, rich with cattle and free from any sign of humanity. The woman must have had strange and extraordinary powers because when she raised her hand the Awash River opened to leave a path wide enough for her people to cross. She led them to this strange land, and under her leadership, the Mohammedan Gallas tamed the cattle and lived on the land as cattle-raisers. They fought battles with the Tigre Christians on their borders. Most of the Gallas were warriors; they chose to return to the Awash, fighting any Christians they met en route. The early Galla settlers were of the Igu and Anna tribes. The Azabos of today (i.e., Mohoni, Machere, Chercher) are descendants of the Anna tribe, and the Rayas (Alamata, Kobo) are of the Igu tribe. Both tribes, however, prefer to call themselves Rayas. Gradually, as their love for fighting with the Tigre died away, the Tigre Christians were welcome to migrate. They inter-married, and it was not long before the Tigre culture predominated over that of the Gallas. The Tigres introduced Christianity and farming, and that is why most of the Azabos and Rayas are Christian farmers today.

The Rayas are able fighters and they love fighting. Before the Italian invasion of Ethiopia, they fought constantly with their neighbours, the Adals, and that was when they practiced the hideous work of testicle-gathering. A man practiced this, they say, just to prove he had killed so many Adals and rightly deserved the spoils, and for no other reason. They would blow their horns and six or seven thousand of them would gather ready to fight the Adals. Four thousand of them would return home while the other two or three thousand were left dead or dying in the wilderness without proper burial. The women would stay at home and cry, and often a mother lost both her husband and children. The older men now recall sadly how unreasonable the whole thing was. All this, they report, was due to their lack of education.

Unlike their Galla ancestors, the Rayas carry no swords, spears, or bows and arrows. They walk about unarmed, but most of them own rifles which they keep at home. They are easy to excite, and with but little influence they can be led to do good or evil. But they are a kind-hearted, generous people.

[1] In 1527, Ethiopia was over-run by the Muslim armies of Imam Ahmed Ibn Ibrahim el-Ghazi, nicknamed by Ethiopians "Gran" which means "left-handed," and popularly referred to as "Mohammed Gran" or "Mohammed the Left-handed."

With a more modern hunting arm, Ato Ghion returns with three partridges for dinner.

Girls do attend priests' schools!

With Korbata as our headquarters, we interviewed men and women in Machere, Igu, Basile, Baro, and various other villages. We tried to continue to Chercher but found the road too muddy. The Governor accompanied us on most of our visits to the various communities, and we found him to be a very helpful and cooperative person. Our work went on smoothly but for one item. Folk tales were simply unheard of! People who claimed they knew folk tales began reciting some sordid experiences they had witnessed during the Italian war, and that was all. The few stories we have collected were contributed by Amharas who had migrated there from Wollo and Gondar.

We delivered Amharic education pamphlets to priest schools in the area. The best of these schools, held in one of the buildings built by the Italians, is in Korbata. The house is almost in ruins, but with proper repair and a few additional school rooms it could accommodate the large number of school-age children in Mohoni. The natives wonder why they pay taxes for education when their children receive none. Indeed they have plans of their own. We were told that in Chercher the natives had raised Eth. $9,000.00 to start a school of their own. Such interest in education certainly deserves help and encouragement.[1]

One serious problem in Mohoni at the present is the rising death rate from some sickness we could not identify. It has spread widely, and whoever is smitten with it cannot last more than two days. Perhaps the help they need might be in the nature of a pest-control project.

Leaving many friends behind, we left Mohoni on August 11 for Alamata via Maichew. Our next step was to interview some persons in Alamata and Kobo and then proceed to Zobel and Rama. We completed our work in Alamata rather speedily and drove to the sub-region of Kobo. Here we were held up for three days because the Governor and the people were simply uncooperative, and we finally had to appeal to the regional Governor, before we could get anything done.

Finally, we rented some mules and proceeded to Zobel and Rama, about 30 and 50 miles east of Kobo respectively. Zobel and Rama, subregions in the province of Tigre, are places of historical interest. Mohammed the Left-Handed is said to have been born in Zobel, and the land was originally inhabited by Moslems. Emperor Yohannes (E.C. 1864-1881) introduced Christianity there, and the small population of Zobel alone (approximately 15,000) supports forty-four churches today. The people, mi-

[2] NOTE: The Ministry of Education sent a teacher to this area in October, 1958, shortly after receipt of this report.

"Time to Read," a school journal published by the Ethiopian—United States co-operative education program, is delivered to a rural school. The journal provides a stop-gap until textbooks are available.

grants from almost every part of the Empire, are one of the most religious in Ethiopia. The land, perched high up on the mountains, is rich with maize, sorghum, teff, and pepper. Small rivers run clear across the mountains and are full the year round.

Here, too, as in Mohoni, we found the same thirst for education. The natives of Zobel had raised money and had built a large thatch-roofed house for a school. But they lacked the teachers, and the house still stands waiting for its first teacher. The only means of transportation to Zobel and Rama is by horse or mule, and it would be excessively costly to open a Government school anywhere in that region. But it would be tremendously helpful if some of the graduates from the Debre Berhan Teacher Training School were to be sent there. The natives will certainly welcome all the help they can get.

Students at priest's school, a 4-year, traditional, rote-learning program which gives children a writing skill in Amharic and a reading skill sufficient to lead them through the biblical book of David.

The farmers in Zobel were terribly depressed because locusts were breeding in the area and they were certain they would lose their crops before any help reached them. We wondered why they could not telephone the Locust Control office in Addis Ababa from Kobo. Oh! No! Even Makale, the provincial capital, could not do that. Even they had to write to the Ministry of Interior in Addis Ababa! No wonder they were frightened. But why shouldn't a telephone call suffice for such an emergency? What is the difference between a fire-brigade and a locust control project? We could not answer that.

After completing our work in Zobel and Rama, we commenced our return trip and arrived in Addis Ababa, ending a very interesting three-weeks' visit to the land of the Rayas and Azabos.

FOOD AND EATING (Excerpts from three essays[1])

In this world of ours, every deed of men is differently handled from country to country and from nation to nation. Even among the members of the same family, the same things may be done differently depending upon the idea and interest of the individual. Now, in this case, let us consider the eating manners of Harrar people.

Harrar is a fairly large city—about 1-1/3 the size of the city of Gondar, or even more—populated with people of different cultural backgrounds, different religions, different languages, and different races. These people are the Amharas, the Kotus, the Aderis, the Somalis, and the Arabs. All these, except the Amharas, are Moslems.

All the Amharas, as far as I know, use a table-like thing called *gebeta* where the *injera* and *wett* are placed. The parents alone, by this I mean the elderly people, gather around and devour the food while the young children are given food only after the parents have finished eating. Nowadays this habit of giving food to the youngsters after the elderly people have finished is dying out. But the youngsters are still given food separately, even if their meal is served at the same time.

Among the Moslems, except the Somalis, the youngsters are fed first, and then the rest of the family eat. But in the case of the Somalis, it is different. All the males of the family, including the father, eat together; the rest of the family also eats together.

All these different groups of the city of Harrar may eat their food using their hands or some cutlery. The Kotus prefer to use their hands and wooden implements having religious background and tradition.

People outside the city have different ways of eating. Once I happened to go to the countryside about one hundred and eighty kilometers away from Harrar with a friend of mine to a small village called Bombas. It was supper time, and a big fire was made in the center of the village. To my great surprise, all the inhabitants of the village divided themselves into three big groups. All the elderly male population sat on one side of the fire, then the children gathered next in one place, and then all the women in one place. Guests are highly respected, and so we mixed with the elderly male group. Then from each house, meals were served to all the three groups, and, after a prayer, the groups happily ate their food, sitting in a circle around the fire.

[1] Authors' names withheld by request.

Any pause on a rural highway quickly attracts curious local residents who enjoy sharing canned and bottled refreshments from the capital with the travelers.

A traveler from Addis Ababa pauses to drink from a gourd in front of a round straw hut in rural Ethiopia.

I asked my friend why the people have this way of eating. He told me that the chief reason was that the people want to help each other; all the people are not equally wealthy, and the villagers want to help those who have nothing to eat by thus eating together and sharing equally what each family has.

I still remember the good morals of those peasants of the village of Bombas and consider their custom something wise and Godly. Every one of these people had all the basic food needed when it was all gathered from the different houses, and all were equally happy and healthy.

In my village, we often eat *injera* and *wett*, which is the favourite food throughout the whole of Ethiopia. The women put *injera* on the *mesobe*, a sort of dish made from grass, and bring *wett*. The older people eat alone. They gather around the *mesobe*, wash their hands, and start eating the *injera* and *wett* with their fingers.

When the older people have finished eating the small children give them water for their hands. The children then wash their hands and start eating the *injera* and *wett*. Since all of us like pepper so much, in each *wett* the women put pepper.

79

During holidays, the villagers prepare themselves a big bread, various kinds of *wett,* and *tella,* which is the famous beer-like drink of the Ethiopians, of which all Ethiopians are fond. Even some Europeans and some Americans drink it once in a while. First *tella* is given. The villagers cut the big bread into smaller pieces and give small pieces to individuals. They then prepare *injera* and *wett.* Since each *mesobe* will contain only enough *injera* for not more than six people, they sit in small groups around the *mesobes.* They also eat raw meat, since the people like it very much.

Unfortunately, in my village, we are not used to drinking milk; even the babies, most of them, lack milk. We do sometimes eat cabbage, but it is not easy to obtain citrus fruits since the parents never bother to buy oranges or lemons for their children.

*　　*　　*

The people in Sidamo live mainly on the food which is a product of the false banana. They call it *inset.* The whole work of extracting the food from this plant and making it into a sort of cake is carried out by the women. The plant usually is planted by the men. After planting, the men have nothing to do with it. When the plant is ready to give the food product, the women build shades in the vicinity of the plant they are to extract the food from and begin the work by cutting the whole plant, layer by layer. The food-bearing layers are those near the center at the bottom. It is considered shameful for any male to watch the women at their work during this time. After the food is extracted, it is buried for a few weeks, sometimes for months. After that, it is ready to be made into cakes and eaten.

The meal is prepared by putting the so-called cake into the fireplace itself, wrapped in a leaf of the false banana. The women, after preparing it, give most of the food or the whole of it to their husbands, and they do not have the right to eat a meal with the male members. They wait for what will be left after the male members have eaten. This food is not eaten alone; it is accompanied by milk. The people of Sidamo tend their cattle more carefully than anybody else in any part of Ethiopia. If a cow dies, the owner of the cow may cut off his little finger or his ear to show his sorrow, even though he may have 50 or more cows.

In some parts of this province, the main diet is meat; these people eat the product of the false banana in addition. Both the female and male members go to the market to buy their share of meat. Most of it is eaten raw on the way home.

In other parts of the province, the people specialize in barley, which they fry, make into a powder, then eat, mixing it with butter.

SYMBOLIC OBJECTS[1]

Shields and Spears: These are inherited by males from the paternal side of the family. They were the main weapons of Ethiopians for many generations, and even now they exist. Our grandfathers used them extensively for war or hunting animals. The shield is used to defend the body against any attack except bullets and the like. The spear is thrown against anything intended to be killed. When these are inherited, the fathers explain to their children all that has been done with them and when they were used. Especially the victories of war and surprise attacks are very carefully told to children in order that they will bear in mind the good history of the weapons and use them as their fathers used them. If by any chance the inheritors go to war, and they are about to be captured, they will not hand over the shield or the spear unless they die.

Sabres: The sabre is used in wars by the cavalry as well as the infantry army. The war coat usually issued to heroes is worn during the war. Both the war coat and the sabre are worn also in celebration of victory days. The war coat can be worn when using the spear and the shield. The sabre and the war coat are handed down to the next generation, usually to males.

Bows and Arrow: These are also important weapons of Ethiopian history. Our grandfathers were clever in painting the tips of the arrows with some kind of poison. The arrows are made with barbs or hooks so that when they are pulled out, they tear out some of the inner structure of the body. The spear also has such hooks.

Bracelets, Earrings, and Beads: These are handed down to male children. They are used as a sign that the fathers of children are heroes, usually for having killed a man or animal. The bracelet is put above the elbow joint or on the wrist, while the beads are put around the neck. As the name indicates, the earrings are put in the pierced earholes.

Skins of Lions and Tigers: To indicate that the father has killed a lion or tiger, and to record courage in hunting, the skin of a lion or tiger is dried and stretched on the wall where it can be seen as one first enters the room.

Other Property: Land, houses, or other property is inherited. This may be distributed by a written or an oral will.

[1] Authors' names withheld by request.

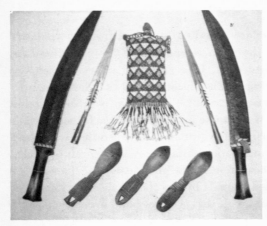

Somali lady's beaded eye-shadow cosmetic bottle is surrounded by Eritrian spear points, Amhara leather-sheathed daggers, and hand-carved wooden Somali spoons.

An elaborate horse-tail fly whisk, a handwritten parchment Bible with wood covers, and a priest's rattle. Bible, in Amharic, goes through the Book of David.

Genealogy Record: A child receives a fully written statement about the genealogy of the family from his father or grandfather. If some of his friends ask about his genealogy, he refers them to the written notice. When he gets new information, he adds it and thus becomes the genealogist of his generation. The genealogy record is also useful for marriage. If a man's family background is not good, he may not get a partner. Besides, it helps a person to guard against marrying someone from his own family or kinship group. The social customs are strict that one shall not marry his blood relations.

Especially among the Gallas, the child is ordered to memorize his genealogy as far back as needed. He will be asked by his friends, from time to time, to repeat it frequently. This makes him unlikely to forget. This teaches him what his past generations have done, their courage and heroic deeds.

Lion headdress, a symbol of courage and bravery, is worn by leader of a male dance group at a festival.

Priest on a visit to a rural home (gojo), outside with housewife and child.

III
Birth Customs
of
Ethiopia

The Garden of Eden, according to a pervasive popular myth in Ethiopia, bordered the lush shores of Lake Tana, source of the Blue Nile, major contributor of the waters that irrigate and bring life to the vast expanses of desert from Khartoum, where the Blue Nile meets the White Nile, up to Egypt where, at flood tide, Ethiopia's Blue Nile waters have been estimated to contribute 85% of the life-giving waters. Thence, the belief among Ethiopians that Ethiopia is the cradle of mankind. Small wonder, then, that birth of a child in Ethiopia is of major significance in the rites, rituals, and customs of this ancient country.

Among the various ethnic groups, customs related to birth vary exceedingly, but everywhere the event is of major significance, both social and religious. Following are some examples of birth customs, selected from numerous essays submitted by Ethiopian members of major and minor tribes. The criterion for selection and presentation herewith was that an essay described interesting differences in birth customs.

SOME CUSTOMS AND TRADITIONS OF THE
ETHIOPIAN CULTURE RELATING TO CHILDBIRTH[1]

Local Customs Affecting the Pre-Natal Period

Everyone likes to have children; therefore, a pregnant woman is considered as a normal woman. Most pregnant women are afraid to show or to say that they are pregnant; this is only for the sake of modesty and not for any superstitious reasons. However, the following things are believed, by Ethiopians, to affect the fetus or to make delivery difficult:

1. Seeing:

The pregnant woman shall not see bad things such as a malformed baby, a still-birth, or a black person, or other things which might frighten her. If she does see one of these things, it is believed that she will give birth to a child marked by the things which frightened her at the time of her pregnancy. Because of this belief, many pregnant women are very fond of seeing beautiful things, hearing pleasant news, and not thinking any very exciting thoughts. In order to give birth to a handsome or beautiful child, a pregnant woman hangs well-shaped goods in her house, and the wall of the house is painted with red and blue colors with a variety of fancy lines which are thought to give beauty to the fetus.

2. Smelling:

If the pregnant woman smells food being cooked, or smells *tej, tella,* or coffee being served, she must taste the food or drink she smelled; if she does not, it is believed that she will give birth to an abnormal child; birth marks are said to be due to this cause.

3. Food:

Almost all pregnant women like to eat foods which they were not accustomed to eat before their conception. Pregnant women often ask for food which is not available in the house. They do not ask for things easily found in the house. The husband or the family have to satisfy her needs if they expect her to give birth to a normal child; cleft palate and harelip are the chief resultant abnormalities.

4. Belt:

A pregnant woman shall not have a tight belt, because saddle nose in the infant is said to be caused by the pressure of the belt on the fetal nose.

5. Charms:

[1] Authors' names withheld by request.

Words written on paper, folded, and covered by leather, then usually hung on the pregnant woman's neck are believed to be a protective measure against the evil-eye. The evil-eye is capable of influencing abnormality in the fetus or making delivery very difficult. Copper plate (metal) is believed to be another prophylactic measure against the evil-eye.

6. Sun:

To be exposed to the sun at midday is said to cause serious illness to the expectant mother, or may cause an abortion.

7. Work:

A pregnant woman must work during her pregnancy; if she does not work, her baby (fetus) becomes very fat and difficult at delivery because the birth-canal may be too small for him. In the last month of pregnancy, certain kinds of foods are forbidden in order to avoid overweight of the fetus.

8. Intercourse:

In the first three or four months of pregnancy, intercourse is considered as essential for the complete development of the fetus. After the fourth month the mother may or may not have sexual intercourse until the seventh month, a matter of choice. The main reason for not having intercourse after the seventh month is because of fear of traumatic injury to the fetus.

At the Time of Delivery

In every area, there are women known as helpers during delivery. They are called helpers during delivery because their help is only at the time of delivery. They do not give any advice to a pregnant woman concerning health of diet, but they are called when the labor starts.

The delivery house has to be protected from sunshine or sun reflection.

In the delivery house, only females are allowed to enter; the midwife gives to the patient a medicine to drink; this medicine is prepared from plant root and leaves. The reason they give this medicine is to quicken delivery; to speed the contraction.

In addition, they give the patient a drink made out of flax seeds with the aim of lubricating the fetus; also, butter is put on the patient's head in order to keep her cool and fresh.

When labor pains start, all the women in the house untie their belts, and they bow down and pray. The praying is directed to Saint Mary because every woman believes that Saint Mary is the best obstetrician in the universe. The midwife massages the abdomen in between contractions and parts the patient's thighs during contraction.

If the delivery is difficult and long lasting, the trousers of the patient's husband will be tied around her in order that her husband's strength will help the bearing down. The necktie of the patient's mother is also said to help the bearing down.

If the labor is a foot presentation, the midwife closes the patient's thighs and raises the feet high up vertically; the back and head are on the bed or floor, only the feet and pelvis are raised up. She then shakes the patient, holding on to her ankles. This is done to let the foot of the fetus into the uterus, hoping it will come back with the normal presentation, which is the head. Meantime, the husband is called in and asked the customs of his ancestors; for example, if at his father's father's house it is the custom to slaughter any kind of animal; if so, he has to do likewise immediately. Manipulation is continued till the foot of the fetus disappears into the uterus. If it does so, they lower the feet of the patient and wait for the head to come; if the foot comes again, they continue the raising and shaking of the feet until the midwife herself is exhausted or the patient dies during the manipulations.

When live birth occurs, there is a thunder of joy; all the women in the house trill at the same time; seven times if the baby is a boy, and three times if a girl. The cord is cut; in some areas it is tied only on the fetal side, and in some areas without tying at all. The newborn is immediately bathed and then fed. When the placenta is delivered, it is buried anywhere outside around the house; formerly it used to be buried, if the baby were a boy, outside the house in the belief that the boy will be a hero and never be afraid outside the house. On the other hand, if the baby is a girl the placenta is buried inside the house; this keeps her always inside the house and, therefore, a good household wife. (Among some groups, the opposite is true, for different reasons.)

If there arises any difficulty in the delivery of the placenta, the following treatments are applied by the local midwife:

a) The midwife carries the patient on her back and jumps up and down rapidly and violently.

b) She, the midwife, gives the patient some things to grasp tightly (e.g., a Maria Theresa dollar was formerly commonly used).

c) The patient is made to sit on a collection of various plant leaves.

d) A plant juice is given the patient to drink.

e) The midwife inserts into the patient's throat her finger, or any smoothly shaped wooden object, in order to stimulate the patient's vomiting reflex, thus helping the bearing down.

f) In rare cases, the cord is pulled.

Following delivery, food is immediately offered to the mother; the food is called Genfo; it is a porridge-like substance made out of *tej* with lots of butter in it. All the women are invited to eat also. Except water, all kinds of drink are given to the mother, including alcoholic liquors; water is believed to cause abdominal cramps at that particular time.

On the morning of the third day, the mother goes out in the morning sun with the baby for a short time; this morning sun is believed to brighten the baby's eyes. The same day, the mother has a bath inside the house. On the seventh day, another bath is given to the mother, and she is allowed to start work; she can go anywhere after the twelfth day of her delivery.

The dried tail of the umbilical cord is put in cow's dung and plastered with this dung on the outerside of the door. In some places, it is hung on the baby's neck. Both customs are believed to protect the baby from a particular kind of evil-eye.

If birth is given to a dead child, there is some degree of sorrow, but no great grief. The baby is buried outside the house within the front yard, and no funeral ceremony is held.

If the newborn does not cry spontaneously, it is considered as a still-birth; the attendants do not give any help to stimulate the breathing, but they wait for some minutes hoping breathing or crying will start spontaneously.

Post-Natal Period

Compliments and admiration are paid by friends and parents. The mother keeps the newborn protected from the sun. The child is also protected from the eyes of strangers, especially if they are handsome or beautiful, because of the danger that they may have the evil-eye.

Feeding

There are no scheduled feeding times. The child is free to suck whenever he or she wants to suck; in addition, he is permitted to suck whenever he is frightened or in pain. To let the child suck the breast of another woman is not socially acceptable, except in cases where the mother dies during the early infancy of the child.[2]

---

[2] An infant suckled by another woman becomes a kin of all that woman's kinship group, acquiring, for example, all prohibitions against marriage with the kinship group.

Cow's milk, butter, and *abish,* (a mustard like substance) if available, are given to the child liberally. As the child grows up, *wett* and *injera,* in addition to breast milk, are fed by the mother till he has learned to eat by himself; then no more breast milk is given. If the child cries, seeking the breast, the mother puts a very sour plant juice on her nipples and then allows the child to suck, after which he will never attempt to feed on the nipples again.

As the child grows older, he is taught to walk, to talk, and to wear clothes. This is the beginning of his social growth. Many artificial methods are used to help the child's physical growth; these include the following:

a) At the age of seven days, the uvula is cut; if it is not cut, it is believed to cause difficulties later in adult life, especially when infection causes it to swell and close the nose and throat.

b) Circumcision is performed at the age of seven to fourteen days. This is important from the sociological and psychological point of view, because an uncircumcized child is not accepted by his friends; he cannot play with other children, because they laugh at him. Because of this reason, children remain isolated due to inferiority complexes produced by the circumcision traditions. An uncircumcized girl is believed to be sexually hypersensitive, and this in turn may cause her to remain unmarried; in some areas this is a tragedy.

c) Tattooing on the neck, forehead, and arms of females and on the gums of males is done to add beauty, and, therefore, to make one more socially admirable.

Parents are responsible for teaching the child morality; the most important of these teachings are the following: courage, obedience, truth, hospitality, sexual relationships, preservation.

Courage:
The father is primarily responsible for development of this trait. He takes his son with him out to hunt animals, teaches him rifle shooting and many other games which require courage and determination. Even the mother is responsible for teaching the child when the father is away or dead.

Here is a good example of a method used by a well known woman in correcting her son regarding courage: Her son was always very afraid to go out of the house after sunset. To correct this, the mother tied the boy against a tree and left him outside the house for the whole night. After this punishment, the boy never again was afraid to go out in darkness; at least, he never showed his fears. And later he became one of the distinguished heroes of the community.

Obedience:

Every child has to learn to obey and respect elders; often a child is severely rejected by his elders and companions for disobedience to elders.

Truth:

Honesty is very important for the child's social growth. A dishonest person's word is not heard by the society. No matter how important the speech or request he has to make, his words fall on deaf ears; or on no ears at all. This is important for technical advisers to know in order to avoid false or uncertain promises to any given community.

Hospitality:

Receiving people with joy and offering them something to drink, then to accompany them halfway back to their homes when they come to visit friends, are important social techniques.

Sexual Relationships:

To discuss sex in front of children is strictly forbidden. The child is told not to play with her or his genitalia, to keep them covered, and not to name them. Other than this, the child learns sexual behavior by observing the elders.

Preservation:

This helps the child to shape his mental life; the child is taught to believe what adults believe, to fear what adults fear, and to accept adult standards of correct relationships with others.

A custom of one community may not be known to other Ethiopian communities. Therefore, some of the customs mentioned here may be local; their mention does not mean that they are known all over the country of Ethiopia.

BIRTH CUSTOMS OF THE AMHARAS OF SHOA[1]
Terrefe Ras-work

When the ninth month of a pregnant woman arrives, she starts preparations for the foreseen occasion. The important item to be prepared is materials for porridge. Porridge for such occasions is usually made of flour from peas, wheat, maize, and barley, the latter being in the largest proportion. Further, the mother-to-be sees to it that her home is in good order and properly provided with the necessary materials, in particular food.

Five or six days before the expected date, the woman takes a purgative to clean her bowels. And if she has her parents nearby, and especially if it is her first time to give birth, she goes to them or the mother comes to her daughter's house to assist her during and after the labour.

When the woman feels her first pain she warns the people with her that the baby is about to arrive, and they call for a woman who is skilled in midwifery. The midwife examines the woman and rubs her belly with butter. She makes her sit on a smooth stone, which has been smeared with butter. Rags or sheep skin are put around the stone for use when the baby is born. One woman is then told to hold the patient by the shoulders, another by the knees, and a third by the waist.

At this time virgins and barren women are requested to leave the room, for, since they have never given birth to a child, it is feared that they may be alarmed at the labour. If there is a man in the house he is told to loosen his belt; all the women, too, loosen theirs so as to have no tightened person around lest he or she influence the body of the patient. Then all the persons who are not holding the woman pray together, saying: "Mary, Mary." Those who are holding the patient pray that the Virgin Mary may come to her.

When they see that the suffering is quite prolonged, they ask a priest to pray over some water by reading or reciting a text of St. Raphael. This water will then be given her to drink. Others take a pair of trousers of the husband and put them on the roof of the house. If the suffering is still going on, they wash the knees of the husband and give the patient the water to drink: all these things are done in the hope that the suffering will be diminished. When finally the baby is delivered and utters its first cry, the women express their

[1] Reproduced from the University College Ethnological Society Bulletin No. 7, December, 1957.

joy with a shout. It is said that the baby cries because an angel makes it taste soil, showing it that it is to die some day. Right away they check whether the baby is male or female, and if the men hear that it is a boy, they fire their rifles seven times, but if a girl, only two or three times, which shows their preference for a boy.

As soon as the mother delivers the baby, she usually faints due to the excessive pain she has undergone, so the people around call her repeatedly by her Christian name and sprinkle a mixture of milk and water over her face until she becomes conscious. If they see that she does not respond, then someone goes up on the roof of the house, and, removing some of the thatch, calls her by her Christian name. Then, standing on the roof, he cracks a large whip, and, again, repeatedly shouts her name until she finally becomes conscious and replies. The person goes up on the roof to call the fainted patient because it is found that usually they answer people who are calling from above rather than from beside them.

The midwife gives to the baby's head, nose, and roof of mouth their proper forms. She raises the palate, using yeast, a practice which seems to have been intended to have the baby taste food on its very birthday. And on the same day also, they make it swallow *koso*, a purgative, with butter to clean its bowels.

It is interesting to note that the afterbirth has special burial places, depending on the sex of the baby. If the baby is male, it is buried inside the house to the right of the door, signifying that the baby will remain home when grown, but, if female, it is buried outside and to the left which indicates her future, namely going out of the family to establish another home in marriage.

Once the baby has been delivered, some of the women get busy preparing the birthday porridge to which all those who have assisted during the birth and those who have been around are joyously invited. While the elders are thus happily consuming the hot porridge with pepper and butter, the new-born baby is fed with fresh butter and the mother is made to drink a soup of flax-seed with honey. When visitors come into the house, they congratulate the mother saying: "Congratulations that Mary saved you." Then either the mother or the people who are inside answer him: "May St. Mary keep you." When people take their leave, they wish the mother as follows: "May the Virgin Mary warm your thighs; forget the pangs of labour, pick up the baby." It should be noted that visitors cannot see the mother unless they are close friends or relatives because a curtain is placed all along the mother's bed precisely to hide the mother and the child from the eyes of some visitors.

Close friends and relatives bring some form of gift when they pay a visit to a woman who has just given birth to a child. The common forms of gifts are a cow with her calf, a sheep, cooked chicken, or the typical big loaf of bread, the most common gift.

The baby is fed only with fresh butter for the first three days, after which it is allowed to suckle its mother's breasts. The child keeps on feeding on the fresh butter for a number of months. The suckling of the breasts usually lasts until the mother is two or three months pregnant again, which may be as long as one, two, or three years. Parents prefer not to give proper names until the baby is six months old for fear of its death; they call a boy Mammo and a girl Mamite which are more exactly common nouns than proper nouns. Also, the baby usually is not dressed in white clothes until one year old, again for fear of death.

The child is bathed daily and is rubbed with butter to strengthen its body. Finely ground clay or burnt dung of cattle is spread in the arm-pits and in between the thighs to prevent chafing. The mother takes a bath every third day, and on her first bathing all those who have assisted during her labour are invited to eat porridge and drink beer.

On the seventh day for girls or on the eighth for boys, after birth, the ceremony of circumcision takes place. It is usually done early in the morning, by a practitioner of either sex, who has the baby held tightly by someone, and then cuts off the foreskin of the organ. Again on this occasion, porridge is served for all those who have assisted during the childbirth. After the circumcision, people who have had a sexual act within the preceding 24 hours are forbidden to enter the house where the baby lies until the wound is cured lest their presence should lengthen the duration of the wound.

It is strongly recommended by the elders, and in fact carefully observed by mothers, that the baby should never be left alone, awake or asleep, until it is baptized; and metal articles especially of iron should be placed at all times beside it. As for the mother, until she goes "outside," she should never be left alone; and until she has the baby baptized she should always have some piece of iron with her; usually she carries an awl stuck in her hair while working. The above precautions are taken for fear either the mother or the baby will be attacked by evil spirits; iron and steel are believed to repel evil spirits.

On the fifteenth or twentieth day, the ceremony of "going outside" is held. The mother bathes herself and the baby and, wearing clean clothes, prepares to take her baby outside the house for the first time. This is also the first time for the mother to go out during the day since her confinement. When it is about nine or ten o'clock in the morning, a male person, either boy or man, goes in front of the mother, who is carrying her child in her arms as they go out of the house. The person who goes in front of the mother has to hold a sword or a knife in his hands in order to chase away evil spirits.

Then the mother sits down in the sunlight and joyously smears butter on the heads of all those who followed her out. After sitting in the sun for a few minutes, she goes back into the house, and all those present are invited to a feast of porridge. From this day on, the mother is able to resume her household routine; usually she slowly starts working, as the number of her attendants, such as her mother and sisters, gradually diminishes.

After a mother has given birth to a child, she and her house are considered to be unclean. For instance, the people who have assisted during the delivery are not allowed to enter a church unless they are sprinkled with holy water by a priest. In fact, if the house of the mother is not sprinkled with holy water, all those who enter that house, even as visitors, are considered to be too unclean to go into holy places. The rule is still more strict on those who touched blood during the delivery of the baby and, of course, on the mother. They are not allowed to go to holy places until the child is baptized. This rule has its origins in the Old Testament, Leviticus Chapter 12, 2-5, where it is written: "If a woman have conceived seed, and born a man child: then she shall be unclean. . . ." Some modifications seem to have been made on this rule concerning women who give birth, but that the prevailing custom is based on it is obvious. Thus the house of such a woman is sprinkled as soon as possible with holy water so that visitors may go into the house to visit her; for, otherwise, they salute her from the door and retreat if they know that the house is unclean.

After the ceremony of "going outside" the family prepares for the baptism when a relatively large banquet is to be given in honour of the occasion. Boys are baptized when they are forty days old and girls are baptized when they are eighty days old.

Some sayings connected with birth:

When a person is unusually slow in leaving his house when intending to go out, it is said that his afterbirth is buried in that house.

Death brags: "If I don't take you at the delivery of the child, I shall take you at the delivery of the afterbirth."

"A pregnant woman desires everything."

"Perhaps so and so has not tasted butter on his birthday, and that is why he is loud talking."

BIRTH CUSTOMS IN JIMMA[1]
Awai Adem

Birth customs among the Jimma-Galla are carried out with rigid and solemn ceremony. The violation of these customs is considered as a direct insult of that which the community considers sacred. In fact, birth customs in Jimma are observed with the same solemnity as marriage and Zari ceremonies. (Zari is a general term used for naming all the invisible spirits who are believed to have the power of bringing good or evil to those who are possessed by them.)

If the pregnant woman is giving birth for the first time and if her parents are alive, she goes to her parents' home a week or so before the baby is due. If the mother-to-be is without parents or is bearing her second child, she gives birth in her own (her husband's) home. Barley, wheat, butter, pepper, spices and other necessary things are bought beforehand. A week or so before the child is born, two experts in midwifery, usually old women, are called to offer their assistance. In most cases these women are paid in cash for their services. On the day of the great occasion, the future mother does not use a bed, but gives birth to her baby on ground specially prepared for this occasion.

Usually before giving birth to the child, the mother suffers very much. When the husband or her parents perceive this suffering, they send for her relatives and for the women neighbors. As soon as the child is born, if it happens to be male, the gathered women shout "illil-illil-ill" five times. If it happens to be a female, they shout it only three times.

At the same time, one of the two midwives takes care of the mother. As soon as the child sees light, she takes hold of the mother and ties her stomach tightly and gives her the necessary cleaning. Then she gives her a glass of lukewarm butter mixed with pounded flax-seeds to drink. This is done to clean the inner organs of any filth remaining within.

Meanwhile, the other midwife takes the child, washes it, and cuts the umbilical cord. Sometimes she uses the blood from the cord to paint the gums of the baby. That is why, they say, the people of this region have more or less pink gums. Then she shapes the baby's head and gives the infant a special kind of raw butter to lick. Finally she puts it to sleep.

---

[1] Reproduced from the University College Ethnological Society Bulletin No. 7, December, 1957.

Then the visitors come and pronounce the usual phrase, "We are glad you are successful." The female visitors are given some porridge, butter, and cheese to eat, but the male visitors leave the room immediately after pronouncing the usual phrase. In some families, especially in wealthy ones, the neighbouring males gather in another room and recite some verses from the Koran or any other Islamic religious books. In the case of the poor, this is impossible because the house usually has only one room. Every woman who comes in eats before leaving. Even if she does not feel like it, she has to taste a little bit for the sake of formality. So ends the first day. If the child is born late in the night, the visitors come the next morning.

For five days nothing special takes place. On the fifth day a different custom is observed with such piety that it can be considered a religious ritual. An animal (sheep or goat) is killed. The spirit Mare, one of the Zari that helps women when they are pregnant and when they give birth, is very much praised. A special kind of coffee toasted with butter is prepared. (The coffee bean itself is toasted with butter and is eaten with a spoon as roasted meat.)

This day is known by the name of "Medicine-Cutting Day." The female relatives and neighbours go out to the woods to cut branches of special trees and herbs. The herbs are often found in the garden behind the house. If the new-born is male, a boy is sent to fetch a kettle-full of water from the spring. If it is female, a girl performs this task.

On their way to the forest and back, the "Medicine-Cutters" sing a special song dedicated to the spirit Mare or Marami. The direct translation of some of it runs as follows in English.

Marami is kind—why should we be bored of begging her?
Oh Mare, Oh Marami, eternal Mistress of the have-nots, have pity.
Mare is better, Marami is better. [2]

What did the cat sacrifice for thee that begets eight?
What did the sterile do that walks in continuous tears?

Oh Mare, grandest child of powerful nature,
Come and witness the great dance held in your favour.

[2] This line is repeated by the chorus after each couplet.

Oh Marami, ever shining sun of the sky.
Oh Marami, the mistress that can take captive elephants home.

Tell me the way that leads to the house of the new-born.
Let me take hot milk for it.

The sterile when I called upon her told me thus:
"Do not go behind my house nor touch my gardens."

A small loaf is better than a big, broken one;
Begetting a female is better than no baby at all.

Oh, Mare, take me to your favour.
Say: "You sterile, beget a baby and suckle it."

Oh, Mare, Sille! Sille![3] A warrior is not bored of fight.
How can women giving birth be annoyed at their pain?

River Goje is praised for its strength and Mare for pain;
I did not experience the pain; for I am sterile, but from the fertile I heard.

Her bedroom is green grass, her child like a green frog.
She says to us: "Do not go to my bedroom nor look at my child."

The husband hates the sterile—she lacks perfume, makes bad broth;
The sterile is looked down upon by relatives—she discontinues the race.

Wallensu when broken becomes double;
Oh, fertile woman, why not offer babies to the sterile?

The mother of five, her death is observed as if she died in the palace;
Thousands will accompany her coffin and hundreds carry her to the grave.

On the other hand, who likes the unfortunate sterile?
Her death is as if in woods and slaves accompany her to her rest.

[3] *Sille:* exclamation of joy.

On their way these singing women prevent any male from passing them; sometimes the men pass by making a pecuniary offering. When the "Medicine-Cutters" come back singing, other women try to prevent them from entering by poking them with spear-like sticks. The "Medicine-Cutters" are permitted in only when they give the women the money (if any) they have received. With this money drinks are bought. On this day, as mentioned above, a sheep or a goat is killed. The local drink is also prepared. All the "medicine," branches of woods and herbs, is given to sterile women to prepare; the others gather and enjoy a heavy lunch. Intoxicating drinks are used only in the less pious families. The sterile women boil all the branches and the herbs together. Then with this water they bathe the mother and the baby—singing and dancing while doing so. This duty is given to the sterile so that Marami (the spirit of birth) may favour them. The remaining wood and herbs are put above the bed of the mother for a few days.

After the heavy lunch is over, the eldest of the visitors thanks the housewife in the name of all present and prays God to strengthen the child and make the baby robust. Then a special song for the occasion is chanted, which means "bear child again." Other folk songs are sung to the beat of the drum. The women sing and dance until the sun sets, and then they go to their homes. If the woman has borne her child in her parents' home, all the expenses of the fifth day are paid by her parents. In this case, a big feast is then prepared by the husband at his father-in-law's on the seventh day. An ordinary husband buys a sheep and prepares drinks. To this feast the same women that came on the fifth day are invited. The same order of singing and dancing as on the fifth day is carried out, but on the seventh day there is no "Medicine-Cutting."

The next important day is the tenth day. This day is called by an Arabic word meaning *purifying*. On this day, a learned Moslem, after reciting some verses from the Koran, washes both hands of the mother. After this day she can eat with her own hands whereas previously somebody fed her meals.

At the end of the fifth day and sometimes at the end of the tenth, the women (neighbours and relatives) talk among themselves to decide their order for taking turns bringing food and drink to the house of the new-born to entertain the parents every morning. This custom, so rigidly observed, is thoroughly enjoyed by the husband! The women extend their morning visits with food and drink up to 40 days, each taking her turn.

The fortieth day is the last and the grandest. New dresses are bought for the mother and baby by the husband or by his father-in-law. On this day, if the mother has been at her parents' home, she returns to her own. On entering the gate of her husband's house she passes over blood of a sheep killed by her husband for the occasion. Then she takes the baby in both hands and goes around the house which is clouded by smoke of frankincense and baddessa (a kind of wood). As she goes around her home, one of her husband's relatives (usually her mother-in-law) puts butter on her head. Each woman accompanying her looks at the child and says: "May you be preserved from evil eyes." Then the circumcision ceremony takes place if the child is a male.

On the fortieth day a few guests (always female) are expected. On the forty-first day, if the baby is male, several women are expected. The male baby is circumcised on the 40th or 41st day from his birth. Females are circumcised when they are seven years old.

On the day of circumcision the two male god-parents are asked. (If the baby is female, females are asked to be god-parents.) The god-parents are the most intimate friends of the father or mother of the child. On this day, they bring money to the parents. If they are wealthy, they bring the child no less than 100 dollars each. As the operation takes place one god-parent holds the baby to his bosom, the other closes the baby's eyes, thus easing matters for the expert operator. Near the place of circumcision a hen or sheep is killed to drench the earth with more blood.

So end the birth customs among the Jimma-Galla.

FROM BIRTH TO BAPTISM IN ERITREA[1]

Birth practices are almost the same among all the Christian people of Eritrea.

The pregnant woman knows the approximate day of delivery; therefore, she will not travel for long distances when the day of delivery approaches. But she prepares for herself food and material such as butter, honey, eggs, flour, etc.

Delivery usually takes place in a room in which there is a little dark near so that the baby and the mother will not face the rays of the sun, and thus risk pneumonia. This isolation in semi-darkness lasts for one week in the case of males and two weeks in the case of females.

[1] Author's name withheld by request.

During delivery most probably the next door neighbor woman will nurse her; if she is able to act as midwife she does so; if not, she may call for help from another woman but she will nurse the mother as far as possible. Immediately after the afterbirth is discharged, they bury it under ground. Then a woman who has a good voice shouts joyfully "Elill, Elill" to express happiness and gladness. If the baby is a male she shouts seven times; if it is a female, three times. After this, everybody who hears the shouting comes to congratulate the father and mother saying, "Let God be praised, and let the mother be strong and healthy, and let her child grow and be blessed"; there is a very poetic expression for the congratulation in the Eritrean language (Tigrigna).

The next day, porridge is prepared and served for all neighbor women. On the third day, maize mixed with some grain and boiled with water is distributed to all houses of the village; this is to let people know that the woman has a child and to bring blessings to the child.

On the seventh day, a group of women, five or six in number, early in the morning go to the river taking some clothes of the mother and the baby to wash; while they are coming back home, they sing and dance. Various drinks and foods are offered to them. On the eighth day, the baby is circumcised as is ordered in the Bible (Lev. 12:1). The mother does not go to the church until baptism of the baby.

In the case of a male, baptism is 40 days after birth. In the case of a female, baptism is 80 days after birth. During baptism, the mother, dressed well and ornamented, goes to the church. After certain prayers, the priest dips the baby three times saying "I baptise you in the name of the Father and the Son and the Holy Ghost"; and he then names the baby. Now the baby takes its first Holy Communion.

After the church service, the father and mother of the baby invite people, especially priests, to their home and offer various drinks and foods. Nearest friends and relatives offer many gifts such as drinks, clothes, even cows, sheep, etc., in honor of the baby. Thus passes the feast, joyfully and happily.

The elders of a village assemble as a court to hear a woman's plea for divorce.

IV
Courtship
and
Marriage

Mating customs, both civil and religious, vary not only from tribe to tribe but also within ethnic groups, particularly if sub-groups within a tribe are geographically separated. In general, marriages are between families rather than between individuals.

Among the Amharas of today, most girls do not marry until they are twelve or thirteen, although they may be betrothed two or three years earlier. Among those ethnic groups which practice child marriage, consummation occurs only after pubescence. The "bride" may live in the home of her "husband" to be trained by her mother-in-law who protects her and treats her as a daughter of the family.

Among some poor families, the boy may live with, and work for, the parents of his betrothed for several years prior to the girl's pubescence, at which time a marriage ceremony is performed.

Marriage "by capture," still recognized as valid, rarely occurs today. Traditionally, a suitor and some male friends abduct a girl whose father has rejected his suit. Occasionally, such marriages may be quietly arranged by both families as an honorable way of consummating a marriage without having to bear the considerable expenses of betrothal and wedding feasts.

Regardless of ethnic group, modern Ethiopian boys and girls who acquire education beyond the elementary level tend to delay marriage until the late teens or the twenties.

BETROTHAL AMONG THE SHOAN AMHARAS[1]
Abebe Ambatchew

The crowning happiness for a Shoan Amhara is to see his child or children married. Because of this, the parents and the nearest relatives of a young man take great pains, before betrothal, to choose a wife for him. The upbringing and parentage of a girl are the two major criteria for selection. Beauty, as such, is of relatively little importance.

A young man's parents, relatives, and other friends pick, at first, two, three, or five girls from among families they know. Out of the chosen girls, the one who belongs to a family of a good lineage, reputation, and wealth is finally selected. In other words, her family must own land, must be known to be kind and respectable, and, above all, must not be smiths, potters, or tanners.[2]

The chosen girl, for her part, is expected to be properly trained in cooking, washing, and making injere (bread), tella (beer), and tej (wine). It is also a point in her favour if she can milk the cows and keep the house tidy. The age considered as proper for betrothal varies from region to region. Usually, it is between seven and fourteen years.

The parents of the young man try to obtain as much information as possible about the girl's conduct before they propose a betrothal. To achieve this, they will send a person with some petty excuse to call upon the girl's parents and, thus, to study the girl and her family life.

The girl, on betrothal day and afterwards, is supposed to be unaware of what is happening. That is, she is not officially informed. Between the time of betrothal and marriage, she is given instructions in house-keeping, cleaning, and making different kinds of wett (sauce or stew). She is most strictly controlled to prevent her having contacts with men other than relatives. This is so as to maintain her virginity and safeguard her against a refused rival who might attempt to abduct her. It is also said that more care is taken to keep her in good health and appearance. For instance, she does no hard work such as carrying water, grinding cereals, or grinding hops. The elderly

[1] Abridged and reproduced with permission of the Ethnological Society of the University College, from Bulletin No. 5, June 1956.

[2] An Ethiopian legend tells of an incident which occurred as Makeda, Queen of Saba (Sheba), was returning from her visit to King Solomon. A band of demons followed the caravan and, one dark night, they abducted and seduced several of the ladies of the entourage. From these unholy unions, were born the first smith, potter, and tanner. All descendants of these craftsmen have the evil eye, and some of them, especially ironworkers, can turn themselves into hyenas at night.—Ed.

women also, indirectly, give her warnings on life after marriage. If a girl for example, neglects stirring wett which is being prepared, the elderly women would scoldingly say: "Why don't you stir it? Don't you know that one day you will be married? Are you going to give your husband badly cooked wett? Never think life would be as simple and comfortable as in your father's home. Besides, husbands do not usually hesitate to give a good, hard beating to a wife as careless as you!"

Very rarely, a contract might be broken. If this happens it is considered as an unpardonable insult. To illustrate, if the contract is broken by the young man's parents, the girl's parents demand, through the group of elders, what degrading qualities have been observed in their family. If they consider the reasons insufficient, they ask for compensation for the money spent in preparing food and drink. They, on their part, return the gifts presented and the marriage payment.

In general, the breaking of a contract creates a lasting and deadly enmity between the two families.

The parents, after making sure that the girl would make a suitable wife, choose three to five elderly men who will go to the girl's parents to propose the betrothal. These men are respected by and acquainted with both families.

A priest is usually included in the group and if one or more of them is a man of higher rank, or more respected than the two families concerned, the task of the group is greatly facilitated. One of the men is chosen as the head of the group, and he serves as the spokesman when the proposition is made. After all the men of the group have been carefully selected, the father calls them together and humbly informs them of intention. A date is then fixed to visit the girl's parents and make the request.

The elderly men go to the girl's home and start a normal conversation for a few minutes. Then, suddenly, all of them stand up. The girl's father acts as if he were bewildered, even if he foresees why they have stood up, and insistently asks them to sit down and explain why they have come. But the delegation refuses to sit down until the father knows fully of their mission.

The spokesman goes forward a little and first points out that the main objective of their mission is to strengthen the ties of friendship between the two families. In addition, he politely speaks of the heavy task assigned to the group and of their confidence in obtaining a favourable reply. The other members, also, now and then add their weight to the task of convincing the father. Lastly, the proposal is made.

The father acts as if he were disappointed, but he politely tells them that he cannot give an immediate consent or answer. He gives the excuse that he will consult the mother and relatives of the girl and invites the men to come back after a week or two. They thank him and leave.

On the next visit, too, the delegation stands and waits for a reply. The father, with one of his selected friends or relatives, asks why they have come. They repeat their request. The father complains that either the mother, brother, or an aunt has disapproved of the proposal, but he informs them that he does not want to disappoint so distinguished a group. So he asks who among the group would be responsible for the girl's welfare afterwards. The man is named, and the father promises to think over the matter again. A day is, apparently grudgingly, fixed for the return of the elders. Later, between the second and third visits, a messenger is sent to inform the bridegroom's parents as to how many people should form the escort. The third visit is the day on which the actual betrothal takes place.

The young man, his father, the elders, and selected friends go to the girl's home, on horseback usually. When they near the bride's home, they slow down. At the gate or entrance, they wait until they are told to go in. But they are not immediately invited to enter, and may have to wait for an hour or more. Meanwhile, servants come in and go out and there is much universal commotion. Then either servants or relatives come and take the horses and ask them to enter.

The group of elders leads the solemn procession; next come the bridegroom's father and friends, and, in their centre, the bridegroom. No woman is included in this procession.

Before eating and drinking or feasting, there is a discussion about the contract. The girl's brother, an uncle, or any elderly gentleman opens this discussion by asking, for the third time, the actual reason that this bond of marriage was proposed. The head of the group of elders, who has promised to take care of the girl as a father, stands and repeats the idea of forming a stronger relation between the two families. Then he makes a speech in order to convince the girl's parents of their daughter's welfare and of the advantages of the marriage. He is then asked what marriage payment his side has brought.

Usually, the bridegroom presents a dress and shemma of good quality to the bride's mother. If, however, the bridegroom cannot afford to make this present, he gives a guarantee and promises to pay later on. The father is given a shemma, a pair of trousers, and a shirt. A dress, a shemma, a shawl for the head, and decorations for the neck and ankles are the normal items comprising the marriage payment to the bride. The two fathers then publicly announce the presents they will give in order to enable the young couple to possess the basic essentials of a home and the means of starting married life.

The presents from the bride's father to the groom are excluded from the contract.

The next step is the writing down of the marriage contract. For a couple who are married for the first time, the contract is based on equal ownership between the couple of implements, animals, land; in a word, most of the wealth of the man. Thus, in conformity to this rule, most of the things that belong to the bridegroom are written down in the contract. The husband can, however, exclude some property, such as land, on the excuse that he has to support an old mother or father. Household utensils, even knives and glasses, are accordingly noted down in the marriage contract. Accurate locations and descriptions of land possessed by the man or to be presented to him on his wedding day are also included in the contract. The names of all the important witnesses present and the name of the family arbitrator and of the bride's new guardian are written down. The contract is duly signed with the prints of their right thumbs or their signatures. The signatures or prints are taken in the name of the Emperor.

The following is the translation of a marriage contract which happens to be that of the author's mother and father:

"When I, Negadiras Dehine, take Ato Adigeh Gobaw's daughter, Mamite Adigeh as wife to my son Amibacew Dehine, I provide the following amount of money and land as their starting means of subsistence:

Five gashas of land:

I. Three gashas at Ada Dalotta

II. Two gashas in Yifirata.

I, also, add five other gashas in the province of Arussi in the region found near Kebid Tig.

I give five pairs of oxen, five cows, three male horses, two stud donkeys, thirty sheep and goats, two mules for riding, one stallion with its riding equipment, three mules and two donkeys for transport with their equipment, and one of the three houses which is found in Arada near Weizero Zerifesewal's property when going down the big road that leads to Mohamed Ali's home. The house with its second room is, for the time being, rented for twenty dollars per month. A monthly salary of thirty dollars from the government, five carpets, decorated pillows for the right and left sides, a kettle and basin, thirty glasses and drinking bottles, twenty horn glasses and fifty knives are, in all, given as common property to both of them.

For the effective execution of the agreement in this contract, Ato Arimide, the gentleman who works with land-engineers, is the chief family judge. The witnesses are: chief priest of St. Rafael's Church, merchant, priest."

WEDDING CUSTOMS AMONG AMHARAS[1]
Kifle Wodajo

The following is an account of the marriage customs as practised among Amharas of Shoa in the past, and in the greater part of Shoa at present. The customs described are typical of the Amharas, and the reporter has discounted the European customs now being introduced in some parts of Shoa, particularly in Addis Ababa.

There are two kinds of marriage practised among the Amharas. The first one is marriage through the church. The bride and the bridegroom receive Communion at their wedding. The second marriage can be called "marriage outside the church." The girl and the boy, with the consent and the arrangement of their parents, can be married without going to the church.

The first kind of marriage is practised among the clergy and the very religious Ethiopians. In this case divorce is not permitted either to the husband or the wife. Even on grounds of adultery, the church rarely advises separation. The husband or the wife who has accepted this kind of marriage can marry again if one partner dies. From the second type of marriage, which is family arranged, divorce is easy. The wife or husband can get a divorce merely by negotiating through the family. If the two members of the party accept, as they say, "to tear the bond of marriage," the marriage henceforth becomes invalid and neither party has any further claim. Both the man and the woman have the customary right to marry again. But if the husband or the wife refuses to break the marriage bond, either can ask the court to grant a divorce. The court has not the right to refuse the divorce, but can decide who is guilty. If the court finds the wife guilty, it can deny the wife's claim to one half of her husband's property, or if the husband is found guilty, the court forces him to give the wife her share of the property.

Whichever type of marriage it is, we can safely sat that marriage among the Amharas is wholly a family affair, and that love marriages are rare. When the girl reaches the age of about twelve to fourteen, the female relatives advise the mother that the girl has reached the age of puberty, and

---

[1] Abridged and reproduced with permission of the Ethnological Society of University College of Addis Ababa, Bulletin No. 2, December, 1953.

suggest that they should find her a good husband. On the other hand, the boy's relatives, when he is seventeen to twenty-three years old, advise the father that before the boy is taken by the wonder of the world they should find him a life-time companion. So the father asks his relatives for prospective wives for his son and chooses one from among the many his relatives suggest. His choice in many cases is based upon the good reputation of the girl's family. The questions the father asks the suggester are whether she is from a Christian family, whether her mother is a good cook, and whether the girl has inherited her father's and her mother's good qualities.

If the answers are favorable, the father of the boy sends some three or four old men to act as intermediaries, asking the girl's parents to give their daughter to his son in marriage. The girl's parents talk over the matter with the rest of their relatives; if they approve of the prospective husband, they will contact the old men and send the answer through them. If they want to answer in the negative, they will tell the intermediaries that they have already given a positive answer to another who came before them. To say "no" is against etiquette.

Once the girl's parents approve, further negotiations continue through the old men as to the exact dates of the engagement ceremony and the wedding. The date of engagement fixed, the girl's parents begin to make the necessary arrangements for the ceremony. They will prepare food and drink in great quantities for the engagement feast. Since all preparations are made at home, at least a month is needed.

On the engagement day, the bridegroom escorted by his three best men, other friends, and an old man who is called the "Negar Abat," literally "father of the affair," will proceed to the girl's home. On arrival, they are guided to a place especially prepared for them, and there the man sees his future wife, to whom he has not previously spoken. (In some cases he may have seen her before.) There they are entertained with dinner by friends and relatives of the bride-to-be, and the drafting of the marriage bond begins.

This bond, in most cases, assures both parties that, whatever possessions are acquired by the husband and wife in the course of their union, belong to both of them, and that, in case of divorce, each is entitled to one half of the common property. Their individual property before their marriage, or property that comes by inheritance during the marriage, is not included in this bond. The principle underlying the bond, namely the right of each to claim from the common property, is called "Habtish Ba Kabte," literally, "Your chance is mine" or "Your property is mine."

On this, the engagement day, the exact date of the wedding will be fixed. This will be, generally, a full three months after the engagement. What is more important, it will be determined whether the marriage is to be a church marriage or not. Then the bridegroom publicly gives his bride a ring and some other jewelry, and henceforth the engagement is considered as effected. Now the girl's and boy's parents begin preparing the wedding feast. Again, food and drink will be prepared in abundance. Usually there is great competition between the two families as to whose feast will be the more attractive. The man seldom sees his fiancee, even in the presence of her parents, during the engagement period.

When the long-expected wedding day arrives, both parents invite relatives, neighbours, and acquaintances, and entertain at a big dinner. At the beginning of the dinner the bridegroom, escorted by his best man, the Negar Abat, and friends, arrives at the girl's home and asks, according to the tradition, permission to enter. When the girl's parents say "yes," he and his escort can enter. After the dinner the man and the girl say goodbye to her parents, and, tears in her eyes, the girl proceeds to the boy's home. Upon the arrival at the boy's home, the couple will be honoured by the company of the family and guests at the dinner.

It is interesting to note that songs, with the verses mentioning the names of the couple, will be sung. Local dances of all sorts, in which the boy's best men are the main figures, are performed. If the songs and the dances are not conducted in the usual manner, members of the girl's party ridicule and insult the boy's best men by hinting at defects in their verses.

Early the next morning, the three best men, with some ten other men friends, go to the girl's home and tell her parents, in the time-honoured way, that their daughter has lived up to their expectations of her virginity. This is indicated by the presentation of a rose and a loaf of bread with Maria Theresa or Menelik silver coins in it. The members of the mission are then entertained at breakfast.

One week later the couple is invited by the girl's parents for dinner. The newly wed couple, friends, and members of the family circle, only, are invited to be present at the dinner. This ends the wedding ceremony, and the routine of married life begins. Such family dinners are given in honour of the couple by all near relatives. Both the girl's and the boy's parents contribute something towards the home of their children. After two months or so, the wife and the husband leave the latter's parents' home and enter their own new house.

WEDDING CUSTOMS PRACTISED IN SHOA[1]
Ezra G. Medhin

Commonly, fathers in Shoa secure brides for their sons when these reach the age of thirteen or fourteen. To insure a lasting married life, the fathers wed their sons to girls who live in villages some eight hours distance, by foot, from the son's village. The fathers are of the opinion that wives coming from distant villages, and not previously acquainted with their husbands, will be obedient to them.

The actual securing of a bride is not accomplished by the father himself, but by some elders, whose help the father humbly entreats. These elders are chosen from people of good repute in their own village.

Early one morning, the elders gather together and go to the house of the girl whom they consider worthy of marriage to their friend's son. They knock at the small wicket-gate, and a servant comes along to ask what their needs are at such an early hour. The elders reply that they want to see the master. The master of the house at once realizes that the elders have come on matters concerning marriage, and he sends back the servant to tell the elders that he is not at home.

The elders return the next morning or some other morning; this time they meet the master of the house, who, on being summoned, quickly steps out of his house as though alarmed. The elders greet him politely and ask him to accompany them to the place where village sessions are held. There they immediately expose their purpose, and wait to hear what the man has to say. At first the man gets angry because he considers it very daring of the elders to approach him with such a request, demanding his daughter's hand. The skill of the elders in smoothing anger comes in very handy at this point. One of the elders stands up and says something to this effect:

"Our dear friend, we are on a very important mission. Do not consider yourself degraded by our asking to have your daughter become wife to the son of our friend Ato so-and-so. You know me personally and, besides, you know that I was once very intimately acquainted with your father. He was a respectable gentleman who, during his lifetime, accomplished much. May

[1] Abridged and reproduced with permission of the Ethnological Society of University College of Addis Ababa, from Bulletin No. 2, December, 1953.

111

the soil under which he lies press lightly upon him. Furthermore, I am convinced that your father's virtues have passed on to you. That, and only that, is the reason which brought these elders and myself here. My dealings are, as you know, honourable and my value in the reconciliation of wives to husbands, and such other social affairs, is not unknown by you. From all this you can conclude that if I undertake an intercession it is only because I consider the man, on whose behalf I am sent, really worthy of my help. Be wise therefore and consent to our request."

These words definitely convince the man, but, as the father of a desirable daughter, he considers that it would be too unmanly for him to yield to the request of the elders without further argument. He therefore angrily says that he will not give away his daughter. He even gets up to leave the session. Immediately, however, the elders surround him and gently coax him into a sitting position. By means of other witty sentences, the elders succeed at last in convincing him that he should appoint a date for further discussion.

At the second session, the man addresses the elders somewhat to this effect: "My sage fathers, I would have been willing to give my daughter to the son of your friend, had I not now found out that her grandfather (her mother's father) with whom she lived for part of her life, has found her a husband. This makes me very sad, but this is what I have learned. Anyway I would like very much to know how much better the social standing of the son of your friend is than that of the person who has been accepted by my daughter's grandfather.

"As you know, I am the son of a gentleman, and I am myself a gentleman, I have always been self-supporting and can claim without any danger of exaggeration a purity of race whose continuity extends over three thousand years. My bones are undefiled by any fractures. Such menial tasks as metal-working, cloth-weaving, hide-scraping and the like have been practised neither by my ancestors nor their neighbours. I would rather wed my daughter to one of my servants than to a man who employs his hands in such servile tasks."

The man continues to aggrandize himself in such vain talk until the time arrives for the elders to describe the ancestry of the family on whose behalf they have been sent. One of them begins: "My son, although we bear no relationship to your daughter, each of us is her father. Apart from your daughters, we would not give even the daughter of your enemy to a person who employs his hands in such servile tasks as you have mentioned. The

112

father from whom we are sent is of the district of Morat[2] of the clan of Debeb.[3] He is a son of Awsabe.[4] These facts alone should suffice to convince you of the greatness of his ancestry."

The man now smiles, and with words that are filled with joy says: "If the man is of the ancestry that you have just described I would not merely say that my daughter had gained a husband, but would consider that she had entered paradise on earth." He then continues to praise the person of such noble ancestry. He invites the elders into his home in the following manner: "My sage fathers, the sun has already beaten hard enough upon you. Let us go into my house and have some beer to drink." The elders, however, remain seated with the excuse that they have not yet been given a direct acceptance of their request. The man then replies: "Is there any other fashion of saying all right? I tell you, from today onwards, my daughter is yours. Give her to whomsoever you choose." After this, the elders accept the invitation to the house where they enjoy a small feast. The girl who is to be wedded serves the elders, and when the father finds occasion he introduces her thus: "My sage fathers, this is the girl, and she is now eight-and-a-half years old." He then talks to the girl in this fashion: "Don't you know these people? They are friends. Come and bow at their feet." All this while the girl is ignorant of what has been going on between her father and the elders.

After the small feast, the elders bless the home and fix the date for marriage. The day must necessarily fall near the beginning of the Lenten fasts or at Easter. Shoan marriages are carried out either in January, February, or April.

Marriage is rarely arranged by Ethiopians for May, because it is widely believed that a couple married in this month will either become poor, or die too soon. When the day has been fixed, the elders salute the master of the house and depart.

The father of the husband-to-be is told of the result of the elders' mission. He begins the complex preparations for the brewing of varieties of tella (beer) by the treatment of grains such as wheat and barley. Unground grain is shared among the people that are going to be present at the marriage feast; they are very willing to help the parents of the husband-to-be by grinding the grain, and on the day of the marriage they bring back not the ground grain, but bread baked from it. This greatly simplifies the

[2] Morat is the name of a district in the province of Shoa.
[3] Debeb is another district of Shoa and the name implies nobility.
[4] Awsabe is the name of a traditional nobleman.

113

preparations for marriage. Nowadays some people, especially around Addis Ababa, bring money when they are invited to a marriage. This practice is of very recent introduction, and in many parts of Ethiopia the parent would consider himself insulted if he were approached with money.

When the actual day of marriage arrives, green branches of trees are cut and erected in such a way as to enclose a ground area of some 600 square meters. A roof of leafy branches is constructed to make a temporary banquet-hall. The bread is brought into the hall and laid out on beds of green leaves.

When everything has been prepared, the feast begins. The young man who is to be married enters with his three best men, his Nagar Abat, and a retinue of some thirty people. Each of the best men has his name: One is called "the best man of the head," the second, "the best man of the feet," and the third, "the best man who is still a lamb or cub." In the hall, the young man receives blessings from the people that are feasting. Some of the rich present him either an ox or a cow. Those who are less rich give him a goat or a sheep. Others wish him a daughter and a son.

Having received these and other blessings, the young man goes to the home of his fiancee (whom, incidentally, he has never seen before) accompanied by his three best-men, his Nagar Abat,[5] and a retinue of some thirty people. Some two or three hundred meters from the home of his fiancee, the bridegroom stops and sits under a tree. For a while he stays there, and sun and wind take their toll of his patience. Soon his Nagar Abat goes to the gate of the bride's home and announces to the Nagar Abat of the bride the arrival of the bridegroom. The Nagar Abat of the girl emerges from the gate and throws a glance at the bridegroom and his retinue. He then goes back through the gate. He thinks that, since he is going to give away such a nice girl, he ought to make the bridegroom bow and scrape for a while.

The bridegroom's Nagar Abat goes a second time and asks permission for the entrance of the bridegroom and his retinue. After a little more delay, the bridegroom is allowed to approach the gate. When he arrives within four or five meters of the gate, women rush out at him, singing a song which can more or less be translated in these words:

> No entrance here bridegroom,
> Outside is your room.

[5] Nagar Abat. Both the bridegroom and the bride have a Nagar Abat each. These are representatives for the husband and wife at the engagement and on the day of marriage. In married life, where cases of disagreement or divorce may come, the Nagar Abats intervene and act as advocates for the husband and wife respectively.

A cone-shaped home of sticks.

As they sing, the women throng the gate, and the bridegroom succeeds in entering only by sprinkling perfume over the ladies or pushing his way through. Once inside, the bridegroom goes into the hall and stands near a group of elders who are in the act of feasting. For at least a quarter of an hour these elders pay no attention to the bridegroom and his retinue, although they see them waiting. After a time the elders inquire "Why have you come?"

The bridegroom and his retinue reply: "We come so that you may be fathers unto us and we children unto you." The elders then ask: "What have you in your hands?" The Nagar Abat of the bridegroom replies: "Rolls of gold and folds of attire." The elders then tell the new arrivals to deposit the beautiful home-made garments and ornaments for the neck, the ears, and the feet. After all these have been deposited, the Nagar Abat of the girl states that he is not satisfied with the number of the presents. The other elders also create a scene about the presents. At last, however, the Nagar Abat of the bridegroom states that the young man has no more presents in his hands and that he would be grateful if he were allowed to bring more at some other time. The bridegroom then calls upon some one to be his guarantor, and he is then allowed to proceed and take his bride.

A more "modern" cone-shaped home, tightly woven.

Meanwhile the bride has been waiting in a neighbouring room, among many girls, dressed in much the same fashion as she is. This is purposely done to confuse the best man, who is supposed to identify the bride, carry her on his back, and bring her to the bridegroom. Much laughter is caused when the best man carries out the wrong girl time and time again.

At last the best man asks one of the women singers to help him in identifying the right girl. The woman agrees to help on condition that she is rewarded. The best man presents her with a precious gift, and the woman begins to dance and sing in and out of the group of veiled girls. She points out the bride by a wink of her eyes or some other sign, and at long last the best man carries out on his back the right girl. He then takes her around among the feasting people and they bless her.

When the girl is ready to leave her home, she must tread over the blood of an unblemished ram. The blood is shed on the threshold of her home and as she steps over the threshold, all the people that have come to the marriage bid her farewell with group songs and "elllllllllllllllllllll," the shrill cry that Ethiopian women emit as a sign of happiness. The girl is then placed on a horse (not a mule) and, among a great din of men's songs and clatter of horses' feet, she is taken to the home of her bridegroom.

116

THE HARRARI WEDDING CUSTOMS[1]
Mohamed Abdurahman
Part I

In order to do full justice to Harrari Wedding customs, I shall try to illustrate the marriage system which was in operation before the Italian invasion; after that, though fundamentally the same, the customs underwent many changes and modifications.

The contract of marriage begins with formal engagement. The boy might have been attracted by a girl he met in the street, or his family might have proposed to him a certain girl. The young man goes in search of her, and, if necessary, he may even drop into her house with some trifling excuse, such as having gone astray, or to ask the residence of such and such a fellow in the neighbourhood. By such means he might make contact with the girl, but will not allow his real purpose to be perceived. If he is satisfied by her posture, complexion, and manner of answering, the boy agrees that his family should arrange his betrothal to the girl. The family, at first, sends an elderly man or woman with the suggestion to the girl's family. They, in turn, may reject or consent to the proposal. If they consent, the elderly messenger is given a day upon which the boy's family may bring a pile of "Qat"[2] as an official promise of engagement. The "Qat" is brought in the morning of the appointed day, and the girl's family adds some more of their own; they distribute it among all their neighbours and kinsmen in the city to announce the engagement. This done, the engagement is sealed, and a new relationship arises between the two families and between the young couple.

Now the girl begins to hide from her bethrothed, perhaps to arouse his curiosity. If she does not hide, he considers it as an insult towards him, and he may hit her; if he does so, he has to send her a suit of clothes. This amusing play of hide-and-seek goes on until the wedding day.

There are other seasonal duties on the part of both. On the arrival of Ramadan (the Islam fasting month), the girl prepares a dish of "Butur," small, spherical, fried biscuits in honey; and the boy, with the help of his friends having emptied the dish, sends it back with a dollar note. On the arrival of Arafa (the biggest Mohammedan festival, at the end of the year),

---

[1] Abridged and reproduced with permission of the Ethnological Society of the University College from Bulletin No. 2, December, 1953.

[2] A habit-forming, but non-addictive, weed cultivated in Harar, and in great demand for chewing, especially among Ethiopians of Arab extraction.

the girl's family expresses gratitude by a present of a bottle of diluted honey and another of milk. This cycle goes on till the wedding day, which is heralded with Zagan, i.e., the presentation of the dowry.

At the request of the boy's family, the girl's family appoints the date for the presentation of Zagan. On the eve of the appointed day, the boy's family, accompanied by relatives and outstanding men of the neighbourhood, solemnly marches to the girl's house, where they are cordially welcomed. Then the eldest of the group begins to present, one by one, the objects comprising the dowry. The dowry varies, but generally it consists of two gowns, two lighter robes, a pair of trousers, a valuable necklace in the shape of a bee-hive, and $100 in cash. The boy's family departs and the things are left in the girl's home where they will remain on exhibition to all the relatives and friends for several days. Then several loads of wood pass from the boy's to the girl's family, heralding the advent Tunaus, i.e., the commencement of the wedding ceremonies. This wood delivery is all done by the boy's friends, who ride donkeys to the nearest forest, chop the wood, and carry it into the girl's home.

The day of Tunaus being decided upon, the girl roams through the city at the head of a group of her friends, who line up in twos and threes, every group clad in a single gaudy mantle. In this way, they frolic through the main streets of the city. This announces her Tunaus and also serves to invite the young men of the city to her house for dancing and amusements. This begins on the day of the announcement. Formerly it continued for seven days, but now lasts for three only.

On that day, the girl chooses three or four of her intimate friends to participate with her in the colouring of the hands with henna (a leaf which, rubbed on the hands, stains them red), and the taking of medicine such as Epsom Salts. [3] On the day of the announcement, these intimate friends go to the boy's house and stick a needle with a highly decorated head on a basket hung on the first pillar of the house. The nearest girl-relative of the boy picks up this needle, sticks it near her temple, and begins to invite all the girls and women among the boy's relatives. The usual form of the announcement is "Mr. So-and-So orders you to crush hops." This traditional announcement indicates that formerly this community did not abstain from alcoholic drinks. When this has been done, the wedding ceremony commences in both families. Smoke ascends sky-high, and the noises begin to attract beggars and to announce the fact to the passers-by. On the day of the announcement,

[3] As a physical purgative. Formerly koso, a treatment for tapeworm, was used.

the girl invites her relatives, together with the young men in her neighbourhood. She goes to their families and announces that she proclaims them
as brothers. These "brothers" have certain responsibilities. They provide the
girl's house with lamps, and they also act as masters of ceremony during the
nights of dancing.

About ten, every evening, when the bride comes back from visiting her
friends and relatives, the dancing starts. It is peculiar to the Harrarians that
dancing is permitted only on such bridal occasions, and that is why we find
this dancing is open to all and sundry of the bachelors of the city. The party
opens with the beating of drums and singing. A group of boys come into the
house and announce, through their song, their wish to have a girl in front of
them. A girl descends from among her friends on the dais and stands erect in
front of the boys, with her back to them, just at the corner of the main pillar.
Slowly one of the boys lowers a corner of the mantle on her head. The song
begins with praises of the girl and then strikes far and wide covering many
themes, all expressed in lyrical terms. The house of Tunaus may be the birth-
place and the source of inspiration of many deep and lovely verses. Such is
the origin of the famous verse which runs:

"Amina Ali Nur, though you may look as ugly as a rat to others,
to me you are as beautiful as a siren."

This verse really voices and enshrines a major trust about love. It
illustrates how blind love is, and how little connection it has with beauty, and
announces the fact that people fall in love in spite of peculiarities evident to
all.

Thus the young men come in groups from all quarters of the city and
have a pleasant time; some may not leave until the day is almost breaking,
still regretting the too-rapid passage of the night in verses such as this:

"The day comes before I am satisfied!"

The bride and all the family spend a drowsy day during which they drag
through their preparations for the next night. The second night is quite
similar to the first. The third, and last, is the jolliest and most active of all.
The girl's friends go to the bridegroom's house with bandages of henna.
After that a famous and melodious chorus begins. The friends of the girl, on
one side of the room, compete with the bridegroom's group across the room,
each group repeating the following verses once:

119

"By the name of Allah the graceful and the merciful,
O bridegroom, you are the successor of Ali.

"The residence of your father is a Hadas (aromatic herb)
Shaded with Ayoban (aromatic herb) roof.

"Your father's residence has Yasin (the most famous chapter of the
Koran read by the prophet during his escape), as its wall, and
Tabarak (another highly valued chapter) as its shield."

When this is ended, the girls among the bridegroom's friends will go in their turn to the bride's house and sing the same song with the girls attached to the bride's party. Then both the groups go to their houses and the jolly singing and the dancing resume. With the dawn of the third day, the dancing night ends, and on the fourth night the marriage takes place. The guild-members and other men pass the day in reading aloud the biography of the prophet. With the advent of evening, activity increases, and soon a whole group of elderly men, friends of the bridegroom, come to witness the ceremony. The marriage oath is taken at the house of the preacher, where both parties will be presented by their kinsmen. With the arrival of the boy's friends, leading a well-decorated mule, the ceremony reaches its close. The girl, entirely wrapped with a robe, is put on the mule, and is shaded by a gaudy umbrella. She is driven to her new home by the boy's friends, who sing and jump in front of her, while her girl friends follow close to the mule, singing different verses all in her praise. By Harrari customs, it is the girl's family which provides all the furniture and fittings for the newly married couple. The new home reached, the bride is carried into the inner recesses of the house, where she awaits the bridegroom. The young man, as soon as he comes, dashes in through her friends, who still swarm around her, and exercises his new mate by striking her three times with a whip, to which all the girls respond by roaring, "Happy marriage," thrice after each lash. They depart, and the bridegroom goes to visit his family and close relations. He leaves a conical basket in the houses of the families closest to him to denote that he expects an invitation at the end of the honeymoon. He returns to his new house, where he is reconciled with his wife. Here ends the first phase of the Harrarian bridal ceremony.

THE HARRARI WEDDING CUSTOMS[1]
Mohamed Abdurahman
Part II

Early in the morning after the consummation of the marriage, a calf is sent to the bride's house to announce the virginity of the girl. As soon as the calf steps in the bustling yard. a cry of rejoicing bursts out. The scared animal is pushed to the kitchen where it is daubed with butter in appreciation of its breaking the good news. Its mission fulfilled, the poor creature is pulled and led back by the messenger to the house it came from. The bride, who has so far obstinately refused to take any food despite the severe measures taken by the groom's helpers, receives a messenger from her family telling her to help herself and to assume a more humane attitude; then she begins to eat. The first of the seven days of the honeymoon is relatively uneventful. The married couple spend their day swarmed by their friends, and occasionally are paid visits by the bride's girl friends.

At noon, when lunch comes from the boy's family, the number of visitors and friends swells. The people sit in circles at two places: one in the bridal room where the young couple lunch with their intimate friends, and the other for the rank and file of the group. The lunch over, the activities decline; at about four p.m., life begins once more; friends from both sides begin to drop in and, as they do, the groom, majestically seated on his chair, blesses with a lash every lass from the girl's party as she flies before him to the darkness of the bride's room and complete security. The girls from the boy's party are similarly treated by the bride. But the wretched boys, no matter whose friends they may be, are lashed by both the bride and groom.

The visitors, mostly young men, are received with lashes, then are accommodated and served with spurring drinks. As the number of the boys increases and the atmosphere begins to grow in fervor, the young bachelors start to sing by couples and gradually, towards the evening, burst out into sprightly and frantic dances to which the whole group joins to build up a song at once fascinating and contagious. The dancing group trots in a circle to rhythmical clapping until a veritable frenzy is attained, and nothing is seen but flying shemmas, brandished sticks, and leaping heads. This goes on until the band drops; for a while, nothing is heard but the clacking of cups and the panting of exhausted figures.

[1] Abridged and reproduced with permission of the Ethnological Society of the University College, from Bulletin No. 3, December, 1954.

As the hardy youths recover their breath, they begin once more to sing by couples, but this time softly and merrily praising the bride and groom. With the advent of supper late in the evening, the merry-making begins to fade away, and the whole song dies down, leaving the young house desolate and dreary. Apart from a few intimates, nobody remains to pass the night in the bride's home. Such is the routine of the seven days.

The "plate of mothers," two big black wooden plates filled to the brims with thin wheat breads steeped in liquid butter and sprinkled with sauces, hails the second morning's offerings from the bride's family. A large group is invited to this unusual meal, but after that all the conventions of the first day begin once more: the same visits and felicitations, the same dancing and merry-making. The seven days of transition are supposed to be eventful and gay, and in fact every new day hails the young couple with rare treats and new surprises.

The morning of the third day begins with a peculiar donation. All those bride's brothers, who acted during the three dancing evenings as masters of ceremony, collectively present several loads of sugar cane and a few baskets of bananas to the young couple. Nowadays plates of dates may be presented instead. In the evening, all the girl-relatives of the groom drop in, each with a basket of biscuits fried in butter or oil, the more distant relatives contenting themselves with the simple present of a gourd of soft drink made of sugar and orange juice. Everybody, over-stuffed, staggers into the room until finally the evening comes with its sprightly dancing and gay songs. Apart from an exquisitely prepared dish of food termed, "Lany Gabata Kaab," from the groom's family, nothing out of the routine occurs on the fourth day. The procession of dishes and plates does not stop here but continues with the dish called "Juma Sirkot" on the fifth day. A dish of sirri, a heavy circular bread steeped in honey, and a basket full of all kinds of seeds accompany the last dish on the sixth day. Those seeds in the old agrarian community symbolize the family's well wishing to the young couple to multiply and sprout as those seeds; the seeds are stored to be sown next season.

At noon, on the seventh day, messengers drop in to invite the groom to meals in his relatives' houses. First, he visits the bride's parents where the mother presents him with a ring, and the father with a book or whatever he thinks appropriate. While the groom is thus roaming, a group of girls comes to the bride; they wash her, comb her hair, and put her in proper shape. The groom, in a colourful attire, trots with his friends to the various homes to which he has been invited, where he eats hurriedly, and receives some presents from his hosts. He dashes from house to house, jumping and singing on the way.

After finishing the rounds, the group comes back to the home once more. Late in the afternoon, ladies from amongst his relatives flock in with a hair-dresser. They encircle the groom, and as soon as the shaving begins they sing ritual songs.

The clean-shaven groom leaves the house to the ladies, and goes on a sojourn to a friend's house or to his parents' home. The number of ladies, elderly and young, increases, and the large group solemnly march from both families' homes into the new premises. It should be noted here that the bride never mixes with the young men but stays during the seven days in her dark private room, while the groom normally stays with his male guests in the outer room, and meets his wife only at meal times, during the night, and perhaps on one special occasion. Now both parties of ladies cooperate in bringing out the young girl from her sequestered room into the main room where they will dress her hair in a new way significant of her ladyship, and dub her a woman. Surrounded by her friends and her parents, the girl sits on a stool and bends to a hairdresser. As soon as the operation starts, the chorus begins to sing songs in accordance with the actions.

Now that she has acquired all the signs of a married lady, the bride has to leave behind all her manners of girlhood and prepare herself for the serious duty of raising a family of her own and of cooperating with her husband to render their lives happier and more harmonious.

On the eighth day the young husband assumes his work, and the wife begins to look after her house. Both families, now that they have wedded their children, give them relative freedom and leave them on their own, but not completely. The boy's mother provides them for at least a year with their food, thus affording more leisure to the young wife to devote to the weaving of baskets for her house. The continuous aid of the parents in all the new phases of life ends with the birth of the first child. As soon as the wife advances in pregnancy, her family invites her for a visit in their house to help her in wading through those unaccustomed painful processes of giving birth. The young mother lives for about forty days after the delivery with her family, while the young father reverts to the solitude of celibacy once more in his house. The young family already increased by one gets accustomed to its new life; cooperation goes a step further, and their independence becomes almost complete. The boy's family provides the wife with all the utensils for cooking and leave her on her own. In addition to her taking the helm of her family, the young mother begins to cooperate with her husband in gaining their livelihood.

While the peasant husband takes care of the muscular work on the farm, the wife participates in converting their product into cash at the market every morning. In this way they achieve happiness and mutual confidence in dividing the labour between them. Similarly at the harvest of the corn, the wife prepares food and drink for the team of harvesters and winnowers. Thus the young couple go on sharing the tears and smiles of life, and contributing to the propagation of the Harrari race.

MARRIAGE AMONG THE KOTUS OF HARRAR[1]

Marriage is the connecting link between two families, and its ceremonies are carried out in different ways in different parts of Ethiopia. In order to have a clear picture of marriage in Harrar, we have to consider the marriage of the Moslems as well as the Christians.

Among the Moslems, there are the "Kotus," those who live in the villages, and "Harrarians" who live in the town of Harrar itself.

When a Kotu is engaged to another Kotu, he has to wait for at least two years before he marries her. The girl has no right to choose her husband; she has to accept anyone chosen by her parents. The man has the right to choose his wife. His parents, unlike the parents of the girl, won't force him to marry a girl he does not like. On the marriage day, the parents of both the bride and the bridegroom will hold a party, and the neighbours are called in. All the people sing and dance. The bridegroom takes his bride home. The bride takes with her all the necessary equipment and household utensils. These will help her when she continues her life with her husband. After the marriage, the bride and the bridegroom will usually have three or four days rest, for they are free from any type of work no matter whether it is important or trivial.

The marriage of the Harrarians is similar to that of the Kotus. But the Harrarian bridegroom takes his bride to his home on a mule's back, and they will be free from work for about a week instead of three or four days.

[1] Author's name withheld by request.

MARRIAGE IN GONDAR[1]

In Gondar, if a man is going to marry a woman, he is not the one who chooses his wife; some of his relatives search for one and choose for him.

In choosing the girl, the following things are taken into consideration: (1) the beauty of the girl; (2) whether her family is rich or poor; (3) she must be of the same race, but any kinship must be at least seven generations back; (4) she must be of the same religion; (5) the character of the girl; (6) the reputation of the family.

After the boy's family or relatives have chosen the girl, they look for a man who has acquaintance with the two families and ask him to tell the girl's parents that they want to have that girl as a wife of their son. The man goes to ask the girl's parents. Then the girl's parents also make inquiries about the boy and his family. If they agree, the two families will prepare the wedding.

On the wedding day the boy will be at his best; he will go to the girl's house on a horse's back or on a mule's back accompanied by fifteen to thirty men. There, before he enters the house of the girl's parents, he will make his oath of marriage in front of at least five old men. Then they enter the house and eat and drink; then he will take his wife with him. There is, of course, a lot of tella (beer), tej (wine), wett (sauce or stew), injera (bread), and a lot of dancing.

During the first or second years, the couple live with their families; after that, they will get their endowment from their parents and will live on their own.

BETROTHAL AND MARRIAGE IN KEREN, ERITREA
Zelleka Tadesse

When a girl reaches the age of seven, she is veiled (purdah) and secluded in her home so that no one can ever see her. She is permitted to reveal herself only to her mother, the female members of her family and females of

---

[1] Author's name withheld by request.

the surrounding area who may come to visit her mother. Shortly thereafter, she is ready for betrothal. According to the customs of the Keren Muslim society, the mother of a boy is the only person qualified to choose a wife for her son. She knows which houses harbor hidden girls of engagement age, and she has seen some of these girls before they were veiled, many of them afterwards. She makes a decision concerning a desirable mate for her son. She discusses her decision with the parents of the girl.

When the parents of a girl have agreed to give their daughter to the son of a woman, that girl becomes the fiancee of the boy, even though he knows little, if anything, about her. The wedding ceremony will be prepared by both families, with help from relatives and friends. Both families invite many relatives and friends to the wedding.

The bridegroom goes to the house of his bride, with his chosen friends, and brings her to the home of his parents. She remains heavily veiled. The young bride spends the daylight hours with her mother-in-law and the other female members of the household. She approaches the bedroom of her husband only after dark and leaves early in the morning before daylight comes. This routine continues until such time as the wife, by the help of nature, produces her first-born child. Then, and only then, may the husband look upon the face of his wife, or the wife look upon the face of her husband.

THE MARRIAGE CUSTOMS OF THE WOLLOMOS
Lulseged Kumsa

Betrothal:

Among the Pagan Wollomo tribe, betrothal is exclusively between the two individuals; that is, the young man and the young girl. When a young man attains the age of puberty, he seeks a wife who appeals to his own tastes and is of his social status. The only means of approaching her is by making contact with the neighbours of his future wife. This system is not very common among the other tribes in the Empire, but since this is the customary rule of this particular tribe, the girl accepts the proposal that has been presented to her secretly through her neighbours. She then quietly makes all arrangements and sets the date of her separation from her family. As a matter of fact, all these processes are supposed to be undertaken in the ignorance of her parents.

The occasion of her desertion from the family is usually a market day when her parents are absent. She plunders her family of everything she can get, such as clothes, rough ornaments (with which women of the olden days decked themselves), and any money she can find. With her plunder, she runs away with her betrothed to her mother-in-law's residence. Because of such great loss of wealth and property, parents who have girls who have attained the age of puberty often take serious measures to conceal their money and protect their movable possessions from a loss of this nature. For example, the mother never leaves the house—especially on market days—without taking with her any money or ornaments which she may not want her daughter to take.

Circumcision:

According to the customs of this tribe, the ceremony of circumcision takes place at the time of betrothal; whereas this performance occurs among Christian tribes at the state of infancy. As soon as the betrothed arrives in the home of her mother-in-law, the circumcision is performed, and then she will be fed with the best foods, so that the wound may heal soon.

Sending of the Elders:

As soon as she recovers, elders of the bridegroom's family, with a group of chosen elders from the community will be sent to the girl's parents to act as go-betweens for the reconciliation of the mother and daughter and to attempt to diminish the vengeance of the girl's parents.

Wedding:

After the reconciliation, the parents of the bride will fix a date for the marriage celebration. At the time of the wedding, the bride and the bridegroom, with a group of elders to accompany them, will be invited to the house of the bride's parents. During this visit, the bride is provided with goods and cattle for her domestic needs and money for the establishment of her home, in addition to those things she has already plundered at the time of her betrothal. All these gifts are considered as her marriage portion as well as the limit of her rights of inheritance on her parents' death.

Her Status During Marriage Period:

Among this tribe the wife is treated like a domestic animal. The husband has the right to beat, to wound, or to do anything of any nature. The wife cannot possess anything of her own. Everything she acquires goes to her husband.

Husband seated outside sleeping quarters safe from flash floods.

Extent of the Husband's Rights:

Polygamy is still practised among this tribe. If a man has sufficient wealth and power, he never limits himself to only one wife. He has the right to procure as many wives as he can afford. The facts that encourage him to engage in multiple marriage are:

1. Since the main occupation of the tribe is farming, the more wives an individual has, the greater the amount of work that is done.

2. To produce posterity in spite of the barrenness of a woman, which results from the excessive labour of women—a fact which the husbands do not realize.

Among the wives of an individual husband, there is the establishment of a hierarchy to settle disputes and jealousies within the family, as in the old Turkish tribes, most tribes of Gallas, of Dembidollo, and the Boaronas of Sidamo. The first wife—that is, the one who united with the husband first—is the mistress of the wives, and the others are bound to obey her in every respect.

Status of the Widow:

If the husband dies, the eldest brother of the deceased marries the widow, and all the children come under the "Manu" (authority) of his brother. Any child born from the woman becomes legitimately the child of brother-husband, and is not the legal son of the deceased.

128

Succession:

The right of primogeniture exists among the Wollomos. The eldest son of the deceased, regardless of the position of the wife in the hierarchy, is vested with rights of inheritance of immovable properties. The only women who have rights of inheritance are those who are unmarried, and their inheritance is limited to movable properties only.

Divorce:

During the period of their union as a husband and a wife, if the husband wishes for a divorce for any reason, the right of divorce has been reserved for the husband. He can repudiate his wife at his pleasure. In the process of separation, the wife has no claim of any kind on the house or other property which they acquired together or to the marriage portion she brought from her parents. Her claim is restricted to the dress she has on and the rough ornaments she is wearing.

Sketch of old Ethiopian man by young Ethiopian man.

V
Death Customs
in
Ethiopia

Whether Christian, Muslim, or Pagan, the Ethiopian, with few exceptions, considers death but a transition from one aspect of life to another, probably more desirable, aspect of existence. Small wonder, then, that wedding and funeral celebrations in many parts of the country are similar in their grandness. Great feasts are a part of both events, but music and dancing, essential at weddings, are deleted from most death ceremonies.

Not infrequently, Ethiopian priests, from the pulpit or in the mass media, advise against too much mourning for a departed loved one, suggesting that such behavior may imply a lack of faith in the generally believed "fact" that the post-earthly existence is superior to that with which we all are most familiar.

Death rites are precisely ritualistic, but details vary from group to group. There is considerable over-lapping of customs, but an effort has been made to select submitted essays which introduce variations in procedures for preparing a human being for the transition from this life to the next.

THE DEATH CUSTOMS AMONG THE AMHARAS OF SHOA[1]
Fassika Bellete

In this short paper I shall describe the funeral and the mourning customs commonly observed by the Christian Amharas of Shoa. The customs are believed to have existed for centuries, although no precise period can be conjured, and many of them are still practised. Where a custom is no longer practised, or is becoming out of date, I shall point that out.

This research is based upon the information of old men, who, over and above their long experience, have been in different parts of the province of Shoa for one reason or another.

To simplify the presentation of the information, I have adopted two divisions: the first part deals with the funeral customs, which start with the death of the person and the burial of the deceased; the second is the mourning customs, which start right after the burial and extend, strictly speaking, up to two years. Generally, we can extend the time up to the fourteenth year after the death of the person.

The Making of the Last Will:

Among the Amharas of Shoa, the last will is made only when the person is very seriously ill, unless he is going to war, or on a great hunting expedition, or if he is very old and it is feared that he will pass soon away. Taking for our purpose a patient who is seriously ill, let us see what is done about the making of the last will. When the person is found to be seriously ill, he is asked by the elders of the village, or the family, to make his will, or the sick person will express a wish to make his last will.

Accordingly, a particular priest called the "father of the soul" of the sick person is summoned. In addition, some two or three elders of the village who have no part in the will are requested to be present. The priest and the elders form the council. With the priest as its head, the council convenes in the chamber of the sick person. The patient then gives his will in the presence of the council, the priest serving as secretary for the occasion, but if he cannot write someone will be called to write the will. The sick person then receives absolution from the priest and says: "Untie me, father"; to which the priest answers: "May God untie you."

[1] Reproduced from the University College Ethnological Society Bulletin No. 7, December, 1957.

132

Ethiopian Orthodox Christian women wear the Coptic Cross. The black head tie and sweater indicate mourning, a period determined by the closeness of the deceased.

From then on, a preparation is made to meet the pending catastrophe (for death is looked upon as such by the common people). First of all, the shroud is bought, if it is not available already. Moreover, supplies of food and drink are prepared in abundance. Further, if the sick person has near relatives in faraway districts, messengers are sent to inform them of the grave condition of the patient. As the state of the patient becomes worse, it is arranged that at least one person remains beside him. When it is observed that the patient is absolutely weak, the near relatives are usually persuaded to leave the sick person's bed-chamber. When it is affirmed that the soul of the person has departed, mainly by feeling the heart and the mouth (the lips), the person examining says to some one nearby, "He has passed." Immediately the people in the death chamber cry out loudly as if to communicate the ill news to the tensely horrified relatives and friends outside. These people then rush into the room, and the room is filled with loud cries and shrieks; some yell, some weep, and others tear their hair, scratch their faces, beat their bodies, and throw themselves on the ground around the bed of the deceased.

Breaking the News:

Let us see how the news is broken to those who should hear it. Amidst this consternation there will be at least one person, usually the head of the family, who makes it his duty to send messengers to the relatives and friends of the family, as well as to those whom he thinks good manners demand that they should be present at the funeral, which takes place towards the evening if the person died in the morning, or next day if he died in the afternoon.

The news-bearers then scatter to the various places either on foot or by horseback according to the distance. In the highland regions, where the people breed horses, the messenger goes on horseback delivering the news from house to house. Along the valleys of the Ethiopian highlands where traveling is difficult, a person stands on raised ground and yells the name of someone living beyond him. If he answers, the former tells him the bad news and asks him to communicate it to so-and-so beyond him, who in turn will pass it on to somebody else till the news reaches the people concerned. This latter procedure is followed in both kinds of localities when requesting the near-by friends and neighbours to come to the funeral. Thus, on the early morning of the funeral day, messengers are sent to inform the neighbours and friends of the death and that the head mourner requests them to be present at the funeral. They climb a hill and cry out as loudly as they can, for instance, on the death of a son: "Ato so-and-so is bereaved of his son and would like you to help in the funeral ceremony."

In the meantime, preparation for the funeral procession takes place and is continued till around nine or ten in the morning. By then, also, the clergy from the church in the compound of which the person is to be buried have been summoned and have started their funeral ceremony which we will describe later. For the moment, however, we shall consider the preparation of the corpse for the burial.

As soon as the death of the person is known, someone who knows how to dress a corpse is given that responsibility. Where the deceased is a layman, someone of the same sex who knows the procedure is given the care of the corpse. He or she washes the body with the cooperation of some others. The

134

body is then laid on the bed and the tying of various parts proceeds. The toes are tied with white thread. The thumbs are also tied together in similar fashion; the hands lie stretched on the abdomen, tied to the body with another thread. If the deceased is a monk or a nun, some of the arrangements differ a bit. The hands are made to lie crossed with the palms resting on the chest. The toes are tied together with a thread. Miniature crosses made of threads are spread along the surface of the body and tied to the corpse. The person who is given the responsibility of shrouding the corpse is a monk in the case of a monk and a nun in the case of a nun.

If the deceased is a priest, although the position of the hands is the same as that of the monk, the thread crosses are left out. Of course, here again, the responsible person to shroud the corpse is a priest.

The body is then rolled from head to foot in a brand new sheet of cloth, and the corpse is scented to destroy the bad odour which may come from it. In some parts of Shoa, the shrouded corpse is again wrapped in a large piece of papyrus. The shrouded corpse is then laid on the bed on which it will be carried to the graveyard, and it is covered by a shemma which was prepared beforehand for this purpose, usually by the departed himself. (To put aside, in time, one's burial cloth, is one of the first acts of a decent aged person.) All is now ready for the funeral procession to the nearest church, or to the one where the deceased wishes to be buried.

The Service for the Dead:

A group of priests and deacons from the church where the deceased is to be buried is summoned in the morning of the funeral day. As soon as the priests arrive, they start praying for the soul of the deceased. The priests and deacons are in their church robes. One of the deacons holds a silver cross mounted on a long rod; one or two of the priests carry censers, while some of the priests carry their dancing-sticks and sistra; also present is a drummer. This group forms a circle around the bed on which the corpse lies and starts the service which is composed partly of reading and partly of chanting hymns. The books used are the *Book of the Dead* by St. Athanasius, St. Paul's *Epistles, Psalms of David,* and the four Gospels. Selections from these are read or chanted according to the status and age of the deceased; that is to say, the service for the laity is different from that for the clergy, each position in the clergy having its own appropriate liturgy.

The whole rite is divided into seven parts. The first part is made in the house of the deceased, and the remaining six are made on the way to the church. Sometimes the whole service is conducted in the church if the clergy do not go to the house of the deceased. This is possible in the case where the house of the deceased may be too far for the clergy to walk, or the priests of the particular church are too few to be spared for such a purpose, or the priests are afraid of the epidemic which caused the death of the person. In these cases they say the ritual prayers at the church when the corpse arrives.

Generally, every Christian Shoa Amhara is given such a funeral; however, we may note a few exceptions to this general rule. No service is said for a person who has suffered death by drowning, by falling from a cliff, by being eaten by wild beasts, or by committing suicide. The reason tradition assigns is that the deceased has not taken absolution from the priest before his death. Even those people who failed to have a confessor are not entitled to such last rites.

The Funeral Procession:

The procession starts at about ten o'clock in the morning. Four men pick up the bed which by now has been brought into the open court for the priests to chant around it. Then the procession starts. The clergy leads the way. Then follow the men who carry the corpse, followed by the head mourners, that is to say, the bereaved such as the wife or the husband, the mother and father, the sisters and brothers (who are above the age of 18). The bereaved are followed by the relatives, friends and neighbours of the deceased or the bereaved. All people present at the funeral procession walk except those who are weak and aged, who are allowed by convention to ride mules or horses; but they form the end of the procession. The rear of the procession is also formed by muleteers and grooms with their masters' mules and horses. Among this last group we may notice some two or three men carrying pots of beer and food. The provisions they carry are the "tear driers," which are given at the end to the group of clergy concerned in the funeral ceremony. The procession stops six times before it reaches the church for the clergy to perform the funeral service for the deceased.

When the procession reaches the church, the clergy read and chant the last service; whereupon the corpse is taken around the temple from right to left once, and deposited on the ground, by the northern gate if the deceased is a male, by the southern gate if a woman; if a member of the clergy, either a deacon, or a priest, by the eastern gate. The last group have the privilege of being taken inside the church. Then a group of people take the corpse up and tilt it thrice by way of making it pay tribute to its Creator. It is then taken to the grave.

At the Grave:

Wherever there is a church, a definite area surrounding it is assigned for graves and living-quarters for monks and nuns. The church usually has a double fence but some may have only one. Inside the outer fence priests, monks, deacons, and people of high rank are buried. A pious Christian, however, no matter of what status or profession, may be buried in this area with the permission of the church administrator. The burial place located on the eastern side of the church and inside the fence is considered as more important since it is near the place where the Holy Communion is prepared. The rules concerning burial in this area are more strict than those concerning other areas. Inside the inner fence on the eastern side people of great importance may be buried.

Inside the church building itself, monks and priests who are known for their devotion and religious service are buried. However, this is uncommon and happens rarely nowadays; it was more common in the past. Emperors, Kings, Princes, and Princesses are buried inside the church.

Laymen and common monks are buried outside the fences, but still on the consecrated ground of the church. Unbaptized infants are buried outside in unconsecrated ground.

What we have said above is not strictly applicable to all churches. For instance, in the towns, where the churchyards are small, the rules may be more strict than in the countryside. Also, the rules are more strictly observed by monasteries and famous churches than by ordinary churches.

Before the procession starts, some people are sent to dig a grave. The spot where they dig is consecrated at the start by a priest who says some prayers and makes a scratch on the spot.

The grave is dug in an east-west direction to a depth of not more than three feet. It is rectangular in shape, but narrows from east to west, and its length is slightly more than that of the height of the occupier. By the time the procession reaches the church, the grave-digging has been completed, and the corpse is taken to the grave and slowly lowered by a rope into the grave.

After the corpse is put in the grave, some priests say the last prayers. The head priest sprinkles dust on the coffin; the grave diggers close the grave, while the tears of the bystanders pour, and the air is filled with the strange cries of the bereaved. The last thing to be done to the grave is to erect a small tombstone if the family of the deceased can afford to do so.

Following the burial, the head mourner sits waiting outside the church to say farewell to those who wish to leave. Each person, one by one, says to the head mourner: "May God give you strength," to which he answers: "May the strength be given to him," (meaning the deceased). When all those leaving have made their farewells, the head mourner, or mourners, rise, and the homeward procession starts. On the way home, no one weeps; the head mourner usually keeps silent.

When they reach the bereaved home, they are met by someone with water for the grave-diggers, as well as for the others, to wash their hands. Soon food and drink will be sent to the house from relatives and neighbours for the guests.

The Mourning Customs:

Strictly speaking, all the bereaved, such as the immediate family, should be in mourning for a year. In earlier days brothers and sisters and even first and second cousins would be in full mourning for a year. With time, one year of full mourning was restricted to the first group only. The half-mourning of the second group starts six months after the death of the relative. The term of full mourning, of course, is extended according to the will of the individual mourner. The half-mourning continues usually for at least another year, but some of the mourning practices are gradually being dropped.

During the period of the full-mourning, no song or any such diversions are allowed in the residence of the bereaved; nor may the bereaved indulge in any pleasurable recreations elsewhere till the term of full-mourning has elapsed.

Let us now see how the mourning, both full and half, is manifested. Weeping is the first and most conspicuous practice of the mourner. There is individual-weeping as well as group-weeping. In the first, the bereaved relatives and friends of the deceased weep, as a rule crying loudly and melodiously such phrases as "father, father!" or "mother, mother!" or "son, son!" as the case may be, or some apt phrase which describes the relationship of the deceased to the mourner, or the kind deeds the deceased has done for him, e.g., my supporter, my adviser, etc.

The group-weeping is rather different. The mourners, usually the women, stand around a certain woman, a lamenter-poet, known as "weeper." This woman begins to sing, in a peculiar and sad tune, praises to the departed, bringing to the memory of the mourners his or her past deeds, upon which the female mourners gathered around her slap their chests and cry: "Waye, waye." Such group-mourning is practised throughout the first three days after the death of the person, usually twice or three times each day.

The full-mourning is maintained for the first three days by everybody attached to the deceased—relatives, friends, and even neighbours. During these three days, the mourners sit around the bereaved either in a large hall or in a tent. As each newcomer arrives from a distant region and enters the mourning place weeping, those inside break afresh into weeping. If the newcomer is a woman and a close relative of the deceased, she comes with her chest uncovered and when she enters the gate she starts to slap her open chest with both her hands; whereupon the other women, their chests uncovered, begin again to beat their chests crying out, "Waye, waye." So hard do these women beat their chests that by the close of the second day their chests are swollen and red. (In extreme cases, the mourners' grief becomes so intense that they brush their cheeks with course material so that the outer skin is scaled off. This is done very rarely and by very few people and cannot be considered as a general custom.)

As it is believed that the eyes of the departed disintegrate on the third day, in the early morning of that day there is a general assembly of relatives, friends, and neighbours at the churchyard where there is intensive weeping. The "weeper" also leads the weeping in the usual manner. By the end of the morning, the weeping is over and a general parting takes place.

By now only the close relatives such as husband or wife, mother and father, son and daughter, brother and sister, are left alone. If they had been using a tent for the general mourning, they now move to a modest room where they will remain for another nine days, that is to say, till the twelfth day after the death. Here they receive visitors, such relatives and friends as are still coming from distant places, since it is necessary that everybody who has a close relationship with the departed should visit the home of the departed. As a rule the house of the deceased is the mourning place.

During the twelve days, the mourners get up at midnight and make lamentation and weeping. On the twelfth day the family of the deceased sends food and drink to the poor and, if they can afford it, to the priests also. After another general weeping, a parting is made among the close relatives who have been staying in the home of the bereaved till that day. This custom is strictly kept by the higher class families. Those who cannot afford to remain for twelve days separate after the seventh day.

Another general weeping is made on the morning of the fortieth day. On this day a large reception is given at which almost all the relatives from both near and far are present. The next morning, a general weeping is made, again with the lamenter-poet present. The "weeper" sings some verses about the departed which remind the mourners of the deceased and incite them to weep the more. To this is added the showing of some object which once belonged to the departed or was a piece of his or her best work, which also increases the weeping. (In modern times, the photograph of the deceased is held high above for the people to look at. This practice of showing the deceased's photograph is performed on the third and twelfth days.)

The tears stop and the grief abates and the people now gather in the court-yard to hear the last will of the departed. After this, the guests and relatives disperse.

The next general weeping is on the seventh anniversary of the death. In the intervening time, between the fortieth day and the seventh year, there are large receptions in memory of the departed. Thus we have a big reception on the eightieth day, after six months, and after the first year. But custom does not demand that there be a general weeping on these days, although some very sad relatives may go off into bouts of weeping.

On the seventh anniversary, however, most of the relatives gather and indulge in a general weeping. The "weeper" will once again be present, and the procedure is the same as that on the morning of the fortieth day.

For forty days after the death, the mourners sleep on the floor, some without even a mattress below them. Some bereaved persons extend the period till the eightieth day, some to six months, and others for the first year; on the other hand, some sleep on the floor for twelve days only. If they usually wear shoes, for the first twelve days, at least, they go without them.

All personal effects such as rings and jewels are put aside until, at least, the fortieth day. Instead of coloured threads, they tie around their necks white threads. The hair is shaved or cut short. In the past, the bereaved was shaved, especially if she was a woman, and did not wear the hair long for at least a year. Nowadays only a few shave, but most of them cut their hair short. If the hair is not shaved off, or cut, it is left uncovered, nor is any dressing such as butter applied to it, with some even after a year. Seldom do they wash the hair, and the men do not shave their beards till at least the 80th day. Some do not cut their nails, as cutting them is considered a decoration.

In the early days the mourners wore their clothes dyed black, blue, or yellow, the first two being predominant. Today, men put black ribbons on their coats. The head covering of the women is also dyed black. The way of dressing among the women is different from the ordinary. For the first twelve days the women wear their clothes below the waist leaving the chest uncovered. They throw a small piece of cloth over their shoulders. After twelve days, they wear their usual clothes and cover their chests.

140

TASKAR OR KURBAN[1]
Debebew Zellelie

Among the various traditional customs that exist in Ethiopia, *taskar* or *kurban* is one of the most important. It is a series of ceremonies to ensure absolution for a deceased person. It had both religious and economic significance among the ancient Ethiopians, and it still retains its prominence with the new generation. Performance of the rites has to be carried out on three occasions: forty days after the burial, one year after the burial, and seven years after the burial.

The rites can be performed on other occasions if it is desired. There can be a celebration on the third day after death, on the seventh day, on the twelfth day, on the thirtieth day, on the eightieth day, and on the one-hundred-and-eightieth day.

On each occasion, the ceremony is essentially the same, the main difference being in the amount of food and drink provided for the feast; there are also slight variations in procedure from one province to another. A description of the custom as practised by the Amharas of Shoa will serve as an illustration.

Some time before the celebration, the family confessor comes to the family of the dead person and discusses with them the form of the celebration, the main purpose of which is not to recall to mind the man or revive the memory of his life to his friends, but to obtain for him absolution, for it is believed by priests and laymen alike that the proper performance of *taskar* or *kurban* will win absolution for the dead person. No *taskar* or *kurban* is performed for a child under seven or for a sinner who has died unrepentant or for a person who committed suicide, since he cannot obtain absolution because he sinned purposely.

The confessor, in consultation with the head of the family of the deceased, directs what preparations should be made. Three days before, the necessary things such as wheat, candles, and incense are sent to the church administrator. The administrator orders the things to be well prepared as they symbolize an offering by which the deceased is granted absolution from his sins.

The day before the feast, the priests get together and pray for the deceased. The prayer consists of the reading of the different chapters from the Psalms of David and of saying aloud some hymns from church books

[1] Reproduced from the University College Ethnological Society Bulletin No. 7, December, 1957.

containing the life histories of different saints. They also read some chapters from a prayer book for the dead written by St. Yared. Every deacon and priest who desires to partake in the feast must be present in the church at the time and pray for the dead person. If one fails to appear but comes the next day to feast with a bright face, as is done by some priests, he is strongly reproached, especially if the deceased was a person of importance in church affairs.

The night before the actual day of the feast all the priests and clergy perform quite an elaborate ceremony. On the feast day, some priests go to the tomb of the person and read a chapter or two from the Book of the Dead. As usual, the common Mass starts in the morning. Throughout the process of the Mass, the Christian name of the deceased is mentioned. In addition, some chapters from the Book of the Dead, which contains the various ceremonies that should be performed for the dead person, are read by the priests. The deacons and wandering religious students—who look to receive a certain amount of reward either in cash or in things (an old coat or a pair of trousers)—read the Psalms of David from cover to cover. After every ten chapters of David, the Christian name of the deceased person is mentioned with a certain common prayer. Its literal translation is: "Oh, Lord of David, rest the soul of your servant so-and-so." Moreover, the priests and the deacons recite an elaborate praise of St. Mary at the end of the Mass.

It remains a tradition that, if the Christian name of the deceased is unknown to those present, as no member of his family can be found, a new Christian name is given to him by the priest who is thought to be most devoted to Holy Orders. Such cases are very rare, for the Christian name of a person is known by the members of his community, unless he is a stranger to the place.

After the close of the Mass, all the priests, clergy, deacons and others who participated in the rite go to a place where a certain amount of food and drink is prepared for them. Generally, the amount of food and drink is limited and often is considered as recompense to the priests.

Towards mid-day, the priests and deacons go to the house of the dead person where they enjoy the real feast. Here, it is the confessor who is the master of ceremonies. He is the one who supervises the preparations. Since the priests are very strict, it is the duty of the host or the hostess together with the confessor to look after the preparations very carefully.

After the full enjoyment of the feast, the eldest priest makes the formal blessing for the family, and the important priests depart. But the deacons, the wandering church students, and the minor priests never leave the house until they have cleaned up the last remnant of the food and drinks, when they express their thanks with church songs. For example:

"May the Angels take the soul of so-and-so to Heaven.
As the father Abraham loved his tribe,
He satisfied us by preparing this meal for us."

But, if the person were poor, the feast would be modest; in such cases the priests do not go to the house of the dead person to feast. That is why the poor church students and clergy are in favour of the death of very rich people, for then they will have plenty to eat and plenty to drink at his taskar. So, we have the common saying which runs as follows:

"St. George, kill only the rich."

The taskar of a deceased person has also social significance. During the taskar all relatives, friends, and acquaintances are called together from different places in order to commemorate the death of their departed friend. The people of the town or village where the person lived are also invited. Then a great banquet is held.

After the banquet, a farewell mourning starts. All the different possessions of the deceased, such as his clothing, gun, shield, stock, sword, etc., are held by different mourners who walk from one side of the room to the other to display them. This external manifestation of the person's property reminds the people of their departed friend, and everybody is ready to shed tears. If there are some professional mourners, they stimulate the people to shed more tears by their rhythmical and very often allegorical songs. Now weeping, roaring, yelling, and chest-beating are at their highest. Everybody present in the hall sheds tears.

After an hour of crying, some subside, and others, especially those who were intimate with the person, continue weeping. At this time, soothers come out from the group and begin to calm the host or the hostess. After some supplication, they all rest in silence, which marks the close of the taskar.

In the minds of the Ethiopians, there is a strong belief—which every Ethiopian Copt either consciously or unconsciously accepts—that taskar enables him to get into the Kingdom of God. They believe that any person of Coptic belief can attain eternal life if part of his money is allotted to the priests and poor people by means of taskar. This idea was undoubtedly accepted by the old priests; but to the more educated priests of today, the purpose of taskar is not mainly for acquiring entry into the Kingdom of God, but rather for helping the economy of the church. The abbot of the *Asabot* monastery (this monastery is situated close to the station of Asabot on the railroad from Addis Ababa to Dire Dawa) told me that the income from taskar covers in part the expenses of his monastery, and that a large number of the monks and nuns living in this monastery are supported by taskar. Also, in Addis Ababa, many wandering church students travel from one part of the town to another in search of taskar. Many of these students depend on taskar exclusively for their subsistence.

Nowadays, the observance of taskar is beginning to be neglected, especially in the towns.

THE DEATH CUSTOMS IN THE PROVINCE OF TIGRE[1]

"When Cain slew Abel, Adam fell into an unbearable grief. But since he did not know how to express it, his face swelled out and his eyes reddened and dilated. So, the Angels of God came to him and, weeping and scratching their faces, showed Adam the art of mourning. Adam adopted that and thus expressed his sorrow and relieved himself of its pain." So runs a Tigrean saying which is told often in the mourning house. Its purpose is evidently to justify the expressions of mourning, and here we shall see the Tigrean way of mourning.

When a person is ill, all of his acquaintances come to him as often as they can and wish him recovery; the family, of course, does its utmost to cure him, and every man who either knows of some remedy or possesses some skill in treating the sick gives his help. But not every attempt succeeds, and death reaps its harvest. When it is known that a person is about to die, the relatives who live far away are sent the message "Catch up the last word," which means, see the dying man before he ceases speaking. In his village, all the neighbours gather together and actually commence the mourning while he is yet in agony. The relatives weep bitterly, but the others try to soothe them: "He is all right, he will recover." But the weeping continues. The elder relatives sit near the dying man separated from the rest by a curtain or maybe by another chamber. They too weep and, naturally,

---

[1] Abridged and reproduced with permission of the Ethnological Society of the University College of Addis Ababa, from Bulletin No. 5, June, 1956.

watch him with the most intensive eagerness. When he actually dies, they hasten to close his mouth, nostrils, and eyes, and then they stretch his body straight and close his legs. The arms are dealt with in differing ways. Those of a layman are stretched straight along his chest and brought together at the lower part of the belly where the thumbs are bound together by a white string. The arms of a priest, or a monk or nun who had been married formerly, are folded crosswise over the chest. But the arms of a virgin nun and a celibate monk are folded in such a way as to let the fingers rest on the mouth. The operation is performed with the greatest speed in order that the corpse will not have time to stiffen.

Meantime, the gathered relatives and neighbours who are weeping outside are told the news, and they now start violent shaking, bitter weeping, merciless hair plucking, and fierce face scratching. The weeping is at its peak at this moment. But the people behind the curtain rather suppress their passions and proceed to prepare the body for the burial. The confession father, or another priest in case of his rare absence, blesses a pot of water which has been brought from the river very recently, and no part of which has been used for any other purpose. The corpse is washed with this water and then wiped and dried. Now begins the dressing. The big toes are bound together with a string taken from the shroud. Then the thumbs are joined similarly, but some men bind them together with the penis; however, this does not seem to be the common way.

The arms of a priest are held in position by a string which is twined around the waist to the back, pulled over the shoulders and over the arms down to the waist, and again to the back where it ends in seven knots that run up to the neck. The arms of a celibate monk and a virgin nun are held in position by a string which is turned around the back and over the chest and the arms. These bindings over, the body is wrapped in a new sheet of calico or muslin usually, but for some people of noble families, in red or blue satin. This shroud may be either cut and sewn from head to toe or it may be left unsewn. When sewn, a long string is folded into two and one of the ends stretched by tying around the neck and at the big toes. The other end is now tied down along this stretched end in a series of knots, each of which is arranged to look like a cross. These knots are merely decorative. For a layman they are seven, for a priest, twelve (the number of the apostles) and for a monk, thirteen (the number of the sufferings of Christ in the crucifixion). When the shroud is left unsewn, as in some districts, the knots are no longer only decorative. The stretched end is in the same position. But the loose end binds the shroud, circling it at the middle of the feet, at the ankles, at the knees, at the hips, at the breast, at the neck, and on the forehead. The knot at the forehead is undone when the body is laid in the grave.

The preparation for burial is done by a person of the same order. A priest shrouds a priest, and a monk, a monk; a laywoman shrouds a laywoman. When a man is mortally ill, it is customary to buy a shroud and keep it ready for the moment of his death; but when his death occurs so unexpectedly that such a preparation is impossible, any neighbour who possesses a new piece of cloth must offer it for a shroud. When such a piece is not available, a couple of young men hurry to the nearest market, and a new piece is secured. No cloth that has been worn or immersed in water may be used for shrouding.

Over this shroud is laid a sheet of interwoven palm leaves which is then either sewn or bound with white string in the same form as the cloth inside. Having completed these operations, the relatives pass over the corpse to the elderly men (or women, if the dead is a woman) of the village and then join the weepers. Here they sit weeping and scratching their faces, and some of them even jump up and drop down.

Meanwhile, the elderly men send for the other villagers so that they may gather. As soon as they arrive, the younger men are set in pairs and told to equip themselves with metallic rods instead of the usual wooden stocks. Each pair is then assigned a series of neighbouring villages to which they must hasten and announce the death. To these villages they will hasten directly, even if it is at night. There they mount the highest hills and yell out the loudest they can, "Ooi! ooi! ooi! Mr. X has died, so Mr. Y (the closest and notable relative) says, 'help us in the burial, at such a church on such a date (the same day)." In Azabo and Raya, the announcers ride horses and instead of shouting from the highest hill, they gallop from house to house shouting: "Life! Life!"

The villages to which the death is thus announced on the day of decease have to be close enough to allow the mourners to reach their homes on the same day. Relatives who live too far away are sent for only afterwards. But the relatives who live in these nearby villages have to come on that very day. When they hear the announcement they have to weep and mourn according to their nearness to the deceased. Their fellow villagers gather around them and mourn with them for a while. Soon after, the trip to the funeral starts. The church must send at least two priests and three deacons with a cross and their ritual vestments. If there are other priests going there, they may take their vestments; of the laity, those who are acquainted with the dead or with his relatives must go to the funeral. Others do not have to go, but usually many of them go to the funeral for the sake of the relatives, who are their fellow villagers. Arriving at the neighbourhood of the mourning house, they halt, and the women arrange their garments in folds customary of this occasion, while the priests put on their ecclesiastical vestments and mount the cross on a rod. Then, weeping, they advance to the house. The women relatives are held by other women to prevent them from hurting themselves with too much plucking of the hair. The men, too, are caught by men, but only if they are so violent that they scratch their faces and fall down violently. When these villagers mix with the mourning family, the weeping rises to a crescendo.

In the house itself, the village priests have come at night and have been chanting the funeral rituals around the coffin. Now, it is necessary to give a brief description of the coffin. A bed, made of wood and leather, which is always kept at the church for the sole purpose of carrying the dead, is brought to the house. It is then inverted and the corpse laid on it. The two ends of a long strap are passed through the bed's holes, pulled over the chest in the upper part, and over the thighs in the lower part so that both ends are parallel. They are then passed through the bed's holes on the other side of the corpse, and then firmly tightened. Since the strap is long there are still pieces hanging loose at both ends. Each of these is tied to two legs of the bed diagonally. Over these is laid a white sheet of homemade cotton fully covering the bed's sides; and above it is spread a multicoloured cloth brought from the church.

Around the coffin, the clergy stand and chant their rituals. For a clergyman, or a layman who had lived a long life, participating in the Holy Communion and having married only once, the priests say additional prayers. In addition to the strictly religious rituals, they chant the "Souvenirs," and they have drum, sistra, and dancing sticks. The ceremony is gayer and longer than that for persons who lived through more than one marriage.

For a child under seven years of age, and adults who committed suicide, there is no ritual at all. An infant is just carried in the arms of its godfather and straight away taken to church for its burial. A child older than seven has the full rituals of a layman, but in the funeral only men from the same village or the closest ones take part. An unbaptized baby is buried in a special court outside the church-yard. Except the mother, or maybe a sister, nobody weeps for an infant.

147

It is said that if the sun has not set, the dead body must be buried on the same day. But usually those who die late in the afternoon and can be kept clean are not buried until the next morning so that there will be a large crowd for the funeral. At about nine o'clock in the morning, the coffin is taken out of the house, and at that moment a pot full of water is smashed. The weeping rises to its highest. The coffin is carried by four men, and two at the feet coming first. It is laid at the gate, and the ritual continues.

A few minutes later, the coffin is lifted up, and the procession begins. In front are the deacons who carry the cross and a priest who bears the incense. The other priests follow them. Behind the priests comes the coffin, and immediately next, the male laity with the mourners in front, and lastly come the women. In some cases, some junior deacons lead the procession bearing some wheat (about four or five kilos) for the eucharistic bread. Among the richer people, three baskets, with about five kilos of wheat in each, are taken.

The coffin is stopped after a few paces. Here a short rite begins and the women start a new way of weeping. The female relatives swing about the most decorative and honorific dresses of the deceased man. Also, the male relatives, usually the more distant and younger, carry his rifle, shield, spear, and head dress. For a deceased woman, the female mourners make a display of her tight purple trousers embroidered with gold fibres, and her fine cotton sheet with a multicoloured broad band of varied pattern at the middle. If the deceased does not have such decorative dresses, nothing will be exposed. In any event, women form into a ring and a lamentor-poet who starts a bemoaning song. She leads, and they repeat the refrain while swaying above the waist and moving rhythmically around her. Usually the mourners stand with her, but there are some who feel better moving around with the others. Each mourner is firmly held by a friend. The men weep bitterly but rather quietly. Those who are so violent that they scratch their faces and fall down are restrained by friends. One man is enough for a man, but for an unconsolable woman mourner, two and even three may be necessary. A lady of higher rank is held by two or three of her more honourable maids.

At the signal of a priest, the weeping ceases. A short prayer is recited, and the coffin is lifted up. The carriers are different from those who had been carrying it before. As a matter of fact, since every friend of the deceased tries his best to have a chance to carry the body so as to manifest his favour, the coffin will have changed hands several times before it reaches the next stop, although whosoever is bearing it tries to continue as long as he can. The next halt comes at a spot indicated by the priests. The same process is repeated here, too. Before it reaches the church, the coffin of a layman and all women must stop seven times; that of the clergy must stop twenty-four times.

Thus proceeding, the funeral reaches the church gate. Here, there may be waiting a bull to be slaughtered. In that case, the procession is stopped until the bull is slain.

The coffin is then passed over some blood strewn in its way and carried into the churchyard where it remains until the slaughter is completed. At the same time the debteras sing the "Souvenirs," or the priests serve the Mass rapidly. At the conclusion of the Mass or the completion of the slaughter, the coffin is brought to the door of the church (to the entrance for women if the dead is a woman). There the corpse is carried by means of the strap to the door of the holy of holies where it is laid and made to worship by inclining the head three times. The men then spread a garment over it and, between two curtains, bring it to the grave.

A priest is already there blessing and incensing the tomb. The corpse is now lowered into the grave where two men receive it and adjust its position. If the tomb is just a grave dug for one person only, the depth is shallow enough for the men to receive the body by hand. But in a sepulchre the body must be lowered down with the strap. Either type of grave is oblong at its floor with its longer sides extending east to west. But the sides of the sepulchre are laid with a single layer of stone, and its western side rises concavely so that the mouth is very narrow. When lowered into this grave, the corpse is held with the strap at the calves and the back. The legs are lowered faster so as to keep the head slightly higher. The two men inside slip off the strap and lay the corpse with its head to the east. Then they come out, and the grave is closed with a large piece of flat stone, the edges of which are daubed with mud. Now, the closest male mourner pours some earth on the slab and everybody follows his example until the top of the grave forms a small mound over which a slab of stone is erected. A single grave is filled with earth because it is for one person only, but the sepulchre is a family burial place, so no earth is poured into it.

The burial over, a priest opens the "Book of Shrouding" and signals for complete silence. The firing of guns, the tolling of the bell, and the loud weeping cease instantly.

He reads a passage which asks the grave to receive the man and says: "He was earth and has been returned to earth." Then the mourners walk out of the churchyard and sit in an open field nearby. This is the usual congregation ground. The women sit under a shady tree, but the men sit mostly in a sunny spot.

The weeping continues for quite a long time. A lamentor-poet now stands up and chants a hymn which she rhymes impromptu, pointing out the greatness and generosity of the dead man's ancestors and praising him for his outstanding deeds and good nature. Although less frequently, a man may be seen chanting such rhymes. The lamentor-poet is just an ordinary woman or man who has the talent of rhyming impromptu death poems. Although they are not professionals and are seldom hired, the greater mourners usually reward them quite well. One or more lamentor-poets may be invited purposely. When the lamentor-poet intones the rhyme, everybody must be silent.

But there are intervals when everybody must weep for a minute or so. Then the poet resumes the intonation and the process is repeated until she has completed. Several volunteers may chant their rhymes.

When the sun becomes too hot for the people, the elderly men will tell the mourners to end the ceremony. Now the eldest priest of the village rises and reads a passage from the "Book of Shrouding" and then blesses the crowd, especially the closest relative, who stands with bowed head. Then the priest bids everybody pray, "Our Father." At the conclusion, the meat of the bull will be laid at the disposal of everyone, and a good portion being carved out for all the clergy. Everyone should take at least a bite or two and then wish a peaceful rest to the soul of the deceased. Finally the mourners and some elderly men separate from the crowd and sit alone. The people from the other villages rise in village groups and by turn come and bow in front of the mourners to whom they offer their condolences saying: "May God strengthen you"; and the mourners reply: "May He not expose you to evil." The people attending the funeral try to show themselves to the mourners, and the latter are very keen in observing who has come and what churches have sent their representatives. They count the crosses to themselves and are angry at any neighbouring church or person who did not appear. Women do the same with the women mourners, but the latter do not change place as do the men.

Finally, only the villagers and the closest relatives remain. These go back to the mourning house. On the return, the women go in front, and the men follow apart. Some of the women disperse on the way to boil coffee and roast some grain which will be taken to the mourning house. The others continue with the mourners up to the house and either stay there or go to their homes. However, all of the elder ones stay in the house weeping and trying to comfort the relatives, and of the men the majority stay with the mourners. They bring boiled coffee and roasted grain or bread and beer.

Every woman who comes into that house should arrange her shemma in the mourning drape appropriate to her district. In some districts, the shemma is folded across its width and suspended at the back from a knot at the neck. In other districts, it is shortened by folding a part of it, and then draped by passing under the left arm-pit to the right shoulder where the two ends overlap. This draping leaves both hands exposed and free for swaying at the funeral. In the towns, another arrangement has been adopted. One end of the shemma is girded at the waist and the other fastened to lie over the shoulders. This is of Amhara tradition.

All acquaintances of the mourning family must either attend the funeral ceremony, or visit the family in the mourning week. But only those acquainted with the deceased have to weep. Whenever a new visitor comes in to offer his condolences he looks grave, greeting or talking to nobody. The conversation ceases completely and the mourners weep. But the soothers advise them to stop it. For seven days, visitors come frequently, and the villagers remain in the house comforting the mourners. Some of the elder priests read books pointing out that it is not death but the loss of the after life which must be feared, that for the virtuous death is peaceful rest.

In the evenings, the neighbours bring their dinners and some extra bread for the family for, during the mourning week, no food should be cooked in the house. At dinner they tell some jokes among themselves that they may distract the mourners. However, the relatives are seldom entertained by that; they prefer weeping, and if they are calm it is just not to worry the soothers excessively. At night, everybody sleeps on the floor. The kinsmen of the dead lie where they sit during the day and dressed as in the day. Every morning very early before day-break, the closest relative wakes up and weeps. The others rise up and join her in the bemoaning which continues up to late in the morning. Occasionally the lamentor-poet rises up and, as usual, rhymes a death hymn endeavouring to draw out the pity of the audience, which weeps vehemently each time she poses.

This is the routine for the entire mourning week. But there are cases when the funeral ceremony should be repeated on a holy day during the week. For men of high birth, for those who died away from home, and those who needed a hurried burial, the funeral ceremony is performed once again; this is known as the *Agober*. Even when the first funeral has been performed normally, the nobility re-celebrate it for two main reasons: First, the *Agober* gives them an opportunity to organize a spectacular exhibition; secondly, their relatives who live far away can have the opportunity of assembling for mourning. This is the more important because the people of noble class are related far and near and known very widely, so that a second chance of

151

gathering together is almost indispensable. For these reasons, the nobles have two ceremonies. Those who die away from home deserve it because all of their relatives and acquaintances should assemble at least once and celebrate the funeral. Besides, this gives a fixed date for all visitors. Of those who die at home, some are buried too hastily; for example, women who die in labour, all persons dying of dysentery or of stabbing or shooting, especially if in the belly. The reasons for the hasty burial is that they cannot be kept clean.

The *Agober* is celebrated not necessarily beside the church, but on any convenient ground. Here the coffin is dressed as though it contained the corpse and is put in the centre of a rich carpet. Around the coffin stand the priests dressed in the best of their church vestments and holding the cross and the incenser. They may chant the funeral rituals or keep silent; for rites without the corpse are strongly opposed by some.

Beside the symbolic coffin is spread another carpet and on it are laid two pillows. A servant bearing the gun of the dead man stands at the foot of the coffin and another one holding a fly-whisk stands at the head, thus symbolically protecting the dead man from flies and other insects. Beside the rifle bearer stands another servant carrying the shield and spear of the man. The rest of his harness is similarly displayed.

In front of the audience appears a row of servants. Some are carrying wine pots which are covered with red veils. Close beside them is a man with a flask of wine at hand; another group displays meat and knives, and still another exhibits the straw work for table and sauce pots covered in red veils. These are the groups that represent their lord's banquet arrangements. Beyond them another group displays the horse and mule harnessed at their best.

The relatives and retainers of the deceased now shoulder their rifles, and, arranging their shemmas at the waist, they advance to the coffin to which they bow very low. Then a master-of-ceremonies calls for silence and the lamentor-poet chants. This time they may be even bards and pipers. The bards and pipers play when there is weeping and when the mourners are going around the coffin.

As soon as the chanting ends, the weeping starts over again, and the procession resumes after a while. These acts are repeated alternately until the end of the ceremony, when the funeral men disperse.

The mourners are far more numerous this time. The announcement has been sent to more remote places, and people who attended the first funeral have been informing others that the *Agober* has been fixed for that date.

They themselves should come back. The mourners are once more keen in observing those who have come, for now, too, the visitors must offer their condolences before departing.

On the *Agober* day, all neighbours and kinsmen of the dead prepare some beer. Under each tree on the return routes, one or two relatives put their pots of beer, and every passer-by comes or is called to drink from the beer alloted to his village.

Once the people start returning from the *Agober* the ceremony has ended, and the mourners go back to the house and continue the mourning. The coffin is returned to the church, and the servants bring the rifle, etc., of the deceased back to the house. However, the meat and wine or any other food cannot be brought into the house again.

An *Agober* is usually held during the mourning week, but sometimes foul weather or fear of disease may postpone the date. When the date of the Agober has fallen within the week, the mourning continues up to the seventh day. On the eighth day everybody disperses. The family is left alone and is expected to resume its normal life. The members of the family will eat and sleep as they did before. But some grief-stricken and heartbroken women refuse to sleep anywhere but on the ground with only a fleece to lie upon. Men are more reserved and would rather resume their normal ways of sleeping. They are also calmer in weeping, especially after the end of the week. Priests hardly weep, for they preach that Christians should not be delirious with grief when the Lord takes the life that He has given and especially when Christians know that Jesus suffered death.

The conclusion of the mourning week does not entail the conclusion of the mourning itself. Whenever a new visitor appears to declare his sympathy the relatives weep, and whenever they recall the deceased they lament softly. Besides, they arrange their hair and dress to signify their grief. A man dyes his clothes black. In the country-side where the dye is not available the bark of a tree called weiba is collected and boiled in water. This yields a yellow liquid in which the entire suit is dipped in order to dye it yellow. For distant relatives, the clothes may just be left dirty for a while. A person of higher rank avoids this dying of clothes. But instead of the softer cotton shemma, he puts on an entire suit of calico which is left white, and sometimes he may even wash it if he wishes. But it must be noted that the majority of the country folk wear calico suits ordinarily; it is only men who normally consider this material below their dignity who wear it for mourning. Also, the clergy do not consider it as a sign of deep mourning; although, very rarely, priests may be seen wearing calico for mourning.

153

A gentleman who contents himself with white calico at the death of one person may be seen wearing a dyed suit at the death of some other person, for example, of a brother or close relative more important than himself. White or dyed, he drapes his shemma on the right shoulder as a sign of mourning.

In the towns, the more sophisticated just fix a black patch either on the left arm or on the breast, or if they are used to wearing shemmas they wear a muslin sheet lined with a black ribbon. Some wash it, others let it go dirty. A normal, everyday practice among many is to shave the head, but there are some who prefer to wear a head of hair; when mourning, however, they *must* shave their heads.

Women, too, dye their clothes, and line their shemmas and robes with black ribbon. In addition, they remove their ornaments. The neck cord, which is normally black, is replaced by a white string; all the rings and crosses suspended on it are put aside. Earrings and finger-rings and other jewelry are taken off and put aside. The women of Azabo and Raya wrap themselves in a sheet of black, coarse sack-cloth fastened with a belt of coarse rope.

As has already been said, men shave their heads as a sign of mourning. However, this manifestation of grief is also carried out by women. At the funeral of a close relative, they tear out a lot of their hair plaits; soon after, they may shave off the remaining hair. However, a broken-hearted mourner keeps her hair until the celebration of the Fortieth Day of commemoration. The idea is to expose herself to suffering, dirt, and lice; she neither washes her hair nor combs nor rearranges it. She just binds the tuft of hair at the back of the neck with a strip of rag and leaves it that way until the celebration of the Fortieth Day, when she shaves it off. Besides, a mourning woman may not apply butter to her hair, or oil, for two or three months, or sometimes for half a year. At the death of her husband, a faithful wife does not use butter on her hair for at least a year.

When a mourner resumes buttering her hair, she has completed her period of grief. This occasion occurs when the neighbours gather together and, having decided to persuade her to end the mourning, they come to her house. They bring with them some fresh butter, and in some districts they bring also a shemma. They pray her to end the mourning, arguing that she has already had a long enough period of mourning and that further prolongation would weaken her health. Somehow they usually succeed in persuading her; failing that, they just seize her hands, and one of the elder women smears her head with butter they have brought along. With that smearing, ends the mourning. The woman resumes her normal life.

HARRARI FUNERAL CUSTOMS[1]
Abdulla Abdurhaman

The following is a detailed description of funeral customs and ceremonies such as are practiced today among the Harrarians, and, with trifling variations, in the Gallan and Aroban areas near Harrar.

Commonly, the death of any person is naturally announced primarly by the lamentations of the relatives, if the deceased person has any. But in the city of Harrar the death is officially announced by an appointed person, a man if the deceased is male, a woman if the deceased is female. The announcer completes a round summoning the master or the mistress of every house as he visits each and announces the death of the particular person. Usually this summoner is the nearest neighbor of the deceased. His task is to assemble the "guild," a group of men who unite for the purpose of burying each other. There are a great many such guilds, since funerals are not commercial in Harrar; in fact, a man or woman who belongs to none will have hardly anybody to bury him or her except hired coolies, and this is considered miserable and shameful by the community. Some of these guilds are ancient and respected associations descending uninterruptedly from father to son, and they have survived competition against others, say, as to the accommodations they offer the deceased and his family, or the skill and the speed with which they bury him.

The burial ceremony begins with the washing of the dead body which is a complicated business including the stuffing of the body orifices and the use of different ointments for embalming and straightening the appendages. This is the task of specialized old women; they perform it behind closed doors.

Clothing will follow the washing of the corpse. For this, the corpse is laid prostrate and is first enveloped in an unseamed white cotton shroud, and then is wrapped tightly in another white sheet which is tied at both ends. A female corpse is clad in a white ankle-long, long-sleeved robe, trousers, and a white headdress.

While this washing and wrapping takes place inside the house of the deceased, outside, in nearby houses, a portion of the men of the guild already called are reading chapters from the Holy Koran aloud and melodiously together, and the women assemble, usually spreading all over the yard and

[1] Abridged and reproduced with permission of the Ethnological Society of University College of Addis Ababa. Bulletin No. 2, December, 1953.

in the street, weeping and mourning. The female relations of the deceased, adhering to the futile and wasteful custom, tear their gowns, which are minutely decorated with colourful hand-knitting, virtually asunder, pluck out their hair by the roots, and cry in touching, lamenting verses.

By the time washing and wrapping are done, and a few chapters read from the Holy Koran, men from other portions of the guild, who have been digging the grave and furnishing the grave implements, arrive with a wooden and leather bed. The cries of the women now culminate into a climax of outbursts. The Holy Koran is closed gently, and men rise to escort the deceased to his eternal resting place. The corpse is tied to the bedsticks strongly, and the bed is shouldered by four men. The procession sets forth towards the burial ground, just outside the walls of the city, singing hymns and repeating the name of Allah accompanied by unison litany. On the way, the heavy bed is constantly exchanged from shoulder to shoulder, and nearly everybody, even an unknown passer-by, gives a helping hand in shouldering the bed for a distance, as a sign of respect to the dead.

When the grave is reached, the bed is placed on the ground, and the body untied. It is left just at the edge of the grave, lying face upward for a moment so that anybody present could say the prayer for the dead man on the spot. This "prayer of the corpse," as it is called, has to be said at one time or another. The relations and neighbours of the deceased may say it for him in his house after the death, but most commonly it is conducted at the graveyard by anybody who wishes to pray. If the death takes place on the Holy Day, Friday, the corpse is carried to the mosque and a mass prayer is said for it; this is always an honour.

The grave itself is an oblong ditch about seven feet by four feet and five feet deep. At the bottom of the grave on the right side as you face north, (since all the Harrar, Moslem graves, on religious principle, are dug facing Mecca) horizontally another oblong cave is dug about the size of the adult man. The corpse is lowered slowly and carefully into the grave, and from this outer grave it is forced gently into the little den, the inner grave, in a sleeping condition face upwards. This chamber is then walled with blocks of stone and mud, to separate it from the outer grave which is then filled with the soil and leveled to the ground. The burial is completed by erecting the grave stones on either side of the grave. These grave stones are usually a pair of flat white blocks, often carved into artistic shapes, one of them slightly bigger than the other. They are erected on the top of the grave facing one another on the north and south ends, the bigger one being located on the northern end, i.e., directly above the head of the buried body. A short epitaph, "God bless his soul," coupled with the date of birth and death, is written on the bigger block. The two main gravestones are then joined by linings of small stones on their adjacent sides in order to show the rectangular outline of the grave. A distinctive, cylindrical piece of stone is inserted in the middle of the rectangle on women's graves.

When the burial is over, everybody goes back home, the men of the guild carrying their shovels, pickaxes, or spades, and the bed. The family of the deceased continues mourning.

The members of the guild, having accommodated their dead fellow-man in a relatively comfortable resting place, and wished him a restful sleep, disperse in the direction of their homes, their spades and pickaxes hanging on their shoulders. Some of them carry important community implements, such as the couch on which the deceased was conveyed, and the shelves, etc., to the house of their chief, under whose care they will remain until required for the next burial.

Though the man may be buried and gone, his spirit, according to the common belief, still demands a lot from the living, in order that it may gain complete peace and tranquility. To be able to understand how the living relatives render the rights and duties they owe their dead, let us follow their domestic activities after a death has taken place.

The first remarkable event, after the departure of the corpse for the burial ground, is the production of "kafara," a kind of unleavened plain bread, baked in small circular shapes (about three inches in diameter) from a ready made, sweetened dough. The cakes, which are baked only at the time of a funeral, are produced only in the case of the deaths of mature men and women, i.e., those over sixteen years of age. No sooner does the male procession, carrying the body of the deceased, leave the gate of the house, than a group of the female kin start a bon-fire in the open air, and set a pan on it. Another group prepares the dough from wheat flour, and still another moulds the small, round cakes. In a matter of minutes, basket after basket is filled with these *kafara;* some are served to the temporary female mourners, who keep them until they go back to their homes to divide them among their children, if they have any; another part is sent to the grave-yard where it is distributed among the paupers and beggars who gather around in multitudes. In some Harrarian societies, this traditional *kafara* is being replaced by some other form of alms, notably dates, because they are handy and sweet. It is not uncommon, on the other hand, for the family or the relatives of the deceased, particularly if these are wealthy, to slaughter a domestic

157

animal, varying from a goat to an ox, and divide the parts among the poor neighbours and mendicants as a rich sacrifice for the dead man.

An outburst of confused noise and lamenting outcries on the part of the female mourners, as they see the first attendants of the burial returning from the cemetery, heralds the end of the funeral ceremonies for the day. The members of the guild address a few words of consolation to the chief mourner and depart. The women force the last tear from their eyes and disperse. But they never cease to cooperate fully in sustaining the relatives of the deceased and in helping them in any way possible. It is, for instance, considered the duty of every woman who lives in the vicinity of the house of the deceased, or who is a member of the guild, to provide the family during three consecutive days with at least one meal, either lunch or supper, the dish being cooked and arranged in an extremely delicious and careful manner. Occasionally they may bring a calabash full of milk, or some other present, to say nothing of the contributions of money, the amounts of which are stipulated by convention established, as we shall see, on ceremonial days.

The nearest blood kinsmen abandon their houses and reside with the family of the deceased, usually for a week or a fortnight, during which period they share the grief of the chief mourner and continue their silent meditation. The men all stay in one room and the women in another, and, for the first days, their main concern is to appear deeply grieved and to receive wholeheartedly the sympathisers who come by scores every morning. In the men's chamber, the chief mourner, wrapped to the head in a white shawl, sits nearest the door, so that it is not difficult for the guests to reach him and to shake his hands. Sympathisers formulate short phrases of solace and well-wishing, while the mourners "Amen" till the end, when they too join in the refrain, which, incidentally, is the first chapter of the Holy Koran.

An informal ritual, known as the *"Fatah,"* is held on the fourth day. This religious ceremony, organized by the family of the deceased with the help of the members of the guild, each of whom contributes the Ethiopian equivalent of twenty-five cents, is attended by the men of the guild and aged neighbours, who all unite to pray God to forgive the deceased his sins and to save his soul from the tortures of hell.

For the remainder of the week there is no special event. The unfortunate bereft still go on with their lamentations, although by now most of them begin to recover. The women dress in black gowns, head-dresses, and tight-fitting trousers, and the girls go out wearing their gowns inside out, gowns which they have, as I described previously, torn to rags. The men have no special mourning markings or clothes.

The end of the first week witnesses the climax of the religious ceremonies that follow a death. A huge ox is slaughtered and a great festival is organized mostly from the private contributions of the family, although the fund raised by a contribution of one dollar from each member of the women's group does help.

This day is a grand day; it marks, to the delight of the relatives, the end of the burdensome mourning formalities. For the occasion, all the men and women neighbours and members of the guild are cordially invited. As every woman enters the house, she tosses a dollar note in the wide basket placed just beneath the threshold for the collection of the contributions, and proceeds to sit among her peers, Harrarian fashion. The principal occupation of the women during the whole day is to look after the kitchen and the cooking, to serve the men and furnish them with their multiple necessities, primarily *"qat,"* a drug which the men must have if they are to do anything worthwhile. Then regular meals and tea follow at short intervals. Besides their kitchen activities, the women mostly gossip about successes and failures of other women who are not present, or reminisce about old times, except when the eldest ones strike up a religious hymn; then they all join in the singing, piously asking salvation for the dead person.

The men, on their side, are exempted from any contributions, but nearly everyone of them has to come with a bundle of the indispensable leaves of *qat* tucked under his arm. This he hands to the master-of-ceremonies, commonly appointed because he is the eldest or wisest of the lot, appointed permanently if he is to stay the day, and temporarily if he cannot.

By ten o'clock, the majority of the invited guests are present, and the master-of-ceremonies opens the *qat*-eating ceremony, called *"Barca,"* dividing proportionately, as he sees fit, the huge heap of the eagerly awaited drug piled in front of him. The youngsters grind the herb with small wooden mortars and pestles, and sweeten it with sugar, in deference to the old who cannot chew it raw. Soon after a few mouthfuls, everybody warms up; the atmosphere becomes light and active. They pass the forenoon thus idly enjoying their *qat*, talking, discussing, and laughing. The master-of-ceremonies sees that the supply of the opiate and its auxiliaries, sugar and the Harrarian beverage, *"ghewa,"*[2] is continuous. At noon, lunch is served only to the few who have not eaten any *qat*, for the addicted consumers abhor any food during and long after taking *qat*. Early in the afternoon,

---

[2] Harrarian beverage prepared from coffee.

everybody feels hot. They stand up, clean the house, wash up, and piously say the mid-day prayer in a group under the guidance of a chosen Imam. When they have finished it, they settle themselves comfortably between cushions and pillows, ready for serious work. Texts of the Holy Koran and a couple of the other prayer books are distributed around. Soon they begin to recite the melodious verses of Holy Scripture, loudly and harmoniously. There is no pause or interruption once they start, and, sweating under their own spiritual enthusiasm for the reverent words of Allah, they complete the entire book, say the long prayer affixed to it, and take on the other books with sustained zeal and vigour.

Around sundown, the ceremony ends and the men, hungry and exhausted, joyously receive their reward in the form of a series of delicious dishes of many types of food, which they eat hastily and freely, in handfuls. Then tea follows, to clear the throat and terminate the banquet. When every man has had his fill, a last God-save-his-soul is said, and everyone takes his leave; a little later the women, who must delay a bit to assist in the cleaning, depart also.

These funeral rites, and their observance, help the emotional read-justment of the bereaved. Afterwards, the male relatives leave, and only a few of the nearest womenkin remain with the family of the deceased after the end of the first week. Notwithstanding the fact that the real ceremonies are now over, these family members and kin will continue to remain idle and wear black mourning clothes for some time. The women acquaintances will never fail to come with a present of some kind, up to the end of the first month. Some families may present a small lunch at the beginning of the second month, and invite the eminent personalities of the vicinity to conduct a ceremony, which is a perfect stereotype of the one I have just described, only on a much smaller scale. And then some may repeat the same ritual annually, renewing their grief and memory of the deceased, year after year.

In my endeavour briefly to describe the Harrarian funeral customs, I have limited myself to customs in case of normal death. I have avoided (as much as I could) out-dated customs, trivial details, and abnormal or emergency cases. But there may always arise simple modifications and slight alterations due to different conditions. For instance, they do not go out to the cemetery to bury a baby less than a year old; whereas, the burial of a cen-tenarian is very ceremonious. The death-tidings of a wealthy aristrocrat may ring far and wide beyond the walls of Harrar, and the demise of a religious eminence may shock hearts and attract multitudes from the remotest distances. It should not, therefore, be surprising if these latter funeral rites differ greatly from those for a friendless pauper or a social out-cast. Among the Harrarians, much of the burial ceremony is simplified, often to bare essentials, by request of the deceased, whose requests are meticulously observed.

DEATH CUSTOMS IN BAHER DAR[1]

My home town is Baher Dar, southeast of Gondar, by the seashore of Lake Tana. In this town there are not many people. There are two religions practiced, namely, Christian and Moslem. The Christians outnumber the Moslems by far. Though the people are of differing faiths, they are united in their social customs.

If a Christian dies, everybody in town is informed of his death, and most of the people come to the house of the dead person, or they go to the church where the body is taken. In the church, the people shed their tears, and the priests perform their habitual songs. After a long ceremony and sorrowful period, the dead body is buried. The head priest, with the sign of the Cross, says a few words to comfort the dead person's relatives. Then everybody disperses for a few hours. Later they bring *tella* or *injera* or coffee to the dead person's house, where everybody sits quietly and drinks. After a few hours, they leave for their respective houses, and that will be the end of the funeral ceremony.

On the other hand, the Moslems bury the dead person in their imperial graveyard outside of town. One Maria Theresa dollar is buried with the dead person. The remorse is the same as among the Christians.

Whenever somebody dies, the Christians and the Moslems participate together in their sorrows and shed their tears equally well together.

---

[1] Authors' names withheld by request.

161

Ancient, primitive carved stones, less than 100 miles from Addis Ababa, of unknown origin. Considered holy.

VI
Religions
of
Ethiopia

Historically, the Ethiopian Orthodox Christian Church is linked to the Egyptian Coptic Church, sharing the monophysite belief that Christ's manhood and divinity are one and single in nature. In other respects, the doctrine of the Ethiopian Church is similar to that of the Greek Orthodox Church. Until 1951, the Alexandrian Church consecrated an Egyptian Coptic to serve as the head of the Ethiopian Church. In that year, *Abuna* (Metropolitan) Basilios, an Ethiopian, became the Archbishop, achieving for Ethiopia the status of an independent national church.

In the fourth century A.D., Christianity was introduced into Ethiopia and has been active, without interruption, to this day, making that country the oldest continuously Christian country in the world. Today, educated guesses estimate that approximately forty-five per cent of the Ethiopians are Christian, forty-five per cent Muslim, and ten per cent Pagan. Elements of all three faiths are often found combined in the religious beliefs and practices of persons and groups, especially in the rural areas. A small number of Ethiopians, the Falashas, are of the Judaic faith and are thought, by some, to be descendants of one of the lost tribes of Israel; however, the Orthodox of modern Israel do not recognize the Falashas as legitimate.

163

THE MONASTERY ON ZUQUALA MOUNTAIN[1]

I. The Church and Stones of Zuquala
Hapte-Mariam Marcos, Jemal Abdulkadir, and Belatchew.

Although the morning was very chilly, we rose early and went out to see the church, which is located at the summit of the mountain. As you approach the western side of the church, you see only the roof because the rest of the church is hidden at the back of the front steps. When you climb up the steps, you see a beautiful, small, hexagonal church, white-washed, but somewhat dusty. Its beauty is accentuated by the stately trees which surround it. As no one can enter the church with his shoes on, we removed our shoes and entered barefoot.

The church consists of three sections: the outer-ringed space where the ordinary people attend mass, the middle-ringed space which only priests, nuns, and those people who receive holy communion can occupy, and finally the inner-circular space where the Holy of Holies is kept, and where the mass is celebrated.

The second section is a rectangular structure whose four walls are covered with paintings representing either characters in the stories of the Bible or scenes from the life-history of the Saint Abbo Gebre Menfes Kidus. A few others represent Emporor Menelik II with his Rases such as Ras Walle, Ras Darge, Ras Gugsa, etc., and their retinues. There is, for example, the picture of a very savage man, described in the Bible, eating the flesh of the human being whom he has killed. In another picture the same man is seen giving water to a leper. Other pictures represent Mary and Christ, Christ gliding down rays of the sun, and children falling down while trying to imitate him; St. George and the dragon are also depicted.

Facing the innermost rectangular structure is the picture of *Abuna* Gebre Menfes Kidus. He is represented as a tall, old man, with a very long white beard and a long pale blue dress. He is seen feeding a dove.

The paintings are quite recent, since the church was built in 1912, and show European influence. There is a self-portrait of the painter with paint pots held up in both hands, at the bottom of which is written, "The Painter, the chief of scholars of Elias." The paintings are open to the public view twice a year, on the days of the Saint, but it is possible to see them at any other time provided the church is open.

[1] Abridged and reproduced from the University College Ethnological Society Bulletin No. 1, May 1953.

Ethiopian religious parade with ceremonial umbrellas at monastery atop the holy mountain of Zuquala, about 50 kilometers from Addis Ababa.

Near the church, at its southeastern part, is a volcanic crater containing a greenish-blue lake approximately half a mile in diameter. It is interesting to note that the lake is regarded as sacred; therefore, no one can swim in it, nor can anyone kill the beautiful ducks that float on it.

Near the lake are places celebrated for their legendary and religious significance, the main ones being the Seat of *Abuna* Gebre Menfes Kidus, the Devil's Tomb, the Wednesday and Friday Stones, and the Atabkignes. The Seat of the Saint is like a very small chair without arms. It is about two feet high, and has a back which is comparatively high. Each year the Gallas put some butter on the Seat. This custom was once forbidden by the monks of the monastery; however, as the belief goes, the Holy Lake dried up for one year after this prohibition, and so the custom was permitted again and is still practised.

The Devil's Tomb is a heap of volcanic stones about four feet high. According to the legend, when the Saint came to Mount Zuquala, there were many devils in the lake who tried to tempt him. He prayed for their extermination, and all but one were exiled to the lake of Bishoftu. The unfortunate one which remained is said to have been killed by the people and buried under the stones at the side of the Devil's Tomb.

The stones of Wednesday (*Rob*) and Friday (*Arb*) are about twelve feet high and six feet wide. They are very steep, which renders them difficult to climb. The story goes, however, that a man who has faithfully fasted on Wednesdays and Fridays is capable of climbing them. Many of the faithful do climb them, and this feat gives them encouragement and helps them achieve their desires.

The two *Atabkignes* are big stone tunnels, each having two to four big stones between which are narrow, low gaps. It is very difficult for tall or fat persons to pass through the gaps. The accepted belief is that men and women who have sinned cannot pass through. The word *Atabkigne* means "a narrow passage between two or more stones."

The most spectacular sight is the Cave, where the monks pray and fast during their retreats. The Cave is a place of seclusion, and nobody is allowed to enter the Cave during the time of retreats.

II. *Life on the Top of Zuquala*

Asseffa Beru, Melake Hiywot Bayssasse, Paulos Asrat, Yohannes Wolde Gerima

Most of the traditional laws governing the life at the top of Zuquala Mountain are more theoretical than practical. According to the customary laws, only members of the clergy are supposed to live in the vicinity of the church. The area considered as the property of the church extends approximately from the top down to the middle of the mountain on all sides.

During the Italian occupation, traditions declined, and most of the customary clerical laws were unobserved. The monastic area became a dwelling place of ordinary peasants as well as of the clergy. Since the liberation of Ethiopia, the laws once again function; ploughing is prohibited, neither trees nor grass on the area belonging to the monastery may be cut except for the needs of the church, no secular songs or folk dances are allowed, unless specially permitted by the authority of the monastery, bathing or swimming in the sacred lake is prohibited, selling *tella* (beer) or any other intoxicating liquor is forbidden. Complying with the above rules, a few groups of laymen live today at the top of the mountain. Although restricted by the rules, the laymen can make their living by growing cabbages, potatoes, onions, hops, and spices, which they exchange for other crops. They breed cattle, sheep, and goats for milk and meat.

High-ranking priest from Zuquala Monastery on a rare visit to Addis Ababa carrying fly whisk and Coptic Cross.

The conditions of life for the clergy, the largest body of inhabitants of the mountain, are similar to those of the laymen. The priests and the deacons, for example, live among their fellow laymen. The manner of life of the monks and nuns, however, should be distinguished. Crippled and aged nuns and monks live in the small houses in the courtyard of the church; here also we find the monks and nuns who are on duty. Otherwise, if well and not on duty, they live in their own homes on the mountain. Previously, some monks used to live in caves near the lake. Formerly, nuns used to live mixed with the monks. Recently, however, they have formed an organized nunnery. For their food, most nuns and monks depend on the monastery. Out of the crop obtained from the land and out of any kind of charity, the monks and nuns receive their support. Some monks and priests make their living in the same way as do the laymen, by farming small tracts, raising cattle, and exchanging their produce with other "independent" monks and laymen.

Now let us consider administrative organization and education in the monastery. The head of the monastery is the *Memhir,* teacher of the monastery. The *Memhir* is responsible for the whole monastery, with regard to its internal administration, as well as its connection with the authorities of the Ethiopian Church. Under the Memhir is the Gebez, who is in charge of the

167

activities in the church. Under him are the *"Lique Deakons,"* Chief Deacons, and other minor officers. The education given in the monastery school is wholly religious. The aim is to prepare men who wish to serve the church. The teachers are not paid. They teach either because they want to teach or because they have no other way of serving the monastery. The latter case applies to the crippled or blind monks who cannot do any work except sit and teach the Bible or other religious books. Students are not grouped into strict classes, but, of course, some students are more advanced than others. Often the teacher instructs the senior students who, in turn, teach those below them. In this manner the teaching system goes down to the beginners. Students flock from distant areas of Ethiopia as well as from the region of Zuquala. The students who come from distant districts make their living either by serving the important monks and priests or by receiving alms.

At Zuquala, life in general is religious. The inhabitants, men and women, old and young, strictly observe the holy days. As a whole, the people are very hospitable.

III. A Short Life History of Abuna Gebre Menfes Kudus or Abbo, Saint of Zuquala
Aklilu Habte

Since most of the historical and religious books were burned during the invasion of Mohammed Gran, the books dealing with the life-history of the Saint were largely lost. It is thus very hard to write a reliable history of his life. It is reported that there is today in the province of Tigre one original book which luckily escaped the hand of the invader; though in which part of Tigre and in what particular church the book exists remain matters of mere conjecture.

There are two views as to where the Saint came from. One point of view, held by the minority, is that he came from Europe, in particular from Venice; the other point of view, held by the majority of the Ethiopian religious authorities, is that he came from Nehissa in southern Egypt. His father, Simon, and his mother, Aquelassia, both were illiterate. Gebre Menfes Kidus was their only child. When the child was born, he was taken by an angel, who returned him to his mother three days later. He grew with-

168

out suckling from the breast of his mother. When he had completed his third year of life, he was taken to a monastery where he studied for twelve complete years, until he was fifteen years of age. He was then taken to the bishop, His Beatitude, Abraham, to be blessed and ordained.

Abuna Gebre Menfes Kidus, from the early days of his youth, was very religious "not caring a dash about his wordly life" as the unknown Ethiopian chronicler of Debre Libanos said. Hundreds of people from many parts of Egypt, Serhe, Nahissa, etc., flocked to see him perform miracles in the name of God. Not only men admired and respected him but also wild animals such as lions and tigers. It is believed by the clergy, though mainly by the least educated ones, that he used to ride lions and tigers when passing from one country to another.

Such was the life he was living when he was ordered by God to go to Ethiopia. He was at first puzzled, for he did not know the way; nevertheless, he was led by the Spirit of God and reached Ethiopia in the twelfth century during the reign of King Lalibela, during whose reign were constructed the magnificent rock-hewn churches in Lasta. He traveled through the northern provinces, then passed to the southern provinces and then to the country of Shogolle, where he performed many miracles. At last he reached Zuquala, but why, when, and how he came to this place are not yet known.

The Saint used to pray persistently to bring the grace of God upon the people. He used to tie his feet with ivy and pray with his head downward. According to the belief, one day Satan, annoyed by his actions, cut off the ivy, and the Saint fell down and broke his teeth. On the ground where his broken teeth fell there grew almond and cocoanut trees. Before he stood up, Satan, disguised as a crow, came and pecked at his eyes, in spite of which he continued to see. Satan and his followers fled, leaving the lake in which they had lived for years prior to the arrival of the Saint. After this, the lake became holy; its waters cured many sick people, and it has remained holy through the centuries up to the present time.

Later, the Saint went to Medre Kebde where another famous church was constructed just like the one at Zuquala. He lived in Medre Kebde for some time, and died and was buried there, at the age of 992 years, as the short Ge'ez history of Gebre Mariam says, or 560 years, as Alequa Meshesha Gizaw, the young Ge'ez scholar, writes. But some among the educated clergy say that it is not established whether he was buried in Medre Kebde or whether toward the end of his life he returned to Nehissa, his motherland, and died there.

ON WORSHIP—excerpts from three essays[1]

It is an historical fact that a few decades ago the only religion which was professed openly and which was recognized by the Ethiopian rulers was the Coptic Christian religion. But nowadays, as everyone enjoys the freedom of practicing any religion that he wishes, in our Capital of Addis Ababa there are many kinds of religious sects, and countless worshipers. Let us consider the most outstanding religious sects and, in connection with them, the worship.

In Addis Ababa, the religion which is professed by the greatest number of people is the Coptic Christian religion; even the Royal family belongs to this religion. The numerous churches which are scattered everywhere in the capital and in its outskirts, and the tremendous number of the Coptic Christians who gather regularly in the churches every Sunday, show that the Coptic religion has great importance in the capital. Even now, a lot of money is spent in building churches and in printing religious books.

A Coptic Christian believes that there is only one God, and he worships Him. There are also a large number of saints whom he honours. Formerly, the greater part of a Coptic Christian's time was spent in his religious practices, and this is true even now in some localities of the capital. A true Coptic Christian must fast during the fasting months; if he does not do this, he is considered to be as bad as the worst sinner.

In churches, he spends the greater part of his time in reading the Bible and the life histories of the saints or in singing religious songs. Saint Michael, Saint Gabriel, Saint George, Holy Mary, Aba Teckle Haimanot, and Aba Gebre Menfes Kudus are the most outstanding saints of the Coptic Church. Many books are written about them, and many churches are built and dedicated to them.

There also are, in Addis Ababa, other worshipers such as the Roman Catholics who are more or less similar in worshiping to Copts. There are also protestants, e.g., Lutherans, Evangelists, Adventists, etc. In Addis Ababa, Moslems are also important. They have their mosques in the middle of the market place, and they perform their religious practices, worshiping God, regularly. It is interesting to see them gathering in their mosques every Friday. They celebrate with great pomp the festival of *Arapha* every year.

* * *

[1] Authors' names withheld by request.

170

I was born and brought up in a little village about one hundred kilometers from Addis Ababa.

The people living in this village have a strange way of worship. What they consider as their "God" is a big tree placed at the center of the village near a market. All the villagers believe that the tree existed in that spot before everything in the universe. Any newcomer has to accept the belief, otherwise he will be shot or considered as the enemy of everyone. Everyone here believes the tree is a supernatural being who can do anything that is wanted by man. All persons (including me when I was a child) used to attend a ceremonial gathering every Friday night. The procedure was the same, week after week and year after year.

Every person brings from his home a big circle of bread, placed in and covered with a many-colored cloth, and a jar of *tella*; all these are carried by servants who pass by the leader's chair and place their burdens near this big tree. The leader then starts to offer some words of thanks which are unintelligible to us, the listeners. Then the group, all together, start praying by a kind of singing. After the praying is done, the leader throws some bread and sprinkles some *tella* on the ground, so that the God will eat and drink. A part of the offering is kept for the snake which lies curled around the trunk of the tree and does no harm to anybody but guards the God's position (i.e., the tree). I have seen this snake with my own eyes many times. The rest of the food is eaten by us; whatever food is taken back to the house, it is said, will produce disease if taken into the body. Since I was afraid at that time, I did not try it once.

After the feast, any person who is sick is brought by bed and placed in front of the priest (leader), who starts to pray to the God by placing his forehead on the ground. The patient seems to be well and is taken back home. After this, the ceremony ends just as the sun sets. The God shows a sign to disperse the crowd by setting the sun and bringing the darkness.

One day, the tree caught fire, and a huge fire took place. The faith of the people was such that some of them sacrificed their lives trying to destroy the fire. Now the tree does not increase in size, but still it is worshiped as a brave God who, as some elders say, is a fire-proof tree. And they say that the God, in order to show that he is the God of fire, produced the fire by himself.

*   *   *

One of the outstanding characteristics for which Ethiopia is known in foreign countries is her ancestral Christianity. Christianity has been firmly established as the main dominant aspect in our history up to date.

171

Begemder is the most famous province for its religion or Christianity. The people inhabiting the region are mostly Amhara, although there are some Moslems, some Israelis, and some other groups as well.

All believe in the living God that created the universe with its inhabitants. The Christians believe in the three Divine Beings: God the Father, the son Jesus Christ, and the Holy Spirit.

Wherever you go, you will find Christian churches every place. To give an idea, there are, if I am not mistaken, over forty-four of them in the town of Gondar, which is a great number in comparison to the few town buildings.

If not all, most of the Amhara people go to churches to worship God every Sunday morning. They directly or indirectly address to God their praises for the good He has done; they reveal their sins to him directly or indirectly through mediators, such as Christ Himself, Mary the Mother of Jesus Christ, Saints, and priests. They do all these things at churches as well as at home in a very solemn and respectful way.

PAGAN BELIEFS AND RITES[1]
Western Ethiopia

Today the Wellege people are predominantly Christian, there being few Moslems. Yet the Wellege still observe some pagan practices in the remote parts of the country. For example, they worship trees and celebrate several pagan ceremonies; the *kalu* is even now an institution common to everyday life of Wellege.

In considering the religion of the pagan Wellege, it is not possible to formulate clearly their idea of God, which they call Waka. Moreover, in our enquiries, it was not possible to obtain either the names or the functions of their various gods. However, whatever their beliefs may be about spirits or the existence of supernatural beings, these are always connected with sacred things, sacred animals, and omens; if we also consider dalu, the witch, the snake man, the rainmaker, and dead parents as sacred, then the spirits are also connected with sacred men, as well as with objects and animals.

The people have a vague idea of the existence of the soul. They believe that there is reward and punishment after life. A good person and a fortunate

[1] Part of a report of a field trip to Nakemte by six members of the U.C.A.A. Ethnological Society, Bulletin No. 6, June, 1957. Abridged and reproduced with permission of the Ethnological Society of the University College.

An American stands by a huge "holy" tree believed to be home of a spirit. Remnants of sacrifices can be seen in hollow base of tree.

person will be rewarded. A bad and unfortunate person will be punished. They seem to have a belief in a kind of predestination, when they say fortunate and unfortunate people. Thus the lucky people who are favoured by the gods are honest, kind, and lead a good life on earth. Consequently they will be rewarded after life. The bad and the unfortunate people are those who are disfavoured by the spirts. They lead a corrupt life on earth and consequently are punished after life. However, the religious rites and the propitiation of the spirits connected with various sacred objects and sacred men are performed mostly for health, for rain, for bearing children; in general, for prosperity in this world rather than for reward in the after-life. Having this point in mind, let us examine various objects connected with worship.

1. *Mountain.* In March, on an agreed day, the villagers, usually only the menfolk, climb to the top of a nearby mountain where they kill a white bull and roast pieces of its flesh. Then they throw the roasted pieces on the mountain in all directions. The remaining meat is eaten raw or roasted. The main purpose of this ceremony is to ask the spirits of the mountain to give rain.

2. *Big Tree.* Under a big tree, a young goat is killed. The parchment-like fat which encircles the entrails is taken out. Then a kalu interprets the map-like lines of the fat. Usually this is done at a moment when people have to decide if they should fight with a neighboring tribe. If the kalu says, "Go, you will succeed," they go to war.

3. *River.* In the months of March or May, if the season is seriously dry, women go to the river and pray for rain. They bring with them leaves of a tree, green grass, and leaves of a creeper. They carry also sticks, somewhat

173

taller than themselves, buttered at the top. They pile the leaves on the western bank of the river and put porridge over them. In front of the piled leaves, turning their faces to the east, they pray to God for rain.

Besides these seasonal ceremonies performed on the top of the mountain, under a big tree, or by a bank of a river, every time people pass by a mountain or a big tree, or cross a river, they cut green grass and throw it in the direction of the mountain, under the tree, or on the river bank, saying, "I ask you for support!"

4. *Large Road.* In the worship of large roads, which also are believed to bring rain, the process is the same as for big rivers. However, in this case men also can attend the ceremony. The shepherds, who are very numerous in Ethiopia, may eat the porridge offered to the river or the road, if they wish.

5. *Snake.* Among sacred animals, the snake is the most common. A man or woman is chosen by the elders of the village to feed the snake. Villagers bring sheep or goats as tribute to the snake and hand them to the old person chosen to perform the ceremony. He kills a goat or a sheep, as he thinks fit, and gives the flesh to the snake. A hollow trunk of wood is provided, in which the snake drinks the blood of the sacrificed animal. The feeder of the snake usually lives close to the den of the reptile, which usually enters the house of the feeder whenever it needs food.

The purpose of the snake-worship is again mainly to secure rain. If the snake suns its body by exposing its ventral side, during the month of April especially, it is believed that there will be no rain; the people say that if the animal moves from its den in search of food, there is a great chance of exposing its abdomen to the sun. Thus, to keep the snake in its den most of the time, the people provide it with food.

A recent story goes that, while digging in her garden, an old woman killed a baby snake unintentionally. Then the woman's hands became full of sores. She was very afraid and told her neighbors what had happened. They warned her that she should ask pardon by paying "the value of the snake's soul." The woman prepared food and gave it to another snake through the man who was detailed to feed it.[2]

---

[2] Editor's note: A charming example of two cultures, a millenium apart, but in juxtaposition, can be found about twelve miles outisde of Addis Ababa. There is a huge, false fig tree under which children in grades one through four sit on crude benches ranged in a square around the trunk of the tree—one side of the square for each class. The teacher proceeds from side to side, from class to class, a preceptor of 20th century education. There is a large hollow space in one side of the trunk of the tree where one can usually see the skull or bones of a sheep, remains of sacrifices, for this tree is also the feeding place of a sacred snake.

THE GOD OF THE DISTRESSED [1]
Paulos Asrat

Half way between Dukam and Bishoftu, in the district called Kurkura, there is an acacia tree which, the villagers say, is over seventy-five years old. This umbrella-like tree, because of its shape and great size, is considered to be sacred. It is called an *Adbar,* protecting spirit.

In September of 1954, I visited the tree with Gebre Rufael, an elderly resident of Kurkura. When we approached the tree, Rufael took off his hat and bowed low; then he said: "Please you, Adbar, the Mistress of Kurkura, protect this young man and me from any illness, from thieves, from the insults of others, and from any danger." He added, putting his hat back on, "Now that I am near death, I thank you for the long life you have given me; please give the same number of years to this young man." Then he turned towards me and asked me to bow with him to the tree. He picked up three or four pieces of green grass from the ground and threw them at the Adbar. I asked him why he threw the grass. His answer was that the Adbar liked green, the symbol of freshness. Then he pointed his finger to show me the twigs, leaves, and grass which had been deposited around the trunk of the tree. The top of the trunk was wrapped with a piece of white cloth. On three or four of the bigger branches were suspended some hand-woven cotton threads. They had all been put there by the villagers, whose wishes had been supposedly fulfilled by the Adbar: having a child after a long period of sterility or getting cured of an illness or even finding a cow which had been lost the night before.

When I approached the tree with a splinter of wood in my hand, just to take some of the streaming gums, Gebre Rufael shouted at me: "Don't touch anything; the Adbar will be angry with you." I smiled and asked him if I could climb the tree; he too smiled and stared at me without saying anything. Finally he told me that the Adbar was not a plaything and that no one should touch the gum of the tree, nor its branches, nor even the dead leaves under it.

"Our Adbar is the god of the distressed," stated Gebre Rufael. "All the inhabitants of Kurkura know that an Adbar is a simple tree, created by God. They may choose any tree and call it an Adbar. They may have as many Adbars in a region as they require, and all Adbars may stand on equal footing with each other as regards worship. The point is that all Adbars are strongly

[1] Abridged and reproduced with permission of the Ethnological Society of the University College, from Bulletin No. 4, December, 1955.

believed to bring good fortune to those who ask them for it."

Gebre Rufael does not know how the tree performs its miracles, nor do his neighbours, but he tried to guess: "You see, this Adbar is a good shelter from the strong sun. All the shepherds of the village come with their goats and cattle and rest under it. Look how majestic, fresh, and beautiful it is. So, we believe that in one way or another it helps those who worship it, not only as a shelter from the sun and the rain but as a protector against troubles." I asked him what the villagers would do if the Adbar did not perform what they wanted from it. He told me that the tree would not hesitate to do good to all who deserve the good which they ask from it. He said: "If the people who ask favour from the Adbar have hit the cow of their neighbour, if they have stolen some grain from the barns of their friends, the Adbar will refuse to fulfill their wishes."

In order to obtain the greatest possible help from the Adbar, the inhabitants of Kurkura organize big and small ceremonies for it. The main ceremonies are held on any day in May and October. In May the villagers sacrifice a white or all black goat, and they sprinkle the blood under the tree. They roast the meat, prepare coffee and bread, boil beans and wheat together, and when everything is ready, they throw some parts from each item to the east, west, north, and south of the Adbar before they invite guests to taste anything. The number of guests attending a ceremony may be from fifty to sixty persons. The guests try to eat everything which is prepared. If anything is left, it cannot be taken home; it must be thrown near the Adbar, and goats, donkeys, or cattle may eat it. Before leaving the Adbar, the guests pray together for their children, for their crops, and for everything they want to be protected from, or for everything they want to be given by the Adbar. The ceremony of October is more or less the same as that of May. The only major difference is that in October a white bull is slaughtered instead of a goat; and thus more guests are expected to come to the Adbar in October than in May.

Gebre Rufael said that fifteen or twenty years ago three or four bulls were slaughtered on every celebration day in May or in October. "Nowadays," he said, speaking calmly, "people are becoming more sensible. They kill only one bull in October and only a goat in May. Little by little they are abandoning the *Adbar*, the protector of the Galla tribe."

Although the inhabitants of Kurkura believe in God, and although they understand that God alone has supreme power over the world, they try to derive benefit from the *Adbars* by making them their guardians against their worries and misfortunes. They have inherited the idea of the *Adbar* from their non-Christian Galla ancestors who originally worshiped trees as supreme gods. Today the people in Kurkura are not as staunch as their Galla ancestors in tree worshiping. The Gallas of Kurkura today think of the *Adbar* as a minor spirit which protects them against most of their troubles. That is why Gebre Rufael called the *Adbar*, "the god of the distressed."

RITES

1. *Atete*. This is a practice in many scattered regions of the country of propitiating the spirit of mothers in case of sickness, childlessness, lack of prosperity, etc. *Atete* is practised by women, and only by sincere believers. The times for *atete* are either a Tuesday or a Thursday evening during the sowing season.

A few days before the *atete*, a very thick beer is prepared. On the eve of *atete*, a thick porridge made of coarsely ground barley is cooked, and coffee beans are roasted. A goat is made ready to be killed at night.

On the eve of the *atete* the woman wears a dress which looks like a short tunic with black and white stripes set horizontally. On her neck she wears small beads of various colours, and red bracelets on her arms. Her hair, her neck, including the beads, and her dress are buttered.

The neighbours gather and sing constantly, clapping their hands. The woman who will celebrate *atete*, i.e., who is is to be possessed by the spirit of mothers, starts to grunt; she turns her head, moves it back and forth, right and left as she grunts rhythmically, all the time remaining seated in her place. Some women do not grunt or move their heads, but sit calmly. While the neighbours sing and the *atete* woman grunts, the drummer moves round her as he beats the drum.

The goat is killed when it is believed that the spirit of the woman's mother, which causes her to grunt and move her head, says' "Kill the goat for me!" The spirit is supposed to speak through the mouth of the *atete* woman. Immediately after the order is given, the people kill the goat. The woman puts around her neck the fatty covering of the entrails of the goat, and keeps it there for five days; the hoofs of the goat she wears on her wrists for

177

five days also.

For five days the woman must stay home. On the fifth day, the fat is taken to the kalu for interpretation of the future, and the hoofs are buried in the floor under the big pots containing the *atete* beer.

2. *Propitiation of the spirit of fathers by men.* This ceremony does not have a particular name, and probably is not so common as *atete* of women. The propitiation of the spirit of fathers is similar to *atete,* the ceremony differing from it in that the man does not dress in a special way, does not butter himself, and does not grunt.

Two pots of a light mead and two pots of a very thick beer are prepared. The pots are kept two on either side of the entrance of an inner apartment of the house.

On the day of the ceremony the neighbours gather. A young goat is killed. The man wears the hoofs on his wrists and the fat on his neck. Moreover, he takes a stick made from the branch of a certain tree, and butters it at the top. While praying, he lays the stick on the mouths of the four pots in turn. Then, holding the stick with both hands, he turns to the east and kneels down between the four pots. Then he prays: "Spirit of my fathers, fulfil my wishes. Give me health and prosperity. By giving this feast I have fulfilled the wishes of the spirit of my fathers." The people eat and drink and, at the end, bless the host, saying, "Let the spirit of our fathers fulfill your wishes."

The man stays five days at home. Parts of the hoof and head of the goat are kept for five days near the pots. On the fifth day, the fat is sent to the kalu for interpretation.

3. *Kalma or Buna Kela.* Literally, *buna kela* means the killing of coffee, but the real meaning is the sacrifice of coffee. *Kalma* is prepared by women for many purposes, such as for the recovery of a sick person. The best days are Sundays. Fresh coffee beans, still in their shells, are washed with water, and a little bit of the shell at one corner of the bean is cut with a knife or the teeth. A clay pan is placed on the fire in which the coffee beans are roasted. Then butter, ginger, some aromatic leaves, and salt are added. When the beans are well roasted and are stirred with a thin stick, they make a peculiar sound: "Toss, toss." People hearing it will answer: "Hatolu, hatolu," which means: "Let all be well; let all be well." It is believed that if the coffee beans do not make the noise, the sacrifice will not be beneficial, and the procedure must be repeated. Finally, roasted barley is added to the coffee, and the whole is served to all the people in the house.

THE ROLE OF THE CHURCH IN COMMUNITY HEALTH[1]

In Ethiopia, as in most cultures, the church is the hard core of resistance to changes. It also plays a key role in community health, since the priest also acts as a doctor. The priests oppose any change of basic cultural patterns. The masses of people are the home of folkways and morals, and the masses change very slowly; they seem to change more slowly in religion than elsewhere, and they change more slowly in religion for one reason—there are no fully satisfactory means of objective verification. Subjective verification? Yes, but not objective verification. Give the priest two different kinds of pens and he can tell you in two minutes which is better. Give him two religious creeds, however, and how can he test them? This simple comparison helps us to understand, in part, why religious changes have been so slow.

Religion has been changing more rapidly with the so-called progressive people. First, modern theories about God, about immortality, about the nature of men, are more and more based upon and made to harmonize with what modern science and philosophy make clear about ultimates of this wide, wide world. This means a decline in the authority of tradition and a decline in the authority of the church and the priests.

If we have a glance at a member of the present generation, we see that nature has taught him to understand and think before starting to do something. This new idea of understanding and thinking is completely opposed by the priests, as they want everyone to take everything on faith without any question.

Science and the Church: One has to think and study the community if one is to start to introduce a new idea to a community. One has to understand the characteristics, traditions, and beliefs of the people before interfering with their business. Most of the church men believe that the causative agents of any disease are God on the one hand, and Satan on the other hand. They also believe that those who are taught the science of Western civilization do not believe in the existence of the Almighty God. Faith has to be assured before a modern health worker can explain and demonstrate pathogenic agents to the priests. Such demonstrations are merely to gain friendship with the priests and so with the community. The community always follows the lead of the priests, since that is what they saw their fathers do.

However, there are some priests who do not oppose, but try to help the introduction of Western medicine. These have realized that Western medi-

[1] Author's name withheld by request.

179

Women attending annual religious pilgrimage to Kalubi, near Dire Dawa, a shrine of St. Gabriel credited with miraculous answers to prayers.

Crowds at entrance to holy place watch formal procession circle and recircle church under ceremonial umbrellas carrying holy symbols, pictures, and relics.

cine is helping people and improving standards of living. They believe that treating and curing diseases is the same as serving God to some extent.

The Family Priest: The family priest is a private priest who teaches the family about the religion. This is like the private doctor or physician. Every family should have one priest who will take care of all their difficulties and give them sound advice. It is the family priest who controls the family fasting and sees that they go to church every Sunday. It is he who gives the Coptic death certificate. This practice has great influence on the community because this priest is not the family priest of only one family but probably of many families.

The Power of the Church: The priests are thought to be highly educated about the church, and for this reason they are respected very much. The community regards religion as the first and most important thing in the world, and so the priests are able to interfere in many of the administrative practices of the state such as demoting a government administrator who is found to be dishonest or who does not serve the church. It is most important, from a public health point of view, that health workers do not oppose the church nor do things that the church does not like done.

The Church Holidays: There are certain days in the month which the church celebrates. The most important of these are St. Michael Day, St. Mary Day, St. George Day, and Abuna Tekle Haimanot Day. During these days, people must not do hard work. The community should go to church. However, on these certain days people do go to clinics because it is then that they have time for treatment; on the other working days, they have to do farming and other hard work. Occasions exist then, and only then, to give public health education as the people come in masses to the health clinics on the holy days of the month. On Sundays, the people go to church early in the morning. After church, they usually visit friends or use Sundays as a day of rest.

Feast for the Salvation of a Saint: On certain church holidays, there are people who invite friends and beggars to their homes in the name of Saint Mary, or some other special saint. On such days, the priests, including the family priest, are present. First, a blessing is given by the family priest, then hymns are sung, followed by some lines of prayer that are common and familiar to almost every layman in the country, and then the feast is continued the whole day.

181

Beggars seeking alms from pilgrims. Beggary is supported by priests who tell pilgrims the amount of alms they must give to support prayers.

One of the "Incurables" at Kalubi receiving alms from a pilgrim.

Fasting: The church strictly demands that everyone within the Empire should fast. No matter what you are, how you are, or where you are, if you belong to the Coptic Church, and if you are more than seven years old, you are compelled to fast. People are said to fast when they do not eat or drink meat, eggs, butter, or milk during the fasting seasons of the year, which total two months and fifteen days in the whole year, plus every Friday and Wednesday. Fasting is especially strict for old men and women, as they are not allowed to eat or drink anything until three o'clock in the afternoon. However, priests do not interfere with medicine. If a patient needs special foods, which the church does not allow, but which are advised by a doctor or physician, he is free to eat them.

Burial Ceremony: The church orders that all dead are to be buried in the churchyard. The family priest must assure that the dead is Coptic before he is free to be buried. If the dead is more than fourteen years old, a burial ceremony will be held. Since the priests are present at the death of anybody, some agreement can be made with the head of the priests so that the death certificate will be introduced to the community.

Mourning for the Dead: Although the community does not follow, the church now sanctions only three days to mourn for the dead. In these three days, friends are allowed to visit the relatives of the dead. This regulation was recently made for the sake of the relatives so that the relatives may not be predisposed to eye diseases or other diseases from weeping for a prolonged period of time. During the burial ceremony, the close friends of the dead do many abnormal things such as rubbing the face with rough material, jumping up and down, beating the exposed chest, and so on and so forth. This is now believed by the priests to be a predisposing cause to disease, and so it is forbidden. Instead of doing all these things, people are directed to mourn for the dead simply by wearing black suits or by fixing a piece of black cloth on the left sleeve of the coat.

Feast for Salvation of the Dead: Great feasts are held for the salvation of the dead of ages twelve and above. The feasts are held on the fortieth, and eightieth days, and on the anniversary of the seventh year. For these feasts, priests, friends, and especially beggars are invited to eat and drink as well as to pray for the dead. These great feasts have led people to economic misery, and they are a social problem as well as a medical problem.

The religious pilgrimage attracts Ethiopians from Addis Ababa and farther away and from all stations of life.

Thousands wait patiently on nearby hillside for a chance to visit holy place and to hear 20th century electronic-amplified messages from religious and political leaders.

Marriage and the Church: Usually the old, well-known, royal-blooded families marry through the church. If marriage is through the church, divorce is practically impossible. In the rare case where divorce is allowed, remarriage is not permitted.

Syphilitic Patient and the Church: A patient who is syphilitic is not allowed to enter the church from the time the first symptoms appear to the time the symptoms disappear. The patient is totally crossed from the membership of the church until he or she is cured. Usually the patient runs for immediate treatment. [2]

The Mother after Delivery: If the mother gives birth to a male, she is not allowed to enter the church for seven days. On the other hand, if she gives birth to a female, she is not allowed to enter for fifteen days. This is because the mother is considered to be unclean or impure. When the time is up, all her contaminated clothes are washed, the priest is called, and some holy water is sprinkled in the room; then, and only then, she is free to go to church. If a friend accidentally visits the new mother during the time of her impurity, he or she should go to the priest to be blessed.

The Couple After Sexual Intercourse: No matter who you are, what you are, or where you are, after having sexual intercourse, whether with your wife or with another woman, you are not allowed to go to church the following day. This is also true for the wife.

[2] Unfortunately, there is an Ethiopian medication which merely, but effectively, masks symptoms.—E. Lord

Religious hermit with his priest's rattle and wood-covered, hand-written Bible (suspended by a thong from his neck).

VII
Medicine and Science in Ethiopia

In the Western world, fortune tellers and metaphysical healers are often labeled by the media they employ: palm-readers, crystal-ball gazers, tea-leaf analysts, etc. A similar phenomenon exists in Ethiopia, but the system is a bit more complex and much more formal. Following are some categories of Ethiopian practitioners of the occult along with their labels, media, and various specialties of function:

Most important is the literate *Mesihaf Gelatch* or *Debterra,* a fortune teller and healer who gives psychological treatment with the aid of some books inherited from his fore-fathers. He refers to these books and predicts the future of an individual, or he orders treatment for the sick on the basis of such books. He writes some philosophy on a long rectangular piece of parchment, sews it with a piece of cloth or hide stained in suitable colors, and gives this to the patient to tie around his neck or shoulders. In addition, he tells the patient to kill a white or grey or black chicken inside his house, to rotate the chicken on his head, and then to throw it in the main road. He also treats persons said to be possessed by evil spirits by doing some charms to drive off the evil. These powerful "magicians" or "witch doctors" operate regionally or even nationally, depending on their reputation.

At the local level, lesser magicians specialize in one or more aspects of the wide general practice of the above-described fortune teller-healer. They

Holy hermit, who reputedly descends from his one-man mountain hermitage only once annually to Kalubi, discourses with pilgrims.

undertake psychological treatments, fortune-telling, etc., but the main difference is that the local magicians are mostly illiterate. They have no books to refer to, and they just use common sense or formulas they have been taught. They predict what will happen and they advise the individual to do certain things as preventive measures within the range of their various specialties. Following are some examples:

The *Chelic Tai* predicts what will happen to the patient and advises him to do certain things with the promise that he will recover from his disease if he carries out what the *Chelic Tai* tells him to do.

The *Mora Gelatch* orders the patient to buy a sheep or goat and kill it. Then he takes out the omentum, reads it, and tells the patient what is going to happen to him, and advises him to do certain things as preventives. The patient usually agrees to behave according to these advices.

The *Sini Defi* are usually females. When coffee is made according to their special instructions, they pour it into small cups, drink it, and read the small granules left inside the cup. Then they tell the person what kind of good or bad luck he is going to have.

The *Itan Wogi* are persons who order the individual to buy some *itan* and put it on a fire. When it gives off smoke, they read the smoke's movements and tell what will happen, nearly the same as the *Sini Defi* does with the coffee grounds.

Tattooing, which is done chiefly by females, especially on the neck and upper gums, is usually done for the purpose of ornament. However, in some communities, it seems to have some medical importance and is used for treatment of bleeding gums and goiter. Among some groups, tattooing is used as an identification mark, especially on males. Their names are tattooed on their arms or legs so that if the individual is found dead he may be recognized easily.

Midwives are old and experienced women who have studied local midwifery from their grandmothers. They begin their service usually at about middle age. They are called, usually by the relatives of a pregnant woman, when labor starts or in case of an emergency. They are not usually requested to help during pregnancy. Some of the procedures which the midwives use during delivery are the following:

1. Prepare delivery area on floor or ground.

2. Allow the presence of elderly female relatives, who can assist in the labor.

3. Palpate the abdomen of the pregnant woman in an attempt to hasten the delivery.

4. If labor persists, they cook some *telba* and some other corn, oily in nature, and let the patient drink it.

5. When the foetus is through the birth-canal, the midwife supports the anus and the perineum by one hand and receives the baby by the other.

6. Then the midwife cuts the cord from the side of the foetus, leaving it a distance of three fingers from the body, ties the rest of the cord around the thigh of the mother and waits until the placenta is expelled.

7. Bury the placenta when expelled; if it belongs to a male, outside, if it belongs to a female, inside the house.

8. The midwife then orders good food for the mother, and orders rest for at least ten to fifteen days. The food consists mainly of butter, meat (of sheep), and soft foods such as porridge prepared in a special way.

189

THE **WOGESHA** AND THE MEDICINE MAN [1]

The *wogesha*, the medicine man, and the midwife differ from one another in the type of work each does. The *wogesha* will be discussed first. He is the simple, local surgeon. His activities are concerned mainly with treatment of fracture, dislocation, and sprain. In addition, he is able to take foreign bodies such as thorns, pieces of wood, glass, and grass from the soles of the foot or the palm of the hand. If something is in the deeper parts, say the nasal cavity, he tries to take it out by dropping fluid such as butter or oil into the nose in an attempt to wet the foreign body and wash it out.

In some cases of abdominal disturbances, he assists a great deal by massaging the abdomen of the patient with butter or some other oily substance. Some more experienced *wogeshas* can suture torn skin, such as the covering of the skull, with gut prepared locally from the small intestines of sheep or goats.

In treating fractures, he first applies some leaves, from a special tree called *kitkita*, just at the site of the fracture. The *kitkita* is naturally plastic and, when applied, supports the fractured limb. He then applies splints prepared locally right on the leaves and then bandages round the splints with pieces of cloth.

He treats dislocation first by applying raw butter on the affected part and then by massaging thoroughly. Some treat dislocations as they treat fractures. If an animal is dislocated or fractured, he treats the animal just as he treats the person. The *wogesha* also cuts off the uvula when it is infected and removes the tonsils as well. If animals or persons get sudden abdominal pain, such as colic, he gives them ground leaves or roots mixed with water to drink. If the individual injures his toes or head due to an accident or assault, the *wogesha* cauterizes the wound with fire; he puts ragged cloth on the fire, and then applies the cloth to the wound. In addition to these procedures, the *wogesha* may also tie around the wound one of the following: white beads, elephants' teeth, nails of a porcupine.

The *wogesha* is not permitted to make any pelvic examination of women. If the woman has a fracture or dislocation apart from her pelvic region, he can treat her. The *wogesha* receives his training from his ancestors. He tries to observe what his father does in every case, and in preparing local medicine from leaves of trees or roots, etc.

[1] Author's name withheld by request.

Some fathers teach theoretically and practically their use of medicine and their methods of administration; whereas, others do not tell their children or any other person about local medicines because they think either their self-esteem will be diminished or the effectiveness of the medicine will be reduced.

The *wogesha* has good relationships with midwives, leaders of the village, and others in the community. However, the relationship of the *wogesha* varies with the educational background of the community. Today, many young and educated persons have no interest in *wogeshas,* while the aged take a great interest in them and trust them.

The leader of the village and other important persons in the community call the *wogesha* to their homes when they need help, but the remaining villagers try to go to the *wogesha's* house, or they may request him to come to their houses. If the *wogesha* lives far, the relatives of the patient pay the fee of his transport or provide him with an animal for transport if they are able. The *wogesha* charges for his treatment in some cases, and in some cases he does not, according to his relations with a certain family or person. If he knows the patient or his friend or his relatives, he does the treatment free of charge. If the patient has no relatives or money and seems a poverty stricken person, the *wogesha* does the treatment as a favor. The *wogesha* is customarily called by the family, relatives, or friends of the patient. But anybody can call the *wogesha* in cases of emergency such as a broken leg or skull.

If there is no hospital available in the community, the *wogesha* is the most important man in the village and is respected by all types of people. The *wogesha* is against Western medicine and modern health workers, because he thinks that his position will be taken and his self-esteem will be lowered. He feels an inferiority complex towards the people concerned. He hypnotises the people in his area, saying that he is the only important man in the community who can do good for them and that nobody else can help them.

If the patient dies after treatment, usually nothing will happen to the *wogesha;* however, in some cases the family of the deceased will accuse him in court. Mostly, the *wogesha* protects himself by saying that the patient did not follow or carry out his instructions.

The visit of the *wogesha* depends on the type of the disease and on the *wogesha* himself. Some *wogeshas* treat once, and they do not need to repeat; so they do not return unless they are especially requested to do so. Some *wogeshas*, on the other hand, make repeated visits to encourage the patient and to alternate their treatments.

The *wogesha* examines his patient by asking the patient or his family how he feels and when the disease started. He feels the temperature just by his hand. After he has confirmed his diagnosis, mainly on the basis of symptoms reported, he gives treatment accordingly.

In addition to the *wogesha*, there are various types of local medicine men. All of them do a good deal of psychological treatment. The functions of some of them are as follows: The priest recites, makes some blessings, scatters some holy water on the patient. He advises the patient to go to a special church for special holy water treatment. He instructs the patient to drink the holy water on an empty stomach, usually in the morning. The priest advises the patient to immerse his whole body in the holy water. The priest makes repeated visits to the patient's house, prepares some holy water by reciting some special words he has learned, and sprays the holy water on the patient and on the house. When a patient is seriously ill and his relatives fear that he will die, they take him to church or call the priest to their house. The priest performs a mass, recites, and gives the Holy Communion for the patient.

Local pharmacists are special people who dig out roots of trees, cut leaves of trees, grind them, and prepare medicines either in powder or solution. Local medicines are also prepared from animals, mostly from wild animals. Following are some examples:

1. Elephantiasis is treated by applying to the legs a dressing of ointment made of omentum of python, genitalia of monkey, and eggs of ostriches.

2. Patients who have difficulty urinating are put in warm water and are given a drink made by boiling water containing a leaf called *insilal*.

3. Those who complain about ear disease—mostly about difficulty of hearing—are treated with the following mixture: goat butter, oil extracted from a special tree, cooked leaves from a special tree called *atuch*.

4. Those who suffer from gonorrhea are given medicine to drink, which is made by grinding together the body of a wajibit bird and a special root called *assirkuch tebete kikush* then mixing the grindings with honey. The patient is then advised not to be visited by anybody for a certain time and to drink *tella* (beer) prepared only from barley. If the patient feels weak, he is given liver of chicken to eat and cows' milk to drink.

5. For treatment of warts, roots from three special trees are put in fire and then used to burn the wart.

6. For treatment of abscesses, *abish*, a bee, and some manure of goats

are ground together and prepared as a thick ointment, which is applied on the abscess as a dressing.

7. Sterile women drink a mixture of horse milk with scrubbings from the teeth of an elephant and from the nails of a mule. After the woman has taken this drink, she is said to be fertile; she is also given rabbit breast to eat.

8. For syphilitic pregnant women, the root of a fibisso tree is dried, ground, and mixed with honey, to be swallowed three times in the morning, especially to prevent the transmission of syphilis to the fetus during the seventh month of pregnancy.

9. For tropical ulcer, the leaves of a gorteb tree are ground and the powder applied to the ulcer.

10. For dysmenorrhea, women drink rabbit teeth which have been ground into a fine powder and mixed with water.

11. The bone of a pig, ground into fine powder and mixed with water, is drunk as a prophylaxis for any disease.

12. For diarrhea, raw meat is given the patient to eat.

13. For distention of the abdomen accompanied by colicky pain, the patient drinks a soup made from dried fish.

SUPERSTITIONS AND FOLKLORE RELATED TO PHYSICAL AND MENTAL ILLNESS[1]

Superstition is unreasonable belief in the supernatural, such as magic, witchcraft, etc. Folklore is an old belief, tale, custom, etc., of a people or a race.

Any disease with a sudden onset, commonly with high fever, headache, vomiting, nausea, sweating, chilling, and sometimes abdominal discomfort is known as *mitch*. *Mitch* is believed to be caused by going out into the bright sun at noon without first washing hands and mouth after taking a meal. The most common foodstuffs which may cause *mitch* are roasted meat, mustard, sometimes *tella* (beer); also, some kinds of face ointment can cause *mitch*. These things release a very strong odor when exposed to heat, and the odor is believed to predispose individuals to contract *mitch*.

[1] Authors' names withheld by request.

People dislike eating or drinking the above foodstuffs, especially at noon time. Also, these foods may cause a person to lose strength and become more susceptible to other diseases worse than *mitch*. This belief misleads people into not eating such foods, and sometimes from their fear they have emotional reactions which upset their minds. If they are sick with *mitch*, they know the cause, and so they do not want to go to a hospital; they may try magic or take local treatment from a *wogesha*, or drink holy water. On the other hand, as far as personal hygiene is concerned, these people will never go outside before washing their hands and mouth, so they are practicing good personal hygiene.

Some people believe that gonorrhea is caused by various factors: (1) If a person urinates towards or facing the moon, he or she is more liable to contract the infection; (2) If the person has contact with the place where a female dog has recently urinated, or if he urinates on that same area, he will get the infection; (3) By urinating on a stone which is hot, the person will get the infection; (4) *Mitch* may develop into gonorrhea.

The people who have the idea that gonorrhea is caused by the above factors think that there is no curative treatment in a hospital, so they may not want to see or consult a medical man. They may try to get other treatment, which may not be effective for their infection, so they keep their infection. However, these attitudes help keep the environmental sanitation in good condition, because the people do not urinate just any place, especially at noon and at night, and never towards the moon. People say that once they have gonorrhea, it reappears or relapses; whenever a new moon appears, they have acute symptoms of gonorrhea. It is difficult to get them to have treatment in a hospital, because they think they know the cause, the time when it relapses, the time when it disappears, and when they will be relieved from their illness for a few days or months; but these attitudes affect the whole body, and they remain sick and sometimes sterile for their whole lives.

If any food or drink remains uncovered over night or for some days and if a person then eats or drinks it, the individual develops a disease which has a sudden onset of generalized symptoms, sometimes located in the abdomen. This condition is known as *megagna*. When the individual is sick with *megagna*, some wise people may aspirate him with a horn or a glass and burn his body with hot instruments. The person then develops secondary infections, and he may die from the complications. People who fear the danger of leaving food uncovered, try to do their best by covering it or cooking or heating it again before they eat it. This is one advantage in holding the belief.

194

If a pregnant woman gives birth to a malformed or an abnormal baby, this means that the mother has been once in special contact with the devil or satan, or she had seen a malformed child during pregnancy. The danger to health is that the woman who has such a belief believes that this anomaly is caused by the devil, so she thinks there is no help or treatment. She will not take the baby to the hospital in order to have some correction made by the doctors. This belief misleads her into leaving her baby without help.

During an outbreak of smallpox in a community, the social groups arrange a special festival day. They decorate the house where the disease is found with fresh green leaves, grasses, flowers, perfumes, smoke of frankincense, and other good-smelling materials. In addition, sheep and hens of different colours are killed. The people perform plays and sing melodies. People have this sort of feast in hopes of having a milder form of the disease. The people do not want to take smallpox patients to the hospital for care. The above treatment or feast pleases the patient for a moment, but it will not cure him. The patient may be cured of his illness or may die from the complications of the smallpox because of his stay in the home of his relatives. Besides, if people congregate when smallpox is present, the disease may spread.

Impetigo is usually believed by some people to be caused by a spider urinating on any part of the body. Since the cause is known, the people do not want to be treated because they think that there is no effective curative treatment. In such cases the patient may die with secondary infections. (On the other hand, the people keep sanitation at a higher level by destroying all the spiders that are found in their compounds.)

Jaundice, with the addition of severe diarrhea, is believed to be caused by the urine of a bat or by a bat flying around a person during the night, or by a person urinating facing a rainbow. The people call jaundice the disease of a bat and a rainbow. They treat, in the case of a bat, by killing this animal and rubbing the blood over the body of the patient. In the case of a rainbow, the person takes the earth in which he urinated and rubs it on the umbilical area.

People who believe that the disease is caused by the above agents try to treat the patient by the causative agents themselves. By luck or by chance, the patient may be cured from his illness, but not by the treatment. He may get his health back because of the resistance of the body against the organisms. Having seen "miraculous" cures, relatives keep the patient at home. They do not want to take him to a hospital, because they have the rigid belief that their own treatment is the one that cures the sick people who have jaundice.

Horny callouses on the heels of the feet are said to be caused when a person steps on the afterbirth of a woman's delivery or when a person steps on the dead-body burial areas.

If an individual spits on fresh or dry faeces, the individual develops a sore throat. It is believed that if a person smells fresh urine, especially the urine of monkeys, he is sure to contract a cold.

A person who is syphilitic will develop the secondary form of the disease on the appearance of the new moon, or when he eats the meat of a goat, or when he washes near the stomach contents of a black sheep; the hidden disease will develop and produce a rash all over the body if he does any of these things.

The people who have syphilis will not be in a hurry to be treated in the first stage; this acute stage will disappear by itself without treatment and will progress to the secondary stage, which, the people believe, only appears whenever a new moon appears. Because of this belief, people are misled; they do not want to seek effective treatment for syphilis; instead, they may wait, expecting that when the new moon disappears, the rash also will disappear. During this period they may give the infection to healthy persons, and an epidemic of syphilis may occur.

If a person drinks water from a deserted spot where a bird has recently drunk, it is believed that the person will develop a goiter. This belief leads to the conviction that there is no treatment, and so the people who get goiter delay coming to a hospital, and they develop chronic diseases of the thyroid glands till they die from suffocation.

If a woman gives birth to a baby with a cleft lip or other anomalies, she is said to have seen persons with such kinds of anomalies during her gestation period. This belief is dangerous for the mother and the child. The mother may become nervous when she sees the child with this condition and she may develop mental illness. The child may remain as he is, untreated.

On festival days (especially a new year) people kill sheep, hens, and goats. These animals, slaughtered on that day, vary in colours. They are usually killed at dawn. The person who killed the animals, right after doing so, must go in and out of the house with a knife in his hand three times. If another person gets in before the thing is done, he becomes frightened when he sees the blood on the floor, and develops aches and pains all over his body; his body becomes immobilized for many days or months, even a year. Moreover, if a person who has been accustomed to killing animals on certain festival days, is unable, due to poverty, to kill an animal, maledictions will be

196

posed over the whole family, who will then develop symptoms of many diseases.

If a person, walking alone in a desert, sees a tall, slender, hairy, nice-voiced, black-dressed lady, that person believes he is sure to get malaria. This lady is not known to be a human being, but some sort of spirit. Some people say that she is mostly found in the forest during noon and at midnight. They have the belief that malaria is treated by eating very old butter; this kills the lady's spirit in their bodies and cures them. Also, they use the white onion (garlic) about the neck as a prophylaxis against malaria whenever they go to a desert place.

The shadow of a hyena causes unconsciousness and immobility to a person who meets the animal at night.

Whenever a hunter kills an elephant, he must celebrate the death of the animal or else he will become a leper or may die soon.

The person who wears the garments of a dead person will soon die. This superstition is a danger to psychological health.

If an individual cuts his fingernails on Sunday, he will develop callouses on the fingers of the hands.

If a person cleans his teeth after sunset, his or her brother will die.

If a person is bitten by a poisonous snake, the people will play, dance, laugh, applaud, etc., all the night in order that the patient may not die.

If a person has a severe headache, people will put a small piece of metal into a glowing fire; when it becomes red hot, they burn different parts of the forehead. The areas which are burnt may become infected; when healed, a large scar results.

If a small, naked child is seen by evil eyes, the child will be acutely sick with fever, diarrhea, vomiting, etc., and the child will remain weak his whole life. People will not allow their children to be naked or exposed to the out doors. This belief is dangerous to the children's lives, since they do not get enough vitamin D, and they remain weak and thin throughout life.

Unless butter is put on the head of a child, the bone of the skull will never be hard and strong. People who depend on the application of butter on the child's head also think that it is necessary to keep the child inside the house, and he will not get any sunlight.

When a person accidentally swallows a fly, he believes that he will get a drink soon, especially *tella* (beer).

If a young married man or girl cuts the fingernails with a razor blade, the first wife or husband will die.

If a person has a sudden onset of abdominal trouble with fever, cramps, colic pains, vomiting, etc., the illness is called *bareya* in men, and *buka* in women. Some people drink a lot of holy mineral water. He starts to vomit, and afterwards he will say that he has seen a very small frog coming out with the vomitus and other small worms, etc. The person believes that he has really seen the causative agents which make him sick.

If a child has the custom of sitting on a stone, his life expectancy is very short. Parents having this belief often will not allow a child ever to go outside, preventing him from getting vitamin D.

If a small child stays outside during rain, it is believed that the child will grow up sooner than those children who have not been bitten by the rain. To the contrary, during this stay in the rain, a child may develop a cold, shivering, and other symptoms which may develop into one of the lung diseases.

If a pregnant woman eats roasted meat or other odorous food stuffs, it will cause an abortion or disease of the foetus. The pregnant woman will not eat meat or these other food stuffs, and she decreases foods which are helpful for herself and for the foetus.

If a frog urinates on the hands or the fingers, the person is sure to lose his fingers. People may not go to the hospital when they see lesions on their fingers, because they think that the lesions are caused by the urine of a frog.

People have the belief that the source of scabies is an evil eye. Because of this belief, people with scabies will usually go to a magician, and the magician may order the treatment. They waste their money without any effect, leave the scabies without any treatment, and cause all the family to have the infection.

On the thirty-first of May, all the villagers will gather together for a celebration. They make some preparations such as killing hens, or rams, and drinking *tella*. The purpose of this celebration is to prevent the entrance of a common cold into their village or, if there is already an epidemic present in the village, a means of getting rid of the epidemic and sending it to another village. They do this also for other infectious diseases, as a prophylaxis.

Atate wekabi is another superstition which is more common among females than males. It is not found in all individuals, but there are certain people who gladly accept this evil spirit as their owner. *Atate* is mostly passed from the mother to her daughter, and sometimes to her sons. If the mother dies and a daughter does not perform the celebration of *Atate*, she is sure to become sick. She shows the following symptoms and signs: No appetite, unconsciousness, weeping, dancing, jumping, throwing something, biting other persons, sweating, tearing clothes, external bleeding, falling down on the ground, laughing, crying, swallowing a hot ember, eating ashes, etc. When the people see these symptoms and signs, they make the diagnosis of the disease. They say she is sick because she has forgotten the things which her mother was doing before her death. At last, the wise men— magicians, witches, and wizards—will tell her that she must celebrate her mother's *Atate*. Following are things to be prepared for the feast: The house will be decorated with differing kinds of green grasses and leaves and other odorous materials. The hostesses prepare bread, *tella*, puddings and porridges. After the preparation, some of the nearest neighbours will be invited to celebrate and make certain that the evil spirit agrees to leave the sick daughter. The people will sit on the floor and beg the evil spirit to leave her and go to another person. The evil spirit will say, after this begging is done, "I left her, and she is free." The people will be glad. They eat, drink, play, dance, sing songs, beat drums.

Those females who are present will put butter on the head of the patient; afterwards, they tie on her neck a different coloured necklace of beads with strings. This necklace, is made of different colours. The material is called *chale*. This *chale* will be put on by the daughter whenever she is sick; on the other days it is kept in a small sack made with good embroidery especially for it. When the ceremony is finished, the women and men will say to the patient, "You should not neglect this *Atate*; you must respect and celebrate as you have now done; if not, you will be sick and will die." She is obliged to keep her *Atate* until she dies from it.

There are certain groups of people in Wollo Province who, although rich by birth, have the following belief: Once each year, they must go, in groups, from house to house between four-thirty and seven a.m.; they must put their fingers in their ears and shout or sing praises to the people in the houses, and then they must beg for money. Any person who fails to do these things will lose his nose or a finger from leprosy.

Mental illness is treated in the following way: The patient is imprisoned at home by parents, relations, or friends and is then treated with holy water and/or a charm. The charm is written on a parchment paper by the church person called *Debtera*, and is tied on a particular part of the body, according to the specific case. Also, mental illness may be treated by group singing and dancing according to the instructions of a sorceror. If a mental disease is believed to be congenital, a ram or chicken is slain, passed over the head of the patient, and thrown away. By this, it is hoped to make the evil spirit vanish like a discontented fairy.

In some communities, there are many taboos against the mentally ill; in other places, the people merely ignore and neglect the sick persons.

Other superstitions related to illness or misfortune are the following:

1. A patient who is bitten by a rabid animal and is treated by a local medicine man, with the *abasha* medicine against rabies, is warned not to cross a river or see any water, even when drinking. Patients acting against this rule are said to die immediately at the sight of water.

2. A man who is dreaming that he has sexual intercourse with a beautiful, strange woman may show abnormal reactions. He will be divorced often because he actually was visited by a beautiful devil-woman while he slept.

3. A person passing through or resting in a cemetery (if not attending a burial) may become mad. It is said that the devil will beat him into madness in the cemetery.

4. Every year, during the famous public holidays, there will be some persons who are fanatics. They will fall into a trance, known as *ado-karibra*. They will dance wildly and act mad. This trance may last one or two days.

5. One of the magic ways to kill a person is to speak some magic words and then stab his shadow. The enemy will die immediately.

6. A person may fall sick, when he, while eating, is stared at by someone who feels very hungry, but lacks food.

7. Sick persons try to find a cure by transmitting their sickness to a chicken. They will swing a red, white, black, or brown cock three times around their head and then throw it onto the main road. If someone else happens to step on the chicken or take it, he will be affected by the disease.

8. If a person who before has invited guests regularly every year, or every month, in the name of a saint or angel, stops this habit to save his money, he will either fall ill or die.

9. A person affected with epilepsy will be regarded as being possessed by a devil, or as having once been beaten by a devil.

10. If a man who is in love with a woman starts acting foolishly or mad it is said that the woman has mixed some love potion into his food.

Other superstitions:

If you don't laugh and be happy on Christmas, you will not be happy for the rest of your life.

If you are merry on Good Friday, you will be condemned.

If you go on a trip on Wednesday or Friday, you will have bad luck.

If dogs get together and howl, somebody in the area will die.

If a crow sits on your house and caws, something bad will happen to you.

If you sew clothes at night, you will be poor.

If you sweep your house at night, you will lose money.

If an owl cries at night, an important person in that area will die.

If a woman crosses your path, you will have bad luck.

If you bite your tongue while eating, somebody you love has remembered you.

If you receive money with your left hand, it won't last long.

If there is an eclipse of the moon, war will break out.

If a big tree falls, an important person will die.

It is believed that worms under the eye teeth give a baby diarrhea; the treatment is to pull the baby's teeth.

Elephantiasis is believed to be a hereditary disorder; therefore, it can't be prevented or treated.

If you cut your nails and don't bury them, you will have an accident.

If you pass urine in water (lake, river, etc.), you will have to separate it from the water after you die.

If a fly falls into your wine while you are drinking it, you will become rich.

If a stone hits your right foot, you will have bad luck.

If a hyena comes while you are sleeping and cries an odd number of times (3, 5, 7, etc.), you will have an accident or some relative of yours will die.

If you hear an owl cry at midnight, you will become sick or have an accident.

If you are going on a journey and see one crow cawing, you should go back; otherwise, you will have bad luck. But if two crows caw on your right side, the journey will be successful.

If you meet a woman carrying an empty water pot, you will be unlucky in the place where you are going. If the pot is full, you will be lucky.

CHANGING OUR CONCEPTS OF HEALTH[1]

Admassu Tefera, B.Sc.

To the older inhabitants of Ethiopia and to some of the young ones, health is the concern of God only, to whom one praisefully prays at night for living through the day and hopefully prays in the morning to give one the strength to pass the coming day. Though this is one aspect of looking at the vast concept of health, there are other angles from which one can tackle the problem. One's health is a gift of God in the sense that God has bestowed on us the intricate and harmoniously working machine which is the human body.

Health is a topic which one does not think about when healthy, but only when sick. Some people feel that thinking about health makes one really sick, perhaps by the release of secretions from stress with accompanying peptic ulcers, anxiety, neurosis, etc.

An Ethiopian of seventy with a sturdy physique, and a hearty appetite, who was an enthusiastic wood-chopper, told me that he never saw a doctor with the exception of the village doctor for cutting out his uvula and splinting a fracture, and yet he felt strong enough to walk to the Church of Kulubi Gabriel a distance of 80 miles and deliver gifts in fulfillment of his prayers to witness his granddaughter's marriage. And what is more striking is that he has a lot of friends who still can recount the battles they fought and the good

[1] First published in *Jesame*, Journal of the Ethiopian Students Association in the Middle East, October, 1958.

old days. Yes, the good old days when men had no soaps and irons to give a shine to their dresses but still lived to be grey-haired and grandfathers. And look at the terrible new era when such devilish maladies as tuberculosis, influenza, cholera, and stomach ulcers shorten one's existence to a mere score of years.

Our grandfathers are right in calling these maladies a recent introduction in the sense that the witch and country doctors, who through the ages have taken as their profession the practice of superstitious medicine, knew nothing about the causes of diseases but dubbed all illnesses as the work of evil eyes and the angry demonstrations of the demon. Their treatment consisted of administrations of the crude extracts of the roots, seeds, leaves, and bulbs of herbs whose identities were kept a secret, and the chanting away of illnesses by presumable communication with evil spirits.

We have no data on the birth and death rates of past generations to assess the toll of death from diseases in general, let alone to know the incidence of a particular disease. But the presence of less than twenty million people in a land whose area is 450,000 square miles, whose climate is friendly, and whose soil is productive seems to be a clue to a greater death rate. Of course, the communal small battles so frequent in our past history may have dwindled Ethiopia's population, but what about the serious epidemics of typhus, malaria, meningitis, and influenza that have time and again wiped out whole villages of people? That epidemics of typhus have caused great numbers of deaths is remembered and authenticated even by the older generation of the good old days. The crowded and poorly ventilated living conditions, the unsanitary methods of preparing foods, the habit of promiscuous defecation in open fields, and the absence of proper facilities of sewage disposal are some aspects of public health which one encounters in all rural areas of Ethiopia as well as in some of the smaller cities. Taking these factors into account, it is sometimes hard to believe that so many Ethiopians survive to adolescence and old age. Our early contact with diseases may have helped us to acquire a good deal of resistance to infection; all the same, some of these diseases, after killing a good many, must leave their marks upon those who survive.

Ethiopia's inhabitants are not robust in physique, and a majority are visibly underweight with no need of confirmation by weighing. The chronic effects of apparently mild infections due to parasites are not fatal but are debilitating and wasting. The yawning, idleness, and apathetic expression observed in some people may not be the after-effects of a party the night before but symptoms of chronic infections. Stimulating oneself to work with cup after cup of coffee cannot be curative but only a money-wasting habit. Many Ethiopians die of diseases whose causes and effects are known to modern medicine and are easy to diagnose, such as the chronic alcoholic who eventually dies of liver disease and mothers who die from infections at birth. But the ordinary Ethiopian, when asked what caused the death of a dear friend, merely answers: "He was well and fine yesterday, but he suddenly died today. So God has 'called' him at last." That is all there is to it. The fact that one's health can be put under one's control is evidently not apparent to most of our countrymen. Therefore, the preliminary task of the public health man is to acquaint Ethiopia's public with the causes, effects, prevention, and cure of the commoner diseases so that whatever steps are taken by the government to improve the people's health are understood, appreciated, and promoted by the inhabitants themselves.

Education has taken its rightful place as the major undertaking that accelerates Ethiopia's progress. The promotion of health is a necessary corollary since an educated man needs good health to work efficiently and realize his ambitions of a happy family life and long service to his countrymen. The Ministry of Education made a significant innovation when it authorized the periodic checking of the eyes of all students in the capital and in the provinces. Trachoma, which was found to be of high incidence, is treated satisfactorily, and a good number of Ethiopia's future intellectuals are wearing glasses to prevent a greater deterioration of their eyesight from taking place. A similar revolutionary step would be to institute the practice of mass chest X-rays for school children. The task of timely vaccination of school children has been proceeding with zeal for the past ten years. In view of the fact that very few Ethiopians go to the hospital for periodic health check-ups, the number of sudden deaths is large; it would be in the interest of the country to see that every employee pays for a health service that periodically checks on his or her state of health.

Some of my countrymen may contend that it is still better to live in the ways of the good old days when there was not much tension and its associated effects of peptic ulcer, coronary thrombosis, hypertension, and cerebral hemorrhage. But before we try to do something about these tension or stress diseases, we have to wipe out the scourge of malaria, typhus, and the other infectious diseases. The era when the African plucked bananas from a tree nearby for lunch, sunned himself all day like a crocodile, and went to his hovel at night to be bitten by bugs and mosquitoes must soon pass away, and this will come about when we become up to date in our health concepts as we are fashionable in our dress and movie attendance.

THE IMPACT OF EDUCATION ON
NON-SCIENTIFIC BELIEFS IN ETHIOPIA

Reproduced from the *Journal of Social Psychology*, 1958, 47, 339-353.

Edith Lord[1]

A. The Problem

Ethiopia, with the technical advice and economic assistance of the United Nations, the United States, and other free countries of the Western World, is making a valiant effort to bridge a thousand-year gap in development. She is investing over one-fourth of her national income in educational programs in the effort to bring about literacy, changes in attitudes, in behavior, and in methods. While technical information and adequate budget are essential elements in achieving the goal of transition to modernity, an equally essential element is knowledge of the people who are involved in the dynamic processes of change. What are the attitudes and beliefs of Ethiopians which motivate their daily behavior? Are there commonly-held beliefs which might interfere with or seriously impede a given educational program or health project? Which of the non-scientific beliefs are affected by learning, and which are resistant to education?

Let us consider some concrete examples of the implied problem: A recent report by an American technical adviser in ceramics pointed out that the Ethiopian pottery vendors in the Dira Dawa market were importing their wares several hundred miles from Addis Ababa despite the fact that good clay exists locally which would permit them to make and sell pottery for half the price or twice the profit. He recommended that local production of pottery be introduced. There is a widespread belief in Ethiopia that all pottery workers are possessed of the evil eye. Would this affect the success of the suggested project? Would an educational program effect a reduction or elimination of this potentially impeding belief? How strong is this belief in Dira Dawa?

The American technical adviser to a newly-opened Ethiopian trades school expressed concern over the fact that most of the students wanted to study electricity, practically no youth was interested in learning such trades

[1] Among the many persons who helped with the translations, administration, and scoring of the questionnaire used in this study, the author is particularly indebted to Weizerit Mebrat Teshale, Ato Lulseged Kumsa, Ato Lakew Mulat, and Mr. Paul Arnold, all members of the Ethiopian-United States Cooperative Education Program, U.S. foreign aid program, Ethiopia.

as plumbing, bricklaying, etc. There is a belief, reportedly stretching back to the days of Queen Sheba, that manual laborers in general, and iron or metal workers in particular, can turn themselves into hyenas at night. Is this a factor which must be taken into consideration when planning a manual arts training program or a trade school?

Malaria is one of the greatest health problems in Ethiopia. American advisers of a malaria-control team have expressed the hope that the disease can be eliminated within a decade. The academic curriculum for the government-sponsored schools introduces the scientific study of malaria in the fourth grade; yet one can hear Ethiopian teachers insisting that malaria can be prevented by eating garlic and that the best treatment for the disease is to eat butter that is fifteen to twenty years old. Will these beliefs contribute in any way to the success or failure of a malaria-control program? Since feelings are facts operationally, must program-planning take into account these non-scientific feelings and deal with them as pertinent facts?

A literate nation is provided with the means for substituting scientific explanations of everyday events—such as death, disease, and disaster—for the supernatural, non-scientific explanations which prevail in developing societies and which have existed in Ethiopia for centuries. There exists in Ethiopia a literate segment of the population which has been introduced to modern education through the government-sponsored schools during the last twenty-five years.[2] The program is modeled largely after the English system, and the curriculum from the primary grades through secondary school is designed to meet the criteria for passing the London Matriculation Examination.

Is this type of modern education having an impact on the non-scientific beliefs which influence attitudes and motivate behavior in Ethiopia? Is it possible to identify any beliefs which are impervious to present educational content and methods, and which may have significant bearing on Ethiopia's desired rapid transition and development?

The purpose of this study is to explore some of the foregoing questions, to discover something about the beliefs and attitudes of the literate segment of the population, and to learn the extent to which the present program of education is having an impact on non-scientific beliefs which motivate attitudes and daily behavior in Ethiopia.

---

[2] Prior to the Italian invasion, education was limited almost exclusively to church schools where students learned to read the Bible in the ancient language, Ge'ez, as well as in the modern language, Amarigna.

B. Procedures

Over 200 non-scientific beliefs were gathered. There was no selectivity in collecting items; a record was kept of every non-scientific statement encountered. Some of the original items were eliminated on the chance that they might be offensive to social, tribal, or religious groups. A few additional items were withdrawn when it was established that a belief was held by only one small tribe or sub-group within a tribe, or that it was unfamiliar to unschooled adults who had proved sufficiently informed in this area of knowledge to be able to give experienced examples of the truth of the other statements. The remaining 132 beliefs were translated into Amarigna and mimeographed under the title "Attitude Survey, Form-S."[3]

Information called for on the cover page of the survey form included age, sex, city, school, grade, and language spoken in the home (as a clue to tribal cultural influences). Subjects were instructed not to write their names on the form. Examples were given of a true statement, a questionable statement, and a false statement, together with directions for marking the form to indicate judgment of each statement as *true, ?, or false.* The forms were submitted to students in the government schools throughout the Empire from Grade 2 through college freshmen, to teachers, to student nurses, and to first-aid workers. This preliminary study reports the results of 1,228 subjects. In addition, 10 selected items were included (for research purposes only) in the 1957 national examination for graduating nurses, which was taken by 24 persons.

Results were tabulated in the three categories of judgment; however, they are reported in terms of two categories: per cent of persons judging an item false; per cent indicating a degree of belief by encircling true or the question mark. It had been anticipated that the question mark might be a popular choice, especially among the more advanced students; therefore, the directions carried the following admonition: "Try to decide whether each statement is true or false. Try to avoid encircling too many question marks." Actually, the question mark was so little used as to become an insignificant category. Some inquiry of advanced subjects plus discussions with Ethiopian colleagues suggested that, where used, the question mark indicated a degree of belief short of conviction.

Tabulations were summed separately for each grade in each school sampled; then results throughout the Empire were grouped by grade; next,

---

[3] See page 220 for a list of the 132 items.

207

results were grouped by academic subdivision: primary, elementary, etc. Results of this preliminary study are reported according to these academic subdivisions. (Results of second-grade students were excluded from this report to avoid the possibility of introducing a measure of reading skill.)

C. Results

A major problem in presenting the results of a study which yields a mass of data is that of grouping the information into small, meaningful units. First, let us view the 132 items as a whole: 76 of the items are believed by 50 per cent or more of the 210 primary students; e.g., 77 per cent of the primary students believe that, on New Year's Day, you must kill the same kind and color of animal customarily sacrificed by your forefathers or you will suffer from trouble of some sort. Attitudes of this sort, which specifically chain the present to the past, may be a force in delaying progress. Sixty-four items are believed by 50 per cent or more of the 381 elementary, or intermediate, students; for example, 77 per cent of this group believe that certain mineral waters can cure stomach trouble by causing a person to vomit worms, sometimes toads. In a land where one medical research study [4] has revealed that roughly two-thirds of the children in school suffer from some sort of intestinal parasite, this kind of non-scientific belief might well contribute to a medically unnecessarily low state of health for the entire nation. Fifty-six items are believed by 50 per cent or more of the 451 secondary school students; e.g., 81 per cent of the secondary school students believe that certain people can read the past and the future from the stars. While belief in astrology probably exists in some degree throughout the world, the concern here is that such a large per cent of the better educated persons in Ethiopia hold the belief, a belief that could lead to resignation about a supposedly fixed future, in contrast to optimism about the power of man to shape his own future, through the understanding and control of natural forces, through the application of modern, scientific knowledge. Thirty-four items are believed by 50 per cent or more of the 96 teachers; [5] for example, 74 per cent of the teachers in this study believe that gonorrhea first came from a female dog. In a country where venereal disease is a major health problem, the non-scientific beliefs of teachers related to any aspect of the

[4] An unpublished study made by the faculty of the Public Health College of Gondar on the school population of that city.

[5] None of the teachers in the population of this study had had college training; hence, in terms of academic background, their level is below that of the college freshmen.

problem become of major significance. Nine items are believed by 50 per cent or more of the 61 medically-oriented student nurses and dressers (first-aid workers); for example, 53 per cent of this more scientifically sophisticated group believe that if a person exposes himself to sunlight after eating fried food, he will get sick. Finally, six of the items are believed by 50 per cent or more of the 29 college freshmen; e.g., 52 per cent believe that a child will grow better if the nerves are removed from under his back teeth. (Incidentally, this primitive surgery is performed by a local person, without anesthesia or antiseptics; it consists of an incision, then the jerking out of the nerve with a tool which resembles a crochet-hook. Children have been known to die from subsequent infections.)

The foregoing statistics give evidence that there is a measurable trend toward increased disbelief in non-scientific statements with increased schooling. Behind this gross observation, however, are some interesting deviations and exceptions. Some of the beliefs are not held by children during the primary grades, but are acquired later, along with reading, writing, and arithmetic. Some beliefs are, apparently, originally brought to school and retained during the primary years, are subject to doubt during the middle-school years, and are reinforced during secondary school years. Seventy items, 53 per cent of the total number, remain relatively unchanged despite education; that is, the variation in per cent of belief is less than 10 per cent for the total group of primary, elementary, and secondary school students. Of these 70 items, 32 are beliefs held by 50 per cent or more of the total population of this study; 38 are held by fewer than 50 per cent of the total student group. As an example of range, within this category of beliefs unaffected by education, the highest is Item 52: 75 per cent, regardless of education, believe that if a bat flies over your head you will get a skin disease; the lowest item is No. 11: only 15 per cent believe that if one cleans his teeth during the night, he will lose his brother. These two items represent extreme range, in terms of frequency of belief, within the category of items unaffected by education. Let us now consider, more specifically, the clustering of items in relationship to academic groups and the shiftings of frequencies of belief.

Perhaps the most important person in any educational program is the classroom teacher. Quite apart from the dissemination of knowledge, teachers indoctrinate while teaching. Laws may be passed making indoctrination a crime, instructors may studiously attempt to avoid indoctrinating as a result of purely personal convictions about the role of the teacher. Yet so long as teaching is done by human beings, the teaching process will be colored by indoctrination. Even the decision of a teacher to refrain ever from making value-judgments results in classroom behavior which conveys a subtle sort of indoctrination. Human beings do feel and believe, and these feelings and beliefs are conveyed to pupils the world over by teachers the world over. Therefore, in a study of this sort, it becomes important to discover which non-scientific beliefs are held by, and hence transmitted or reinforced by, Ethiopian teachers.

A slight digression is necessary at this point to present some facts about the teaching population of Ethiopia. During the school year 1956-57, there were 3,003 teachers in Ethiopia conducting classes from Grades 1 through 12. Of these, 406 or 14 per cent were foreigners, of which 218 or 54 per cent were Indians. These foreign teachers function primarily as secondary school teachers and as headmasters. Ethiopian teachers—the possessors and conveyors of local culture, including non-scientific beliefs, represent 86 per cent of the total teaching population.[7] Their work is concentrated at the primary and elementary school levels, with Grades 1 through 8. Roughly 30 per cent of the Ethiopian school teachers have had no more than four years of academic training. None of these teachers were included in the present study. Thirty per cent of the remaining Ethiopian teachers have had anywhere from five years of academic background to eight years plus from one to four additional years in a teacher-training program. The teachers used in the population of this study were drawn from the latter category; i.e., Ethiopian teachers with five or more years of formal education, capable of using the English language as the medium of instruction. Let us look at the beliefs, the non-scientific beliefs, which are held by teachers, and therefore presumably reinforced in the classroom situation in Grades 1 through 8. Again the grouping of data becomes a problem. The following categories appear to be convenient ones: items related to (a) the Devil or Evil Eye; (b) Death; (c) Disease; (d) Disaster; (e) Danger; and, of course, the always necessary category of (f) Miscellaneous. Another reporting problem: What shall be considered significant? Let us arbitrarily say that if 50 per cent or more of the teachers believe that a non-scientific statement is true, it is an important item. By these criteria, we find that, of the 34 items believed by 50 per cent or more of the teachers, 16 are related to disease, the cause, prevention, and

[6] These figures were obtained from Mr. Paul Arnold, U.S. foreign aid education adviser in research and statistics.

cure. In other words, in a country where the life expectancy is estimated to be between 30 and 35 years, the largest number of false, or non-scientific, beliefs held by native teachers has to do with the problem of diseases, their cause, prevention, and cure. The Ethiopian Government, The World Health Organization, the United States foreign aid agency, and other groups are earnestly endeavoring to change the health picture in Ethiopia. Surely this finding should take some place in their considerations.

To dramatize this point, let me introject an example or two. An Ethiopian colleague, a former teacher, warned me against drinking water in a certain provincial town on penalty of my catching malaria. He was challenged thus: "You are one of the better educated persons in Ethiopia; don't you know the cause of malaria?" He quickly, and eruditely, gave all the known scientific facts about malaria. Then he added: "You people from the United States and the United Nations think that this (the scientifically established cycle) is the only way to catch malaria. We Ethiopians know better. We know that one can *also* catch malaria from drinking the water in places where the anopheles breed." Well, this is all to the good. So this chap is unscientifically over-cautious. This will do the country no harm, even though his attitude is, in part, unscientific. But let us look at another aspect of this same problem. A little boy, aged 10, developed gonorrhea. When he first brought his painful symptoms to me, he stated that he had consulted the school health worker, locally called a dresser. He had told the child that the disease from which he suffered was contracted from having urinated on a stone warmed by the sun; he neither treated the boy nor referred him to a doctor. This first-aid worker is on the payroll of the Minstry of Education; he is in a position even more important than that of the classroom teacher wherein such problems as venereal disease are concerned. Let us remember that this health-worker was giving to this child his best advice—not as it had been taught to him by instructors in the dressers' course, which he had studied and passed, but as it had been taught to him by his father and grandfather, before he went to school. The dresser at a local hospital-clinic, well trained enough to take slides and administer curative hypodermics, explained to the boy that the disease was not contracted from a sun-heated stone on which urine had been passed. He laughed at this as an old superstition; rather, he told this boy, such a disease could be contracted from the secretions of a person who also had the disease. To quote the child, he said: "Someone in your household has this disease; he has perspired, or he has shed tears from his eyes. The perspiration or the tears have touched you. That is how you contracted the disease."

211

Unless the instructors and trainers of nurses, dressers, and teachers are aware of the local superstitions and take them into account in curriculum and instruction planning, progress toward greater health for the nation will be considerably impeded, I believe.

Three of the items believed by 50 per cent or more of the teachers related to the devil or the evil eye. They read as follows: (1) Manual laborers, such as pottery makers, usually have the evil eye. (2) There are some skillful persons who can summon the devil at will. (3) If a child eats bacon, he will be protected from the evil eye. (It should be noted here that eating pork in any form is prohibited by the Ethiopian Orthodox Christian Church.)

Among the five items on danger, disaster, and death believed by 50 per cent or more of the teachers, we find the following belief: If a person has an electric shock, the wires will immediately carry his blood to the dynamo at the headquarters of the electric power company. Actually, 67 per cent of the teachers believe this statement; yet they are teaching text-book science well enough that, on the 1956 Ethiopian 8th Grade General Examination, a national examination, 77 per cent of the 8th grade students correctly answered a question concerning convection, radiation, and conduction of energy. It is not too strange, then, to discover that students who have passed this 8th grade examination with sufficiently high marks to be accepted in secondary school still cling to a non-scientific belief so widely held by their former teachers: 66 per cent of the secondary school students indicated belief in this non-scientific statement about electrocution. This is but one of the many bits of evidence that acquisition of information does not necessarily increase knowledge, does not always bring about a shift from non-scientific to scientific attitudes.

The 61 nurses and dressers used in this study represent persons of varying academic background. Some of the dressers had had as little as four or five years of formal schooling prior to taking the dressers' courses. The nurses had had from 6 to 10 years of general education before entering nurses' training. Despite this meagre academic equipment, this medically-oriented group proved to be second only to the college freshmen in their rejection of non-scientific beliefs. Only nine of the 132 items are believed by 50 per cent or more of this specially educated group. In terms of influence for change within the culture, this scientifically trained group is of particular importance. It therefore becomes of special interest to explore the impact of education on their non-scientific attitudes.

Six of their nine widely believed items are specifically related to medicine; three are miscellaneous items. These significant six items were combined with four additional medically-related items which were believed by 40 per cent or more of the medically-oriented group. The 10 items were included (for research purposes only) in the 1957 National Examination for Graduating Nurses. Of the 24 nurses who took the examinations, eight had been, as junior students, part of the population of 61 medically-oriented persons comprising the category of this study. Results, at that time, were made known to the nursing school faculty. We therefore have a small sample, within our group of 24 graduate nurses, who presumably had some specific instruction around particular non-scientific beliefs known to be held by student nurses. Let us look at the results.

The belief that beautiful couples produce ugly children remains relatively unaffected by general or special additional nursing education. Inquiry revealed that genetics is not taught in the schools of nursing. Sixty-two per cent of the original group of 61 medically-oriented persons indicated belief that certain mineral waters can cure stomach trouble by causing a person to vomit worms, sometimes toads. Only 42 per cent of the graduating nurses believe this, but there is little difference between the eight specially tutored nurses and the 16 untutored ones; this may be called a persistent, resistent belief. Both mental hygiene and psychiatric nursing are included in the curriculum; nevertheless, 33 per cent of the graduates believe that too much charity leads to madness. Twenty-five per cent of the tutored, as opposed to 37 per cent of the untutored, cling to this belief as graduate nurses. This, however, is in heartening contrast to the 51 per cent of the total medically-oriented group who believe it.

If a person exposes himself to sunlight after eating fried food, he will get sick. While one-fourth of the graduates believe this, only 13 per cent of the tutored nurses held to the belief. Returning to the causes of mental illness, we find that 44 per cent of the untutored graduates believe that too much learning results in madness; whereas, none of the tutored graduates indicate belief.

The most dramatic shift of belief, within this group of 10 items, occurs with the statement: The deaf, the dumb, and cripples can be cured by bathing in, and drinking, the mineral water which causes a person to vomit worms or toads. Seventy-one per cent of the 61 in the medically-oriented group believed this. Only 19 per cent of the untutored, and none of the tutored graduate nurses believe it. The remaining four items in this group were believed by 44 to 46 per cent of the medically-oriented group. None of the graduate nurses believe either of the following two: A child will grow better if the nerves are removed from under his back teeth; the best treatment for malaria is to eat butter that is 15 or 20 years old. None of the tutored group believes either of the remaining two items, but the untutored group believes, 19 per cent and 12 per cent respectively, the following: If a person kills a cat or lizard, his hand will shake forever after. If a bat flies over your head, you will get a skin disease.

The foregoing data suggest that dresser-training or nursing-education is superior to academic secondary school education, and only slightly inferior to college freshman education, in its impact on non-scientific beliefs. Further, there is evidence that tutoring specifically related to non-scientific beliefs has greater impact than merely more general nursing education has. Also, it must be noted that, of the 132 items of this study, only one, that related to genetics, is held by 50 per cent or more of the graduate nurses.

Now let us look at the six items so resistant to academic education that they are believed by more than half of the college freshman students. The widespread belief in demonology, mentioned earlier in connection with teachers, again appears. In addition to believing that skillful persons can summon the devil, these college students believe that if you go into a room which has been closed for a long time, you will be attacked by the devil. Three of the remaining four items are ones already cited as resistant even to medically related education (and also believed by more than half the teachers): Items relating to the cure of stomach trouble, the removal of the nerves from children's teeth, and the relationship between charity and madness. The final item of belief held by more than half of the persons in this most advanced academic group (and shared by 63 per cent of the teachers) is that a person in malaria country can prevent infection by eating garlic.

Having considered the special groups, and special kinds of education, represented in this study, let us now turn our attention to the children in the primary, elementary, and secondary schools. What is the nature of the beliefs which reflect a steady decrease in belief with increased years of education? Eighteen items fall into this category, only 14 per cent of the total. Two are related to the devil; only one is related to death; two are related to disease; eight, the largest category, are related to danger or disaster, and five are miscellaneous. This would suggest that those non-scientific beliefs which are most amenable to correction and change through academic education are related to phenomena of danger or disaster. Does this mean that education is giving these children some sense of personal, internal control over their environments, as opposed to a sense of impersonal, external control? May we even assume a causal relationship here? Is it mere chronological growth rather than academic education which contributes to the decreasing belief? As mentioned at the outset, these non-scientific beliefs are widely held by unschooled adults, which permits us to hypothesize that education is the force at work for change; however, additional research must be done before this hypothesis can be expressed as a conclusion.

Let us consider eight items which, unexpectedly, reflect a steady *increase* in belief with increased years of education. Two of the items have to do with stopping the rains. Those who have lived in places where there is no word for drought, where seasons are marked by the onset and cessation of the rains, the little rains and the big rains, those people can perhaps identify with students who, as they mature, give increasing interest to the phenomena of rain. It is only regrettable that this interest manifests itself, in part, by increased belief in non-scientific concepts about ways and means of stopping the torrents. Astrology and the meaning of dreams creep into belief slowly and grow with years of education, accounting for two of these beliefs which increase with the years of learning. Two other items relate to the curative powers of certain waters, beliefs already cited as persistent. Possibly beliefs in this area are related to increased religious awareness as students grow older; the mineral waters which bring the miracle cures are highly regarded because of their holiness rather than out of any consideration for their chemical content. One belief, within this group of increasingly held beliefs, is that gohorrhea first came from a female dog. Possibly this merely reflects a physical growth factor which makes the problem, and a desired explanation for it, of increased concern with age. The academic curriculum does not touch the problem, and, as previously noted, school health workers are not prepared to contribute anything toward a decrease in the particular non-scientific beliefs associated with this disease. The remaining item which increases in belief with education seems to be beyond explanation; it would fall under the category of miscellaneous: A person can eat more bananas if he has his feet in water while eating them. One exceptionally bright Ethiopian student, now abroad on a foreign study scholarship, repeatedly offered to demonstrate the truth of this strange, non-scientific statement. He did not believe it as a child (22 per cent of the primary school children do not believe it). But in secondary school he decided to test the hypothesis, and his experiences eating bananas with feet in and out of water led to his conviction (like 61 per cent of the secondary school students) that the statement is unquestionably true. It is noteworthy that most of this group of beliefs show little increase in belief from primary to elementary school but show marked increase in belief at the secondary school level.

And now we come to perhaps the most fascinating group of non-scientific items in this study, those which show no change in frequency of belief with education, those which are resistant to education, those which children bring to the first grade of school with them and retain persistently, unchanged, through 12 years of schooling. Seventy items, 53 per cent of the total, fall into this category. In other words, more than half of the non-scientific statements explored in this study are impervious to present-day education in Ethiopia. The state of constancy implied by the phrase, "no change in frequency of belief with education," was arbitrarily determined as being a variation of less than 10 per cent in frequency among the three academic groups: primary, elementary, and secondary school students.

Thirty-eight of the items in this unchangeable (or at least currently unchanging) group are items of relatively low frequency of belief; that is, fewer than 50 per cent of the total group believe the item, and the variation among the three academic groups is 9 per cent or less. (It must be mentioned that nine of the 38 loosely-called low-frequency-of-belief items crowd this arbitrary cut-off point of 50 per cent, the highest being an item believed by 49.6 per cent of the total group.) One cannot call any of these persistent, non-scientific beliefs insignificant, but one can direct his major concern, at this point in the development of a country, to those persistent, non-scientific beliefs which are held by *more* than 50 per cent of the literate group sampled, and which show little (less than 10 per cent) or no reduction in frequency of belief with years of education.

Let us direct our attention to the 32 items believed, with approximately equal frequency, by 50 per cent or more of the 1,042 children, regardless of grade-level. Thirteen are related to disease; for example, if a person spits on a toilet, he will have a sore throat. A person who has tape worms will not suffer from amoebic dysentary. If a man urinates facing the moon, he will get gonorrhea. If a frog urinates on a person's hand, that hand will become infected and rot away. Cancer of the throat is caused by wearing a scarf around the neck, or a turtle-neck sweater. Members of certain tribes must shout praises once a year or they will suffer from leprosy and will lose parts of their bodies. In a land where life expectancy is pathetically short, is it of no importance that education is having no measurable impact on these naive beliefs about the causes of disease?

Then the devil again raises his leering head. In addition to persistent beliefs already mentioned in other context in this study, such as that pottery-makers have the evil eye, we find that such a statement, as, "A copper anklet will protect an infant from the evil eye," is impervious to education. Of some possible social, perhaps even political, significance is the fact that among the non-scientific items of high-frequency of belief which are resistant to education is the statement, "A person with thin lips is dangerous."

Thirty-six of the 132 items in this study defied classification into any of the meaningful categories thus far discussed. One might merely call them anomalous as a group; however, close scrutiny reveals that there are three patterns within this group of items. Fourteen of the items reflect a decrease in belief during pre-secondary education but little or no change with secondary education. Nine items show little or no change with pre-secondary education but reflect decrease in belief with secondary education. Thirteen of the items might, most properly, be called anomalous: 10 of them show decrease from primary to elementary but increase from elementary to secondary; three show increase from primary to elementary but decrease in belief from elementary to secondary. If there is a logical grouping of these items which apparently *are* affected by education, but affected in varying ways, that logic escapes this researcher. These thirty-six items spread, in context, among the devil, death, disease, disaster, and luck, both good and bad. The over-all frequency of belief ranges from a mere 20 per cent of primary school students who believe that "If three persons light their cigarettes from a single match, one of them will die" (a familiar, world-wide superstition) to a high of 87 per cent of the secondary school students who believe that: "There are some skillful persons who can summon the devil at will."

D. Discussion of Results

Both clinical and test evidence exists to support the thesis that Ethiopian children are as heavily endowed, intellectually, as are the children of other lands. The presentation of this evidence is the proper subject-matter of another volume, but as a quick datum to illustrate the sort of evidence referred to, consider this finding: Over 200 Ethiopian children were given parts of the Binet and Wechsler Intelligence Tests. If one bases judgment of results on a sub-test such as drawing a diamond, the average American youngster is mentally two years in advance of the average Ethiopian child; if one bases judgment of results on a sub-test such as correct counting of pencil-tappings on a table, the average Ethiopian child is mentally two years in advance of the average American child. In America, a child is given a pencil, and introduced to its use in the reproduction of forms, before he is weaned from the nursing-bottle; pencils are somewhat rare in Ethiopia. But in Ethiopia, a child's birth is heralded with rhythmic drum beats, and heard-

rhythms are a part of his daily life. The littlest Ethiopian lad can identify various tribal rhythmic patterns (which the present writer, an observer of this phenomenon, cannot do despite a musical education and several years in Ethiopia).

Intelligence is not the problem! And the problem cannot be solved through intellectual or intellective approaches alone. Yet these approaches must not be ignored. The data of this study strongly suggest that education is capable of making an impact on non-scientific beliefs. Further, the data suggest that this impact has been quite marked when it is specifically related to the problem of unscientific beliefs, quite marked when within a medically-oriented curriculum, measurable with about half the items studied, and with the other half, somewhat feeble. There are probably infinite reasons for the regrettably low relationship between acquisition of academically sound scientific information and the relinquishment of non-scientific beliefs. Unquestionably, many of these reasons can best be explained in terms most familiar to the cultural anthropologist or the social psychologist. But let us look at some educational aspects of the problem.

How closely is the present curriculum related to the real needs of Ethiopian children? It was mentioned earlier that study of Malaria is introduced in Grade 4. The American educator is somewhat shocked, however, to note that the curriculum cites the cause of the disease as a gnat. Mr. Webster's admirable volume is somewhat reassuring with the explanation that in England the word *gnat* is frequently applied to mosquitos in general. Leaving semantics aside, this suggests that the curriculum is related to needs in science in Ethiopia. But with the knowledge of needs as revealed by this present study, let us look further into the present science curriculum: By the 5th year, Ethiopian children are studying the earth's crust; astronomy is paramount in the first half of the 6th year (with obviously little impact on beliefs in astrology), and physics and chemistry are the major concern of the second half of this 6th year. Do not underestimate the Ethiopian schoolboy; he is, in fact, studying, learning, and passing examinations in astronomy, physics, and chemistry by the end of the 6th year.

No one would quarrel with the statement that education must begin where the learner is, not where the teacher or adviser thinks he should be or wishes he were. Subject matter introduced above the level, or different from the level, of the learner's orientation is a mere abstraction. The new learnings are rooted in air; they do not take hold, root, bud, or blossom. They can be memorized and regurgitated at examination time, but they do not effect changes in attitudes or behavior. Without such changes, no meaningful learning of a sort worthy of a nation's subsidy has taken place.

This study has demonstrated that education can have, and in some measure is having, an impact on the non-scientific beliefs which motivate attitudes and daily behavior of Ethiopians. The study has further demonstrated that more than half of the superstitions herein considered have proved impervious to modern educational procedures in Ethiopia.

E. Implementations of Results

In order to close this paper on a happy note, let us look at some of the ways in which the results of this study are being used: During the summer of 1957, every Teachers' Vacation Course in Ethiopia (an inservice training program with compulsory attendance) will include a work-shop on every-day science, based on the findings of this study, especially the findings with reference to the non-scientific beliefs held by teachers. One hospital with a dressers' training program has already revised its curriculum on the basis of the results of this study. Perhaps most important, the Director of Curriculum and Research of the Ethiopian Ministry of Education is planning a series of primers for children and a series of radio and newspaper articles for adults designed to attack the persistent non-scientific beliefs revealed by this study, and he is also taking the results into consideration in a contemplated revision of the curriculum.

Education has had, and is having, an impact on non-scientific beliefs in Ethiopia. It is hoped that this identification of specific beliefs which are amenable to or resistant to present educational methods will bring about activities which will increase that impact.

Non-Scientific Beliefs Held by
Ethiopian Teachers, Secondary School Students, and Medically-Oriented Groups Presented in Descending Rank Order of Frequency of Belief by Teachers

Item No.	Belief	Per Cent of 96 Teachers	Per Cent of 451 Students	Per Cent of 61 Medical
53	Certain mineral waters can cure stomach trouble by causing a person to vomit worms, sometimes frogs and toads.	81	88	62
54	The deaf, dumb, and crippled can be cured by bathing in and drinking the mineral water which causes a person to vomit worms or toads.	80	84	71
35	There are some skillful persons who can summon the devil at will.	78	87	62
56	Gonorrhea first came from a female dog.	74	79	41
73	The best treatment for malaria is to eat old butter (15 or 20 years old).	74	64	44
52	If a bat flies over your head, you will get a skin disease.	69	73	44
68	If a pregnant woman exposes herself to sunlight after eating fried food or spices, she will lose her baby.	68	63	34
94	Cancer of the throat is caused by wearing a turtle neck sweater or a scarf around the neck.	68	79	49
58	A child will grow better if the nerves are removed from under his back teeth.	67	68	46
67	If a person exposes himself to sunlight after eating fried food, he will get sick.	64	71	53
98	If a person possesses a hyena's foot, he will be able to run swiftly.	64	63	38
75	A person in malaria country can prevent infection by eating garlic.	63	71	38
80	Too much learning results in madness.	61	60	54
21	If a person has an electric shock, the wires will immediately carry his blood to the dynamo at the headquarters of the electric power company.	60	66	43
62	Certain people can read the past and the future from the stars.	60	81	51

Item No.	Belief	Per Cent of 96 Teachers	Per Cent of 451 Students	Per Cent of 61 Medical
49	If you step over fried grain or a killed chicken which has been wrapped around the head of a diseased person as a cure, then thrown away, you will suffer from a disease, or may even lose your life.	58	57	34
72	Butter rubbed on a baby's head will go inside the head and cause the eyes to be bright and the head to be strong.	58	62	25
78	A man who has skill in stopping rains must not eat or drink while he is performing the ceremony to stop rain, or he will be unsuccessful.	58	64	44
102	Too much charity leads to madness.	58	74	51
3	Beautiful couples produce ugly children.	56	62	64
16	A man with bow-legs is a dangerous person.	56	51	33
34	Manual laborers, such as pottery makers, usually have the Evil Eye.	55	55	47
74	The center of memory is the heart.	55	50	41
77	The members of certain tribes have the inherited ability to stop rains.	55	65	33
14	If your eyelid twitches, you will soon see a person whom you have not seen for a long time or have never seen before.	54	57	44
59	If a man urinates facing the moon, he will get gonorrhea.	54	57	25
46	Some magicians can tell you the correct color of the animal you must kill for a feast in order to avoid madness or some other disease.	53	68	33
61	A boy who smokes wishes his parents would die.	52	49	51
71	The organ for thinking is the heart.	52	45	46
114	If a person laughs at a man who has leprosy, he will catch the disease.	52	54	21
6	If a person who has been bitten by a mad dog crosses a river after being treated, the medicine will not be effective.	50	58	36
40	A person who has tapeworms will not suffer from amoeba.	50	58	31
47	On New Year's Day, you must kill the kind and color of animal customarily sacrificed by your forefathers or you will suffer from trouble of some sort.	50	70	39
100	If a child eats bacon, he will be protected from the Evil Eye.	50	47	29
83	If a frog urinates on a person's hand, the hand will become infected and rot away.	49	53	29

Item No.	Belief	Per Cent of 96 Teachers	Per Cent of 451 Students	Per Cent of 61 Medical
55	The members of certain tribes have the power to turn themselves into hyenas at night.	49	39	23
84	If you go into a room which has been closed for a long time, you will be attacked by Satan.	49	57	29
123	If a person goes weeks without taking tapeworm medicine, his face will become dry and chapped.	49	41	23
18	A person with thin lips is dangerous.	48	54	41
82	If a person hears a sound while drinking *abisho,* he will become mentally confused.	48	61	29
96	If a baby boy dies, the next boy born will survive if he is given a girl's name and always addressed with feminine forms.	48	59	33
13	If the sole of your foot itches, you will soon take a trip.	47	50	44
36	There are persons, known as *tenquai* or *ofaboko,* who inherit the power to read the past and to foretell the future.	46	61	34
44	If a mother loses several babies through death in infancy, her next baby will live and grow if friends can manage to get her, unknowingly, to eat a part of the ear of the new baby.	46	31	33
51	Malaria has the appearance of a tall, thin woman with much uncombed hair; she can be seen in the desert at midnight and noon.	46	37	33
92	If you catch the reflection of a burning house, or other object, in a mirror, the fire will go out.	46	46	36
95	Butter in the mouth of a new-born baby will prevent his voice from becoming shrill.	46	57	23
122	A copper anklet will protect an infant from the Evil Eye.	46	58	28
20	The person who dreams of a beautiful, light-skinned woman, has, in fact, had a visit from St. Mary (The Virgin).	45	58	44
115	If a man dreams that a cow or some other animal eats the sleeve of his coat, he will become ill or die.	45	56	25
29	If your shoulders twitch, you will have new clothes.	44	46	43
30	If the palm of your hand itches, you will receive money.	44	59	44
88	To cure hiccups, one should call the names of friends whom he suspects are talking about him; if he calls the right name, the hiccups will stop.	44	44	39

Item No.	Belief	Per Cent of 96 Teachers	Per Cent of 451 Students	Per Cent of 61 Medical
112	If a hyena howls once only during the night, an important or titled person will die.	44	48	18
32	If a person can get possession of a hyena's eyebrow, he can remain awake indefinitely.	43	60	25
126	Itching skin is caused by the Evil Eye.	43	40	23
69	If the first born child is a girl, the parents will have good luck.	42	47	44
129	If a person possessed by the devil (epilepsy) falls down, anyone who helps him up will catch the disease.	42	41	21
132	In order to avoid being killed by the devil, a well-cleaner should kill a fowl and leave it beside the open well; the devil will come out to lick the fowl's blood and will not attack the man when he enters the well.	42	48	15
38	If a bee enters your house, you will have visitors.	41	58	31
93	A person who smokes is a subject of the devil.	41	50	36
116	A boy with a cow-lick on the front of his head will always be alone and will bring bad luck to his family.	41	51	29
117	If a snake, cat, or hyena crosses the road in front of you, you will have bad luck.	41	44	16
118	If you dream of kissing a woman friend, you will never be friends again.	41	54	21
121	A gift of a used handerchief will break friendship unless the recipient gives the donor a coin.	41	53	28
128	A person may get rid of a devil which possesses him by being so frightened by a moving car that the devil leaves him.	41	47	21
131	If a person crosses a river at noon or midnight after using perfume, he will catch leprosy.	41	41	18
48	If your face itches, you will soon weep.	40	47	16
87	If a person hiccups, it is a sign that some of his friends are talking about him.	40	51	38
106	If a person swallows a queen bee, he will have a beautiful voice.	40	47	25
120	A man with hair on his toes or the back of his fingers, is a lucky man.	40	55	26
124	A person who sits on a grinding stone in the night and strums a *kirar* (harp) will become an expert player.	40	38	16
19	Satan will never visit the home of a man who owns a black dog or cat.	39	34	29

Item No.	Belief	Per Cent of 96 Teachers	Per Cent of 451 Students	Per Cent of 61 Medical
28	If you eat in the dark, the devil will dine with you.	39	36	25
81	If a person drinks liquid made from *abisho* seeds, he will be brilliant.	39	50	29
85	If a person kills a cat or a lizard, his hand will shake forever after.	39	52	46
101	If a person worries on the first day of the month, he will worry all that month.	39	48	26
10	If a person spits on a toilet, he will have a sore throat.	37	49	33
108	It is bad luck to meet a single black crow.	37	43	25
109	A girl born with temporal baldness will become rich.	37	46	21
127	A piece of brass attached to the front of a truck will prevent the devil from harming the truck.	37	41	15
7	If a person cuts his nails on the Sabbath, the cuticle on his fingers will become infected.	36	43	34
105	The person who buries his fingernail parings will be able to use them for firewood in heaven.	36	46	16
110	If you pass a man carrying a weaving machine, you will have bad luck.	36	38	18
25	If a man keeps a dog which has a white spot on his forehead, he will have bad luck.	35	39	21
50	If people do not boil grain, make coffee, and eat under a tree during October, the community will suffer cold or disease.	35	54	33
76	If a cock crows in the evening, a high official will be deprived of his power.	35	43	25
99	Members of certain tribes must shout praises once a year or they will suffer from leprosy, and will lose part of their bodies.	35	47	23
107	A black spot on a person's body is a sign that the person has been kissed by St. Mary (The Virgin).	35	45	34
113	If an owl hoots on the roof of a man's house, that man will die soon.	35	46	21
119	If you meet a person guiding an unloaded donkey, you will have bad luck.	34	37	18
125	If a grandchild holds the knee of a grandparent, that grandparent will die.	34	41	15
22	A man who smokes will not be attacked by Satan.	33	35	26
70	If a person urinates on a stone which has been exposed to sunlight, he will get gonorrhea.	32	38	18

Item No.	Belief	Per Cent of 96 Teachers	Per Cent of 451 Students	Per Cent of 61 Medical
97	If a person pays out money on the first day of the month, he will continue to pay out all month.	32	40	16
1	If two brothers cross a river together, both will be drowned.	30	23	34
65	If a man, on leaving his house, sees an empty water jug, he will have bad luck.	30	49	·26
79	In the olden days heaven was so close to earth that man could communicate easily with God, but a mule kicked heaven high up in the sky; as a punishment, mules may not reproduce their own species.	30	41	28
103	If a fly gets into a drink, the drinker will have good luck.	30	35	15
104	If you kill a spider, you will be buried without a shroud.	30	27	20
39	If a fly gets into your mouth, you will soon receive a drink.	29	49	29
43	If a colony of ants comes into a house through the door, the family living in that house will have good luck.	29	47	15
91	If you run out of water while washing your hands, your relationship with that household will be ended.	29	29	16
111	If you pass, or cross between, two large vultures, you will have a long life.	29	40	23
8	If a person is quick enough to swallow his saliva three times before a shooting star fades, he will have the voice of a great singer.	28	30	18
17	A person with wavy hair is dangerous.	28	34	26
42	A man who kills an elephant must provide feasts in honor of the dead elephant, or he will go mad or be maimed.	28	43	25
130	It is dangerous for a woman to marry a man whose wife has died, for she, too, will die soon.	28	31	23
23	If a merchant sells anything on credit in the early morning, he will have to sell on credit the whole day.	27	35	28
26	If a truck driver gives a ride to a lone priest or a lone woman, an accident or other misfortune will occur.	27	31	33
33	Ironworkers often take the form of hyenas at night.	27	42	26
86	If you see yourself in a mirror in the night you will become a fool or an idiot.	27	30	18

Item No.	Belief	Per Cent of 96 Teachers	Per Cent of 451 Students	Per Cent of 61 Medical
89	If you hang a horse's hoof on your door, you will have good luck.	27	36	20
66	If a man, on leaving his house, sees one person alone, he will have bad luck.	26	35	18
15	A man with a hairy body has good fortune.	25	37	26
4	A man who dresses in a dead man's suit will soon die.	25	20	23
64	If a boy stands in the rain, he will grow tall.	24	40	23
90	If someone in a group sneezes while you are talking, it means that you are telling the truth.	24	44	25
2	If a farmer fails to kill a dark sheep yearly, all of his animals will die.	23	20	23
9	If it rains during bright sunshine, a hyena will be born.	22	41	21
24	If a flock of crows fly in the air, there will be a war.	22	32	21
57	A person can eat more bananas if he has his feet in water.	22	61	23
60	The rains will fall on a person who eats the hind part of any animal.	22	36	34
45	If three persons light their cigarettes from a single match, one of them will die.	20	28	11
63	A young boy who sits on a stone will not grow tall.	19	30	13
27	The blow of a strong wind is the sign of the death of a well-known man.	18	25	25
37	If a man with low intelligence sits on a grinding stone during the night, he can easily become a brilliant scholar.	16	29	15
41	If a Christian does not wear a string around his neck, the food he eats will not nourish him.	15	28	15
12	If you close your fist while rain falls in bright sunshine, you will be the Godfather of a newly born hyena.	13	14	15
31	If a person's photograph is taken, part of his blood is taken from him and goes into the picture.	11	25	20
5	If a person cuts his nails in the evening, his uncle will die.	8	13	8
11	If one cleans his teeth during the night, he will lose his brother.	8	13	10

STORY THEMES IN ETHIOPIAN FOLK TALES

One thousand and eighty-six stories with identifiable themes, told or written by Ethiopian children in grades 2 through 8, reveal the following frequencies and percentages of recurrence of themes. (Computed from data reported by Russell G. Davis, Hassan Mohsin, and Brent K. Ashabranner):

Theme Statements	Frequency	Per Cent
1. Cleverness pays	290	26.68
2. Honesty is good—dishonesty bad	95	8.74
3. Stupidity brings destruction—harm	75	6.90
4. Avoid bad companions	53	4.88
5. Cruelty is bad	44	4.05
6. Destiny is inescapable	39	3.58
7. Kindness is good	36	3.31
8. Disloyalty is bad—loyalty good	30	2.76
9. Greed and miserliness are bad	29	2.67
10. It pays to be cautious and careful	29	2.67
11. Tyranny is bad	24	2.21
12. Adultery is bad	23	2.12
13. Prayer and faith in God help	20	1.84
14. Education pays	17	1.56
15. Cooperation and unity pay	15	1.38
16. Married life is good	15	1.38
17. Envy is bad	14	1.29
18. Patience is rewarded	12	1.10
19. Pretence and sham pay off	12	1.10
20. Hard work and industry pay off	11	1.01
21. It pays to be powerful	11	1.01
22. Gratitude is good	11	1.01
23. Over-ambition brings destruction	10	.92
24. Vanity brings punishment	9	.83
25. Justice will prevail	8	.74
26. Vengeance is necessary and satisfying	8	.74
27. Respect your elders (parents)	8	.74
28. Avoid strange people and things	8	.74
29. Men are faithless (untrustworthy)	8	.74
30. Drunkenness is bad	8	.74
31. It pays to be courageous	8	.74
32. Don't ignore good advice.	7	.64
33. Vengeance is a bad thing	6	.55
34. Obedience is necessary	5	.46
35. Over-confidence brings destruction	5	.46
36. Women are faithless creatures	5	.46
37. Miscellaneous themes with four or fewer occurrences	78	7.18

Architecture from another era. One of the several Gondar Castles built in the 17th century by Ethiopians and Portuguese, relics of the splendor of an ancient Ethiopian civilization.

VIII

History
of
Ethiopia

A scholarly saint could not present any such review of historical high-lights and escape criticism, for source books are in frequent disagreement. The criterion for inclusion of a datum, A.D., was the existence of an extant document to validate the event; however, some of the precious, early, original, extant documents were not available for examination, requiring reliance on secondary sources.

ETHIOPIA—PAST AND PRESENT[1]
by Tekle Michale K. Mariam

Throughout the three thousand years of Ethiopia's independence, her contact with the outside has been limited to her neighbors either in the form of war or in the form of commerce. In the earlier part of this period, waves of Semitic, Hellenic, and early Christian civilizations reached Ethiopia (when Europe was still pagan and semi-savage) in turn only to ebb away again.

[1] First published in *Jesame*, Journal of the Ethiopian Students Association in the Middle East, October, 1958.

However, in the succeeding centuries after the birth of Christ, the Axumite Kingdom[2] had strengthened both militarily and economically. Under her formidable naval power and in possession of the Red Sea ports, trade was flourishing as far as India. Her military might was more than a match for the Yemenites in the Arabian peninsula, and she pushed inland as far as the gates of Mecca. Later, defeated, she withdrew from the Arabian peninsula, but her prestige in Ethiopia proper was still undiminished.

The following decades witnessed the birth of Mohammed and the consequent spreading of his doctrine known as Islam. A French historian calls the periods succeeding the rise of Islam "centuries of historical night." He says, "Encompassed on all sides by the enemies of their religion, the Ethiopians slept nearly a thousand years, forgetful of the world by whom they were forgotten." This was marked by the decline from the height reached by the Axumite Kingdom.

It has been generally true that Ethiopia was completely isolated from the time of the Moslem advance that began in the seventh century and spread up to the sixteenth century. This was the time of Ethiopia's Dark Age—a period in which institutions which had taken shape changed very little until recently.

Europe was dimly aware of the existence of Ethiopia. Rumours of a Christian Kingdom were of special interest to the Portuguese sailors around the coasts of Africa. This resulted in an expedition towards the interior under Christopher Da Gama. (With the help of the Portuguese, the impending danger of Gran Mohammed under the Turkish suzerainty was checked off, but meanwhile, for all her past glories, Ethiopia lost to the Moslem armies all her ports and the coast lines along the Red Sea.) The expulsion of the Portuguese shortly after and her perpetual warfare with the neighbouring countries, especially the Turkish Empire, gave her no time for peaceful development.

Not only did the Ethiopians in the latter period refuse to welcome any foreign state aid, but they bitterly resented it. They had been intensely jealous of any foreign interference, whatsoever, in their domestic affairs. During the last hundred years, despite treaties and public professions of faith on the part of European powers to support Ethiopia's independence and development, suspicion, however, remained as a strong factor. The Ethiopians saw that all Africa had been partitioned out among the European

---

[2] During the first century A.D., the Kingdom of Aksum, the first Ethiopian state, flourished in the area approximating the present province of Tigre.

In Asmara, Eritrea, Dr. Edith Lord administers screening examinations to the 200 qualified applicants competing for the 25 places in nurses training course, Empress Menen School of Nursing, an Ethiopian-United States cooperative education project.

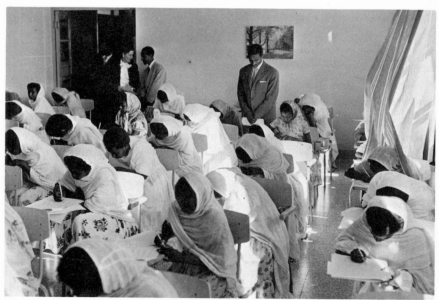

A group of girls taking entrance examinations for admission to nurses' training.

powers, and even though they had hitherto been "an island of Christians in the sea of pagans, they struggled to remain an island of independence in the sea of conquest."

No wonder then, the result was to remain in obscurity and seclusion behind the hills of Ethiopia, which paralyzed communication and transport development. Thus, she had to nurse a type of culture which became characteristic of the Ethiopians. (During the sixteenth and seventeenth centuries, waves of influence, whose effects were resisted and limited, reached the country.)

The story of its ancient fleet trading with India, the asylum it afforded for the Prophet's family when he was persecuted, the disastrous efforts of the Italians to subjugate her, the connection she had with the one time rivalry between France and England on the Nile—all these dramatic events brought her before the world. Nor were these all; the greatest was yet to come.

In the last hundred years or so, while the rest of the world was advancing materially, Ethiopia, outside the radius of Addis Ababa, remained almost unchanged until this generation.

In 1935 Ethiopia faced one of the most cruel acts of Mussolini's aggression in modern history. Her history as an unconquered Ethiopia for thousands of years had to suffer the short, unpleasant interruption. With her Emperor Haile Selassie's dramatic struggle, she was liberated in 1941. Many of the barriers between Ethiopia and the rest of the world, both physical and mental, were broken down to a great extent. Ethiopia has now come out once more on the international scene, and the full tide of world influence has broken in upon the country.

Indeed, although the Ethiopians are torn between their intense nationalism and conservatism on the one hand, and the realization of the need of influence and stimulus from foreign civilized nations on the other, the Emperor and His assistants are determined to open more intellectual windows for development of national life. What can be seen in Ethiopia today is a hectic attempt to make good the lost centuries of development. The effort is to bring about a more rapid and comprehensive change than history has hitherto recorded.

A modern centralized state structure with complete administrative and economic devices is introduced. One of the immediate problems which is being faced is the supply of trained staff for such an elaborate and highly articulated state service. The need to extend an efficient and well-regulated form of administration has been understood. To meet this challenge of administering a modern state, the Emperor is assisting the education of many young men who are determined to carry out His policy with responsibility, loyalty, and efficiency.

The prospect of real success does not seem to have a long road to travel, though the road may be dangerous in this troubled world.

A SWEEPING GLANCE
AT HIGHLIGHTS OF ETHIOPIAN HISTORY
B.C.

Moses takes an Ethiopian[1] wife (Septuagint, Numbers xxii.I).

Ethiopia is identified as a son of Ham (Septuagint).

Hamitic peoples from North Africa populate Ethiopia; some immigration from Nubian tribes from the Upper Nile regions.

10th C—Makeda, Queen of Saba (Sheba), visits Solomon and conceives a child, Menelik I, who is subsequently annointed King of Ethiopia by Solomon.

? 1000-500 ? —Immigration of Semitic Arabs from Yemen, bringing with them a more advanced culture.

3rd C—Ptolemy II and Ptolemy III of Egypt establish trade and hunting stations in Ethiopia, through agreements with Ethiopian rulers.

c. 270—Ptolemy II of Egypt authorizes Septuagint (Old Testament) from Greek originals; *Ethiops* and *Ethiopians* written, as opposed to other translations which write *Cush* and *Cushites*.

A.D.

1st C—Kingdom of Aksum flourished in area approximately that now known as Province of Tigre.

1st C (late)—Red Sea port of Adulis, just South of Massawa, developed under King Zoscales; foreign trade established.

3rd C (late)—Kingdom of Aksum extended to include part of South-Western Arabia.

---

[1] Ethiopia of the ancient world was the middle-Nile region south of Egypt, later called Nubia. The Aksumites began to call themselves Ethiopians only after conversion to Christianity in the 4th Century.

325-350—Reign of King Qezanas; culture is trilingual; Greek, Sabaean, and Ge'ez (ancient Ethiopian). (Qezanas is often spelled Aeizanas or Ezana.)

Aksumite Kingdom has currency system with gold coinage.

4th C (c. 330)—Ethiopia converted to Christianity with conversion of Qezanas.

451—Council of Chalcedon; decisive break between Greco-Latin Church and Syrian-Armenian-Egyptian Church.

6th C (early)—Ethiopian territorial expansion in all directions.

6th C—Hebraic influences from Jewish Arabia are fixed on one group of Ethiopians, the Falashas.

6th C. (middle)—Reign of King Ella Atsebeha, known as Kaleb.

7th C—Ethiopia landbound and ringed by forces of Islam.

8th C—Adulis destroyed by Moslems; remnants of Christian Aksumite kingdom isolated in mountains.

c. 850—Church formally condemns polygamy.

9th C: With decline, coinage currency system disappears. Barter reappears with use of blocks of salt (still in use in Tigre), iron, and lengths of cloth.

11th C (late)—Church formally condemns polygamy again.

1093—Nile fails to rise; Egypt's dependency on Ethiopia's Blue Nile recognized.

12th C—First written legal code, *Fetha Negast* (Judgment of Kings), which is primarily a collection of church laws translated from Arabic.

c. 1150—Zague dynasty to power, claiming descent from Moses and Ethiopian wife. Aksum destroyed by usurping northern Queen Judith (Yodit or Godith).

1178—Saladin, Sultan of Egypt and Syria, gives Ethiopia the chapel of the Invention of the Cross, Church of Holy Sepulchre, Jerusalem, and a station in the grotto of the Nativity in Bethlehem.

1270 ff—Zague dynasty ejected; Solomonian dynasty re-established by Emperor Yekuno Amlak, who decreed that one-third of all lands would forever be reserved for the support of the clergy. Second Tekla Haymanot founded monastic order in Debra Libanos. The rule was established that the *Abune* of Ethiopia must always be an Egyptian, not an Ethiopian.

12th C—Under Lalibela, Christianity flourished; the famous rock churches of Lalibela were hewn.

13th C—Solomon-Makeda (Sheba) story written into Ge'ez records, making it a religious "fact."

13th C—Although Ethiopians continue to repulse forces of Islam, losses are suffered; for example, what is now Shoa became largely a Moslem sultanate.

1325—Emperor Amda Tsiyon threatens to make Egypt a desert in response to attempted persecution, by Sultan el Nasir, of Coptic Christians.

1314-1344—Emperor Amda Tsiyon wars against surrounding Moslem kingdoms; outcome indecisive.

13th-17th C: Literary Renaissance, church-centered, somewhat sporadic.

14th C—Ancient Christian Ethiopian-Nubian civilization obliterated by Moslem Arabs.

14th C (early)—*Kebra Negast* (Glory of Kings) translated into Ge'ez from 1225 Arabic text; discusses Solomon dynasty in Ethiopia.

14th C—Establishment of office of King's scribes to record official annals, act as chroniclers and contemporary historians.

14th C ff—Invasions by Islamic forces from eastern plains.

1441-1442—Ethiopian delegates from the monastery in Jerusalem attend council of Florence and there submit Ethiopian church to Roman Catholic domination, but this act is not recognized or accepted by priests or people of Ethiopia.

1487—King John II of Portugal sends Peter de Covilham as envoy to Ethiopian King to propose alliance against Moslems.

1508—Emperor Lebna Dingil to throne under regency of Empress Helena (Eleni); institutes system of contemporary chronicling of events which has lasted to present.

1512—Queen Regent Helena sends Ethiopian envoy (an Armenian) to . Portugal.

1520—Emperor Lebna Dingil welcomes Portuguese Embassy to Ethiopia; embassy remains six years. Emperor gives Portuguese Priest Alvarez letter to Pope declaring submission to Roman Church. Emperor cedes Massawa to Portuguese King Manual as naval base in return for various craftsmen and physicians.

1520—Introduction into Ethiopia by Portuguese of matchlock fire arms.

1526—Ethiopian Ambassador to Portugal leaves Ethiopia to assume post; is neglected in Portugal.

1527—Ahmed ibn Ibrahim el Ghazi (Mohammed) Gran overruns Ethiopia, destroys churches and monasteries; Ethiopian Chronicles report nine out of ten were converted to Islam (probably only nominally.)

1540—Emperor Lebna Dingil, in hiding, sends Portuguese John Bermudez to Portugal to request help.

1541—Christopher da Gama (son of Vasco), with 400 Portuguese volunteers, lands at Massawa.

1542: Portuguese "rescue forces" routed by Ahmed Gran.

1543—Emperor Claudius (Galaudeiros), with regrouped Ethiopian forces and regrouped remnants of Portuguese army, attacks Ahmed Gran at Darasgay, near Lake Tana, kills him, routs his troops.

1543 ff—Emperor Claudius reconquers and rebuilds devastated Ethiopia.

1557-58—Turks occupy Massawa; Ethiopia landlocked.

1557—Jesuit Oviedo and mission sent by Pope to Ethiopia to Romanize Ethiopian Church; Emperor Claudius rejects his authority.

1559—Emperor Meenas outlaws Roman Catholicism for Ethiopians, including wives and slaves of the Portuguese.

1563—Emperor Meenas dies; his son, Sertsa Dengel, succeeds him.

1597—Emperor Sertsa Dengel dies; his son Jacob (Yaikob) succeeds, but succession is disputed; his nephew Za Dengel is successful successor.

1603—Spanish Jesuit Peter Paez arrives as missionary; opens a school.

1607—*Abune* releases Ethiopians from oath of allegiance to Za Dengel, who has been converted to Roman Catholicism by Paez; Za Dengel is killed.

1607—Sisinnius, nephew of Sertsa Dengel, is crowned; Paez converts him to Roman Catholicism. (Sisinnius is also spelled "Sosneyos" or "Susenyos.")

1612—Sesla Kristos, brother of King and Governor of Gojjam, is converted to Roman Catholicism and establishes a Jesuit mission.

? 1612—The *Abune* excommunicates Emperor Sosneyos; a series of rebellions follows. The Pagan Gallas move northward to the Blue Nile.

1622 ff—Paez dies and is replaced by Spanish Jesuit Alphonzo Mendez who suspends all Ethiopian priests, directs that they must be reordained by him, the people must be rebaptized, churches reconsecrated.

1632 ff—Following many revolts, Emperor Sosneyos restores Ethiopian Church then abdicates in favor of son , Fasilades, who establishes capital at Gondar and builds castles. Jesuits are deported; Ethiopian Roman Catholics are banished or executed.

1655 ff—Emperor John I (Yohannes) burns all books remaining from Jesuit period, forces Moslems to live in restricted areas of towns.

1680—Emperor John I dies; his son, Joshua I ("Iyasus" or "Eyesus"), Joshua the Great, succeeds him.

1680 ff—Emperor Eyesus re-establishes supremacy of crown over Church, introduces numerous administrative reforms, condemns graft and malfunctioning of government employees. He sends Murad, a Moslem Armenian merchant, to the court of France as an Ethiopian envoy. (Eyesus is often spelled, "Iyasu.")

1704—Emperor Eyesus is assassinated by his son, Tekla Haymanot, who assumes the throne.

Emperor Tekla Haymanot I is assassinated by nobles of the court; his uncle, Taywofilos, ascends to the throne.

1709—Emperor Taywofilos dies. Succession is disputed among nobles; contender from Solomon dynasty is defeated. Justus of Tigre succeeds him, but is not widely accepted by the Ethiopian people.

1714—The army rebels and instruments the crowning of David (Dawit), son of Eyesus.

1719—Emperor David (Dawit) is poisoned; Atsme Giorgis, nicknamed Bakaffa, another son of Eyesus, succeeds David.

1729—Emperor Atsme Giorgis dies; his infant son, Joshua (Eyesus) II (Joshua the Little), is crowned; the Queen-mother Berhan Mugasa is named regent.

1753—Emperor Joshua II dies; his young son, Joas, is successor, but the Queen-mother Wibeet, a Galla, rules for him; she appoints many Gallas to important government posts.

c. 1753 ff—Michael Yesuhul, Governor of Tigre, arranges murder of Joas, ousts Gallas from Government posts, arranges for crowning of John, aged (over 70) son of Eysus the Great. After a reign of several months, Emperor John II is poisoned; his son, Takla Haymanot II, is crowned. Empire is disunited by numerous rebellions and civil wars; various *rasses* (chiefs) are crowned in different parts of the country.

1800—There are six different "Emperors" of Ethiopia in the nation.

1813—Reign of King Sahla Selassie of Shoa (Grandfather of Menelik II).

1840—England-India Company buys a coastal strip of Ethiopia, opposite Aden.

1849—Ras Ali of Gondar and Walter Plowden sign England-Ethiopia trade treaty.

1850—Maria Theresa dollar (Austrian) becomes the standard coin of Ethiopia.

c. 1850 ff—Civil wars among followers of claimants for crown from Tigre, Gondar, Gojjam, and Shoa. Ali of Gondar and Goshu of Gojjam are killed.

1855—A "dark horse" named Kassa becomes Theodore (Teywodros), King of Kings.

1856—England attempts to effect peaceful transfer of Massawa from Turkish to Ethiopian rule.

1860 ff—Emperor Theodore suppresses Tigre Rebellion, tries to convert Gallas to Christianity, expels Moslems, attempts to establish Ethiopian embassies in England and France.

1862—Turkey appropriates Ethiopian territory, especially along Red Sea coast.

1862—Turkey states that Ethiopians are Turkish subjects (like Egyptians) since both Egyptian and Ethiopian Copts are under the same Patriarch.

1864—Theodore imprisons over 60 British subjects for political reasons.

1868—Emperor Theodore commits suicide, by gun shot, to avoid capture by 3,400 British troops under Sir Robert Napier, sent to Ethiopia to rescue British subjects from political imprisonment.

1868—Napier leaves Ethiopia with ex-prisoners, the *Abune's* crown, Theodore's crown, and the Royal copy of the *Kebra Negast*.

1868-1872—Civil strife over successor to Theodore.

1869—Tekle George (Giorgis) succeeds, rules for three years.

1869—Suez Canal is opened, making Red Sea Coast of increased importance.

1869—Assab trading center is purchased by an Italian Company.

1872—Ras of Tigre crowned John IV; his chief rival is King Menelik of Shoa.

1872-1876—Egypt's Khedive Ismail makes unsuccessful attempts to conquer Ethiopia.

1878—Emperor John (Yohannes) IV grants King Menelik nearly autonomous rule of Shoa; they betroth their children; John recognizes Menelik "heir apparent" to title of King of Kings.

1882—Italian Government buys Assab from private company; trade treaty with Menelik is signed.

1883—Empire of Egypt collapses following Mahdi uprisings.

1884—Egyptians retreat from Harrar, Ethiopia, defeated by Mahdists.

1885—Italian military units take Massawa, move inland; skirmishes result.

1886—King Menelik builds Addis Ababa and designates it capital city.

1887—Ethiopians, under Emperor John, fight successfully at Dogali; Italians routed from all inland posts.

1888—Italian mission offers Menelik military aid and Tigre in exchange for help against Emperor John and possession of Asmara.

1889—Emperor John dies in battle against Dervishes; he is succeeded by Emperor Menelik II of the Solomonic line.

1889—Treaty of Ucciali executed by Emperor Menelik II with Italy; unsigned Italian translation implies Ethiopia is an Italian Protectorate.

1890—Rebellion by Ras Mengesha of Tigre is suppressed by Emperor Menelik II.

1890—Russian and French emissaries visit Emperor Menelik; Italy objects on basis of Treaty of Ucciali; Menelik clarifies wording and intent of treaty.

1890, January—Italy announces that the Italian settlements in Ethiopia shall be called a colony named Eritrea.

1891—Anglo-Italian agreement recognizes Ethiopia as under Italian "sphere of influence."

1891—Ras Mengesha of Tigre treats with Italians for support in secession from Ethiopia; project is unsuccessful.

1893—Emperor Menelik II denounces Treaty of Ucciali.

1894—Ninety-nine years concession granted to French for Addis Ababa-Djibouti railway.

1895—Italians defeat Ras Mengesha and occupy Adua. (Also spelled, "Adwa" or "Adowa.")

1895—Ras Mengesha of Tigre joins with Emperor Menelik to repel Italian invasion.

1896, March 1—Italians, under Baratieri, attack Menelik's forces near Adua, (then capital of Tigre); Italians defeated.

1896, October—Italian-Ethiopian peace treaty; Treaty of Ucciali is annulled; Ethiopia is recognized as a sovereign and independent nation.

1896—Emperor Menelik gives railroad concession to *Compagnie International des Chemins de Fers Ethiopiens;* Djibouti link toward Harrar completed; funds depleted.

1897, January-March—French diplomatic delegation to Addis Ababa; English mission to Ethiopia, which achieved borderline agreement between Ethiopia and British Somililand; envoys from Russia and Turkey arrive; many overlapping concessions given to foreign persons for plantations and mining in Ethiopia.

1897-1908—Emperor Menelik settles Ethiopia's boundaries with England, France, and Italy, except for Ethiopian-Italian Somaliland border (which is still undetermined).

1898—Ras Mengesha of Tigre rebels against Emperor Menelik; defeated by Menelik's forces, led by Ras Makonnen.

1898—Emperor Menelik orders all Ethiopians to be vaccinated against small·pox.

1902—French Government buys control of railway line; Menelik is angry; progress on railroad stops.

1902—Boundary Treaty with England includes agreement that Ethiopia will undertake no construction work across Blue Nile, Lake Tana, or Sobat River that would obstruct flow to Nile.

1903—Electric lights and telephones installed in Addis Ababa.

1905—Italian Government takes "trading" colony of Benadir, Somililand.

1905—Bank of Abyssinia established as concession of National Bank of Egypt.

1905-1910—Archeologists from Germany, directed by Erno Littman, explore Aksum.

1906—France, England, and Italy execute Tripartite Treaty; French win rights to build railway to Addis Ababa; Menelik not consulted, is angry, critical, indignant.

1906—Ras Makonnen of Harar, father of present Emperor, Haile Salassie I, dies.

1907—Emperor Menelik, ill, names Lij Eyasus, grandson of 12, as his successor with Ras Tesemma as Regent; Menelik forms Council of Ministers to help him govern.

1908—Emperor Menelik II establishes first government school in Addis Ababa.

1908—Railway concession transferred to a private French company.

1908-1910—Empress Taitu presses claim for Regency with Menelik's daughter Zauditu as Empress.

1910—The *Abune* accuses Ras Tesemma, Regent for Eyasu, of breaking his oath to Menelik.

1911, July 30—Ras Tafari Makonnen betrothed to Menen, daughter of King Michael of Wollo.

1911—Ras Tessema dies; Lij Eyasu reigns without regent, with guidance of Council of Ministers.

1913, December 13—Emperor Menelik II dies after severe illness of six years.

1916—Lij Eyasu adopts Islam, claims descent from Mohammed, not from Solomon; decrees Ethiopia religiously subject to Turkey.

1916, September—The *Abune* excommunicates Lij Eyasu and revokes loyalty oaths to him; Eyasu goes into hiding.

1917, February—Menelik's daughter, Zauditu, is made Empress with 25-year-old Ras Tafari Makonnen, Governor of Harrar, named as Regent and Heir Apparent.

1918—First railroad trains travel between Djibouti and Addis Ababa.

1918—Empress Zauditu dissolves Council of Ministers, established by Menelik in 1907.

1919—Ethiopia's application for membership in the League of Nations is rejected because of the slavery conditions in Ethiopia.

1923—Ras Tafari Makonnen arranges application for Ethiopia's membership in League of Nations; Ethiopia receives unanimous vote for membership September 18, 1923.

1923—Ras Tafari Makonnen visits Aden and takes first flight in aeroplane.

1923, September 15—Empress Zauditu and Regent Ras Tafari Makonnen proclaim death sentence for buying and selling slaves.

1924, March 31—A new slavery law is promulgated by Empress Zauditu and Regent Tafari Makonnen with provisions for freeing slaves and their offspring.

1924—Ras Tafari Makonnen visits England, returns with Emperor Theodore's royal crown, taken by Napier in 1886.

1925—Ras Tafari Makonnen founds Tafari Makonnen school in Addis Ababa.

1926—Ethiopia signs League of Nations International Slavery convention designed to suppress slavery in all forms.

1928—Twenty-year Treaty of Friendship signed with Italy; treaty includes allocation of an Ethiopian free-zone at the Italian port of Assab.

1928—Regent Ras Tafari Makonnen founds school of religion in Addis Ababa.

1929—Merab, former Emperor Menelik's doctor, estimates that between one-fourth and one-third of the population are slaves.

1930—Penal Code is compiled.

1930—Ethiopia signs Arms Traffic Act with Britain, France, and Italy.

1930, April 2—Empress Zauditu dies.

1930, November 2—Ras Tafari Makonnen is crowned Emperor Haile Selassie I; many foreign diplomatic guests attend coronation. (He is the 225th Monarch of the Solomonic line of Ethiopian Emperors.)

1931, July 16—First Constitution is granted by H.I.M. Haile Selassie I; Parliament, including Senate and Chamber, "designated by provinces."

1931—Emperor issues radical decree against slavery, which frees children born of slaves and frees slaves on the death of their masters.

1931—Empress Zauditu Memorial Hospital opens in Addis Ababa under sponsorship of Seventh Day Adventists' Mission of America.

1932—A Slavery Bureau is established in Addis Ababa with the directive to eliminate slavery in Ethiopia within two decades.

1933—Sudan Interior Mission establishes a Leprosarium in Addis Ababa.

1933—Emperor introduces a series of copper and nickel coins, on decimal system, to improve currency system.

1933—His Imperial Majesty orders freedom for 3,000 slaves of deposed Ras Hailu of Gojjam.

1934—Sixty-two local Slavery Bureaus exist in Ethiopia to process emancipation.

1934—Parliament Building is opened.

1934, September 29—Rome reaffirms 1928 Treaty of Friendship with Ethiopia.

1934, December 5—Local battle with Italians from Somaliland over territory around water wells at Wal Wal and Wardair; dispute is referred by Ethiopia to the League of Nations, which delays action.

1935, January 7—France agrees to give Italy seven per cent of her shares in Addis Ababa-Djibouti Railroad.

1935—League of Nations' efforts to settle Ethiopian-Italian boundary dispute are unsuccessful: "The Wal Wal incident was an accident. . . ."

1935, September 29—Ethiopia issues mobilization orders.

1935, October 3—Italian forces, under General De Bono, cross Eritrean border into Ethiopia.

1935, October 5-7—Council of League of Nations states that Italy has resorted to war, disregarding its covenants.

1935, December 12—Ethiopia requests meeting of League of Nations for aid as a victim of aggression.

1936, March 3-April 22—Ethiopia appeals to League of Nations for aid as a victim of aggression.

1936, April 8—Mussolini declares that annihilation of Ethiopia can be "neither averted nor delayed."

1936—Emperor leaves Ethiopia for Geneva to meet with League of Nations.

1936, May 9—Italy formally annexes Ethiopia to Italy as part of Italian Empire.

1936, June 30—His Imperial Majesty Haile Selassie I warns Assembly of the League of Nations that failure to act on the problem of Italy's aggression in Ethiopia will not only destroy the League but will also precipitate a World War.

1936—*Abuna* Petros is shot by Italians in the Addis Ababa market place.

1936, October-December—Italian conquest of Ethiopia is recognized by Germany, Austria, Hungary, Japan, and Switzerland. (France and the United Kingdom followed suit later. The United States, Canada, and New Zealand never recognized this conquest.)

1936, December—Italy declares that all of Ethiopia is under its control; guerrilla fighting is widespread.

1937, February 19—General Graziani massacres thousands in Addis Ababa, including most of the young men who had been educated abroad.

1937-1939—Continuous resistance fighting by isolated Ethiopian guerrillas throughout Ethiopia.

1939, Spring—Ethiopian resistance fighters form Committee of Union and Collaboration to combine resistance activities throughout Ethiopia.

1940, July 3—H.I.M. Haile Selassie I arrives in Khartoum from London.

1941, January 20—Emperor enters Ethiopia.

1941, May 5—Emperor Haile Selassie I enters Addis Ababa.

1941, January-November—British Armies of Liberation with Ethiopian Patriot Forces battle successfully, and gradually force surrender of all Italian forces in Ethiopia.

243

THE FORTIES

Since the liberation of Ethiopia in 1941, the history of the country has been quite well documented in the world's newspapers and journals. Recent progress and innovations have been so numerous and so varied that any attempt to enumerate them in this "Sweeping Glance at the History of Ethiopia" would require more pages than all of the other pages in this book. Therefore, this somewhat detailed historical chronicle ends as of the Liberation; however, there are added a few data in summary form touching highlights of the decades since Liberation.

Within a year following the Liberation, the British collected and evacuated 50,000 Italians, and British troops were withdrawn from Addis Ababa. The Emperor officially decreed that the name of the country is Ethiopia, not Abyssinia, and the *Negarit Gazeta* was introduced as the official journal for the printing of all laws.

A Council of Ministers was established to meet under the chairmanship of the Emperor or the Prime Minister to serve as advisers on matters of state. An Imperial proclamation designated twenty electoral districts, with notables and land-owners as electors to elect deputies. The Emperor decreed that there would be a Governor General for each of the twelve provinces, and He defined their responsibilities and authority. A High Court, provincial courts, and regional and communal courts were established and their functions defined by an Administration of Justice Proclamation. The State Bank of Ethiopia was established by Imperial Proclamation, and Parliament was reopened by His Imperial Majesty Haile Selassie I. In further defining powers of ministers, His Imperial Majesty stated, "All Departments and Ministers of Our Government will carry out their duties under the direction of Our Prime Minister who is subordinate to Our Orders." The Ministry of the Interior was made the central agency responsible for Provincial Administration.

His Imperial Majesty reopened Haile Selassie I Hospital in Addis Ababa, which had been closed during the Italian occupation. He issued a proclamation "To Provide for the Imposition of the Death Sentence in the Case of Armed Robberies," and another, "To Provide for a Tax on Land." A customs schedule was published in the *Negarit Gazeta*. The United States made a loan of silver to Ethiopia, and a new currency was issued. Employees of the Franco-Ethiopian Railway formed Ethiopia's first modern trade union.

A special technical school was established in Addis Ababa which, in the 1950's, was expanded to a full four-year secondary school. An Air Force Training School was established at Bishoftu with help from Sweden. General Wingate Secondary School, under British sponsorship, was opened in Addis Ababa; also, a teacher-training school and Haile Selassie I Secondary School opened in Addis Ababa. Buildings for an agricultural school were completed, and the University College of Addis Ababa was inaugurated. By the end of the decade (the 1940's), approximately 250 government schools were in operation with an enrollment of around 35,000 pupils. A Government memorandum on education defined policies on mass education, education for girls, the language of education, the use of foreign staff, the role of the church in education, and financing of education.

A delegation was sent to Egypt to request autonomy for the Ethiopian Orthodox Church. A monument to *Abuna* ("Pope") Petros was unveiled in Addis Ababa. A second delegation was sent to Egypt seeking autonomy, but the Coptic Synod in Egypt refused Ethiopian demands for autonomy of the Ethiopian Church. However, toward the end of the decade, Alexandria granted additional powers of self-government to the Ethiopian Orthodox Church. The Coptic Holy Synod proclaimed Ethiopia an Archbishopric of the Coptic Church with power to elect her own Archbishop and form a Holy Synod. The Patriarch of Alexandria reserved the right to consecrate Bishops and to control religious schools in Ethiopia.

Ethiopia was the first of the member nations to pay its contribution (in gold) to the newly formed International Bank. The 1942 Agreement and Military Convention with Britain was revised to allow other than British advisers to the Ethiopian Government. British military authorities returned management of the Ethiopian railway to a French railway company, and the British permitted Ethiopia to resume administration of the Ogaden, an area occupied primarily by Ethiopian Somalis. At the Paris Peace Conference, the Ethiopian delegate demanded return of the "lost provinces" of Ethiopia (Eritrea and Italian Somaliland), access to the sea, and full reparations from Italy, and the Emperor issued a formal statement of Ethiopia's claims to Eritrea and Italian Somaliland.

Ethiopia invited a United States economic commission to visit Ethiopia. Subsequently, an oil prospecting concession was granted to Sinclair Oil Company of the U.S.A. The Ethiopian Airlines was established under an agreement with Trans-World Airlines.

Ethiopia was among the fifty founding nations to sign the World Security Charter in San Francisco on June 26, 1945, establishing the United Nations Organization. The Imperial Ethiopian Government and the Food and Agriculture Organization of the United Nations signed an agreement whereby FAO would provide Ethiopia with a liaison officer, three veterinarians, two bacteriologists, and two cotton experts. Twenty-one veterinarians and biologics experts from FAO began a campaign against rinderpest and for the control of other cattle diseases. With parochial leadership from Alexandria, the Theological College of the Holy Trinity Church was opened in Addis Ababa.

THE FIFTIES

Early in the 1950's Eritrea became an "autonomous unit federated with Ethiopia under the sovereignty of the Ethiopian Crown." The Ethiopian Parliament opened with an elected Chamber of Deputies, the first under the Constitution of 1955; two women were among the elected Deputies. The Government reported that two million citizens voted in Ethiopia's first Empire-wide national elections for the Chamber of Deputies. A New Penal Code was promulgated, and urinating and defecating in public were legally prohibited. The Development Bank of Ethiopia was established, replacing the Agricultural Bank of Ethiopia, and the Imperial Ethiopian Mining Board was established. The Emperor promulgated a revised and expanded constitution.

During the latter part of the 1950's, drought led to famine in Wollo and Tigre Provinces, reportedly leading to the death of 100,000 persons. Twenty thousand metric tons of American wheat were shipped to Ethiopia, and proceeds from the sale of the wheat were granted to the Ethiopian Government for economic development projects. Among projects assisted by the United States under The General Agreement for Technical Cooperation were (1) the establishment of the Agricultural Technical School (secondary) in Jimma, and The Imperial College of Agriculture and Mechanical Arts, (2) provision of three sprayer-equipped Piper Cub aircraft to aid in work against desert locusts, (3) aid in military training and equipment, (4) establishment of an Audio-Visual Services Center and a Public Administration Advisory Service, (5) a water-well drilling program in Shoa, Harar, and Wollo

Provinces and in Eritrea, (6) introduction of a Livestock Improvement Project, (7) establishment of the Cooperative Education Press and, (8) in Asmara, Eritrea, a Vocational Trade School, (9) inauguration of a campaign to protect the people of Ethiopia against malaria, (10) a special program in secondary teacher education at the University College of Addis Ababa, (11) opening of the Imperial Ethiopian Mapping and Geography Institute, (12) introduction of a Work Unit System of Coffee Processing, which increased Ethiopian coffee sales prices by $14 to $52 per quintal, (13) establishment of a vaccine laboratory, (14) a Vocational Building Trades School in Addis Ababa, and (15) the Imperial Ethiopian College of Agriculture and Mechanical Arts at Alamaya, (16) allocation of $160,000 for construction of a printing plant, (17) establishment of a Veterinary Assistants Training Center and (18) the Debre Berhan Community Education Teacher Training Center, (19) start of the Public Safety Program including police equipment, (20) aid in establishing a radio network, (21) a Women's Vocational Education School in Addis Ababa, and (22) the Haile Selassie I Public Health College and Training Center at Gondar, (23) beginning of a survey of the Blue Nile Basin, (24) introduction of a vacation course for teachers at University College, (25) provision of milk to supplement the diet of over thirty thousand Ethiopian school children, (26) development of a Communications Media Program, and (27) establishment of the Itegue Menen School of Nursing in Asmara, and (28) provision for advanced jet training in the U.S.A. for sixty Ethiopian Air Force cadets.

During the 1950's, His Grace *Abuna* Basilios, first Ethiopian Archbishop, was elected as spiritual head of the Ethiopian Orthodox Church, and the Alexandrian Patriarchate invited representatives of the Ethiopian Church to participate in the selection and consecration of the Patriarch. The Primate of Ethiopia, *Abuna* Basilios, was crowned Patriarch of Ethiopia in the presence of His Imperial Majesty Haile Selassie I, in Cairo, becoming the first Ethiopian Patriarch in the history of Ethiopia.

The Government issued a Legal Notice entitled, "Statements of Policy for the Encouragement of Foreign Capital Investment in Ethiopia." Between 1951 and 1959, the United States provided over $100 million for Ethiopia in the form of loans, grants, economic and military assistance, and aid programs. During the year 1959 alone, loans to Ethiopia from communist countries totaled the equivalent of United States $140 million. A Swedish Building College was opened in Addis Ababa, and Sweden inaugurated a five-year medical program for Maternal and Child Health at

Princess Tsahai Hospital. The Gandhi Memorial Hospital for children opened in Addis Ababa. The Ethiopian Government ratified the Italo-Ethiopian agreement relative to the construction of the Koka dam and power station on the Awash River as reparations. The Federal Republic of Germany and the Ethiopian Government signed a technical and economic assistance agreement for about seven-and-a-half million dollars. Egypt and Ethiopia completed a trade agreement. During the last year of the decade, the Government made public, for the first time, a five-year economic development plan for the years 1957-1961, prepared with the assistance of Yugoslavian advisers, and His Imperial Majesty Haile Selassie I returned from a two weeks' visit to Moscow with a long-term, low-interest credit equivalent to United States $100 million for agricultural and industrial development. Sinclair Petroleum Company left Ethiopia after investing ten million dollars in dry holes.

A United Nations Commission investigated the political sentiments of the people of Eritrea and concluded that a majority favored association with Ethiopia. The British Military Mission to Ethiopia (largely advisory in function) withdrew. The Haile Selassie I Naval Base and College opened in Massawa, Eritrea. Ethiopia became a member of the International Council of Nurses, and the Emperor offered African students from other African countries two hundred scholarships, fifty annually for four years, at the University College of Addis Ababa. The State Bank of Ethiopia opened a branch office in Khartoum. Agreement was reached to change the French-Ethiopian railway to an Ethiopian company with headquarters in Addis Ababa. The Sudan and the United Arab Republic reached agreement on questions related to the Nile; however, Ethiopia, source of the Blue Nile, did not participate in the negotiations. Crown Prince Asfa Wosson paid an unofficial visit to the United States. In May of 1957, His Imperial Highness Makonnen, Duke of Harar, second son of the Emperor, was fatally injured in a highway accident; the entire nation mourned.

The Kagnew Battalion of Ethiopia participated in the Korean War as part of the United Nations forces. His Imperial Majesty contributed $19,000 to the United Nations Fund for refugees. Ethiopia participated in the Conference of Independent African States held in Ghana, and Ethiopia joined the International Geodetic and Geophysical Union as an official program-participant through the observatory of the University College. In the closing month of the decade, fighting broke out between Somalis of

248

Italian Somaliland and Ethiopian frontier guards over a disputed international border.

During the 1950's the United Nations and related agencies played an active role in Ethiopia including the following activities: The International Civil Aviation Organization sent experts in aviation, radio maintenance, meteorology, and aircraft maintenance; WHO and UNICEF helped the Ethiopian Government to start a Venereal Diseases Control Project; WHO initiated a program for vaccination (BCG) of Ethiopian school children against tuberculosis; the Food and Agriculture Agency assigned home economics experts to Ethiopia; United Nations experts organized training courses in the Telecommunications Institute in Addis Ababa; the United Nations agreed to establish an Economic Development and Public Administration Institute in Addis Ababa; UNESCO sent two experts in adult and fundamental education to help establish the Community Development Teachers Training Center at Majite; the Food and Agriculture Agency established, in Addis Ababa, a Regional Locust Secretariat to help coordinate locust control in Ethiopia, the Somalilands, the Sudan, and Kenya; the International Children's Emergency Fund cooperated with the Ethiopian Ministry of Health in creating a broad program for the treatment of patients with Hansen's disease (leprosy); the Economic and Technical Assistance Council selected Addis Ababa as the site of the headquarters for the new United Nations Economic Commission for Africa.

During the decade, Ethiopian institutions of higher education graduated the first class of students with Bachelor of Education degrees, the first class of cadets from the Imperial Ethiopian Naval College of Massawa, 190 Community Education Teachers, community sanitarians, health officers, and community nurses from the Public Health College and Training Center at Gondar, the first Bachelor of Science graduates from the Imperial Ethiopian College of Agriculture and Mechanical Arts, among other accomplishments. As the decade closed, Ethiopia had approximately six-hundred government elementary schools, thirty post-elementary schools, and six institutions of higher learning with a total enrollment of about 160,000 students.

In March of 1957, Richard Nixon, Vice President of the United States, made a two-days' state visit to Ethiopia. During the decade, H.I.M. Haile Selassie I made state visits to the following countries: The United States of America, Canada, Mexico, Yugoslavia, Greece, the United Kingdom, France, the Netherlands, West Germany, Sweden, Norway, Denmark, Switzerland, Austria, India, Burma, Japan, and the Soviet Union.

249

The decade of the sixties began with increased domestic and international expansion. Czechoslovakia signed a technical assistance agreement with Ethiopia and established a trade and aid relationship. Russia signed an agreement to implement economic aid, gave Ethiopia an IL-14 aircraft, and constructed exhibits in Addis Ababa and Asmara. Ethiopia contributed 1,800 men to the United Nations forces serving in the Congo, and began negotiations with the Sudan for trade agreements. A Conference of Independent African States was held in Addis Ababa. Border skirmishes continued between Somalia and Ethiopia, and British Somaliland united with Somalia to form the Somali Republic.

The Emperor created an Agricultural Development and Settlement Board to effect land redistribution, farm credits, and relocation of persons to develop uninhabited lands. Plans included assistance from Yugoslav, Israeli, and United States technical advisers. Construction of an electric power plant was begun on the Blue Nile, to serve the Gondar area.

In December of 1960, the Emperor departed for state visits to West African countries and Brazil. During his absence, officers of the Imperial Guard attempted to seize power, led by the Commander of the Imperial Bodyguard, the Chief of Security, the Governor of Jijiga, and the Police Commissioner. The rebels announced the formation of a new government under Crown Prince Asfa Wossen who, on radio, deplored the stagnation of Ethiopia and vowed to serve "in accordance with the Constitution." Students from University College and the Engineering College paraded with placards supporting "our country's peaceful change"; they were driven away from the headquarters of the loyalist army at bayonet point. The Crown Prince publicly announced the appointment of Ras Imru Haile Selassi (then Ambassador to Moscow) as Prime Minister and Major General Mulugeta Buli as Chief of Staff. On the fourth day of the insurgency, the rebellion was defeated by army and air forces. Before they could escape from the Palace, about fifteen hostages were shot by the rebels; they represented high government officials who, at the outset of the rebellion, had been tricked into going to the Palace under the pretext that Empress Menen was seriously ill. On the fifth day, the Emperor returned from Brazil to Addis Ababa via Asmara, and a week later the Senate and Chamber of Deputies, in joint session, reaffirmed allegiance to the Emperor's Government.

The decade of the sixties solidified the gains Ethiopia had made since the Liberation and the end of World War II. His Imperial Majesty increasingly has emerged as a stable force in Africa, a leader to whom other African leaders more and more look for guidance in solving the numerous, persistent, and continentally disruptive problems new nations are facing. The Organization of African Unity, for example, appointed the Emperor to head a group of African national leaders to seek a solution to the Nigerian-Biafran civil war.

On an international level, both economically and politically, Ethiopia has become the center for present and future activities. In 1961, the United Nations Economic Commission for Africa moved into its present permanent headquarters in Africa Hall, Addis Ababa. The building, situated near His Imperial Majesty's Jubilee Palace, was a gift from the Emperor to the United Nations.

The Economic Commission for Africa represents the majority of African states and has the task of coordinating the economic development of the developing countries of that vast continent. Other agencies of the United Nations with offices and programs in Ethiopia are the Children's Fund, Educational, Scientific, and Cultural Organization, Food and Agriculture Organization, International Civil Aviation Organization, International Telecommunication Union, Technical Assistance Board, and World Health Organization.

In May of 1963, most of the African heads of nations met in Addis Ababa for a Heads of States Conference. From this meeting there emerged a Charter creating the Organization for African Unity. The following year a second conference was held in Cairo, and the African Heads of States decided that the Secretariat of the Organization for African Unity would be permanently headquartered in Addis Ababa. This decision conferred on Ethiopia the honor and responsibility of being the political, as well as the economic, center for the majority of African states.

During the third decade of the Twentieth Century, as Regent, a youth in his twenties grasped the contemporary destiny of Ethiopia. As his Imperial Majesty Haile Selassie I, he ascended the throne on November 2, 1930, the 225th monarch of the dynasty established by King Solomon and the Queen of Sheba. As Ethiopia enters the final decades of the Twentieth Century, this elder world-renowned statesman is still in command and has the distinction of serving as a chief of state longer than any other chief of state in the world. He set a record in 1969 by becoming the first state visitor to the United States to have been received at the White House by four Presidents.

AN ARUSSI MAN

ETHIOPIAN MOSAIC

Main entrance of Haile Selassie I Hotel, one of many so-named in provincial centers of population.

IX
Suggestions from Ethiopians to Foreigners in Ethiopia

The suggestions contained in this section, including the following "Introduction," were gleaned primarily from students in the University College of Addis Ababa. Ethiopian teachers and colleagues also contributed. Considerable editing has been done by the author to avoid excessive repetition—although some repetition exists for emphasis where due—and to increase clarity, but no changes in substance have been made in the contributions of the Ethiopians.

INTRODUCTION: In my opinion, the best way of helping foreigners would be to give them information dealing with the people's social and religious customs and with the nation's political and economic situation. I think a foreigner would be psychologically more at ease in Ethiopia if he is told what to do than if he is told what not to do. Once the foreigners have been made familiar with our customs and traditions, with our social and political situations, it will be wise for them to have the following points in mind:

1. Many Ethiopians (just as Black Americans) get offended when they are called "negroes" by westerners. Perhaps it would be wise for newcomers to know our racial origin.

Taken in Addis Ababa. Note center of picture, mule driver; to left, horse-drawn surrey; right and left, Volkswagens; and plane in sky! Four eras in transportation.

A camel train, "The Ship of the Desert," walks along a paved highway past an electric light pole, a common sight in Ethiopia.

2. Ethiopians are described by most foreigners as polite and hospitable. No wonder then that we like polite westerners.

3. Most Ethiopians get furious when westerners ridicule our "Taboos." It would, therefore, be wise for foreigners to have a deep respect for our Church and religion as well as for our social traditions.

4. Westerners often forget that we are in the process of modernizing our ancient country. The country is not yet modernized. Perhaps it would be well for foreigners not to mistake Ethiopia for their already "modernized" homeland. Our streets are narrow and crowded, our electricity is weak and unsteady, we do not have big concert halls, nor are our ministries efficient. I suggest that foreigners take things as they are. Nevertheless, we always welcome sympathetic and constructive criticism.

5. Some westerners seem too fond of generalizations. They say Ethiopians are this and that. My advice here would be "wait and see"—do not hurry to conclude—first have enough data.

ADVICE OF A GENERAL NATURE: The newcomer to Ethiopia should not quickly intrude with criticism of the country's culture, the habits of the people, the religious beliefs of Ethiopia, or the Government of the country. Some foreigners gather false information about Ethiopia before they come. Once I remember there was a teacher who told us everything he had heard about Ethiopia before his arrival—that the Ethiopians are un-civilized people, badly clothed, who live in caves and caverns like primitive people. This is false. All who come here should be ready to give up early false information and treat Ethiopians as they are, not as they were reported to be, or as one read about Ethiopians before coming to this country.

These are the things foreigners should study and know about Ethiopia and Ethiopians: the educational background; the country's environment; natural resources; main traditions and customs of the people; the fact that modern education is very new in Ethiopia; the fact that we most want you to show us how to develop our country economically.

People from abroad should not interfere with our religion; they should not have bad attitudes toward us, such as discrimination; they should not take pictures of our people dressed in rags.

257

Visitors to Ethiopia should observe the following things: Try to understand the social inter-actions of the many people in this country; beware of introducing religious beliefs and political beliefs. Do not behave like the Spaniards of ancient Peru who, under the pretext of helping, merely collected treasures. Foreigners will probably have problems adjusting to a different culture and tradition and being comfortable with a lower standard of living. If they would try to understand us, we would try to help them to understand. We might even take them to our homes to meet our parents, then they might be able to understand.

In any reference to the Church or the Royal family, the foreigner should show reverence. Further, he should avoid referring to anyone by his tribe; especially, he should never call anyone a Galla, even if the man is a Galla, for everyone likes to be called an Amhara. Besides, the meaning of Galla is not good; it means pagan, unchristianized. (Editorial note: *Galla* more closely means "unconverted to Islam." The tribal name of the Gallas of Ethiopia is *Oromo*. The Oromos were a Pagan tribe at the time Ahmed (Mohammed) Gran (16th century) tried to impose Islam on the peoples of Ethiopia. The Oromos were so resistant to conversion that, finally, Gran—hearing of the large numbers killed and the small numbers of conversions—called off his troops with an Arabic phrase meaning, "That is enough!" which loosely sounds like *Galla.)*

A foreigner should never change the facial expression he first shows. That is to say, if a foreigner meets an Ethiopian and shows him a smiling face and friendly talk, and the next time offers no smile and a black face, that at once will suggest that his intentions are not those of a good man.

A person coming to Ethiopia should at least know that there are many different cultures among the people here; that the strengths of the various cultures are important factors in our major culture, and that each cultural group acts differently and must be handled differently. Foreigners should not assume that all Ethiopians are ignorant. They should avoid misunderstanding things in Ethiopia which are different. For example, if an Ethiopian boy is calm, it does not mean that he is ignorant nor bad. In this country, boys are taught to be calm and quiet.

A foreigner should understand something about our class system in Ethiopia, for if he understands the classes of people he will be better able to deal with them accordingly. There are some who feel superiority and some who feel inferiority; this is something of which foreigners are not aware. Under no circumstances should a foreigner show his feelings about the superiority or priority of one Ethiopian tribe over another. No one should ever mention names of various tribes in making comparisons, and no colour discrimination should be shown.

Visitors should understand that Ethiopians come from different homes of different tribes who speak different languages, and they should work against discrimination in race and religion. Let everyone be frank towards all Ethiopians and they will enjoy their days in this country. They should be careful about their behavior; even for curiosity's sake, they should not appear in tej-houses or other bad places.

CUSTOMS AND CHARACTERISTICS: Among educated Ethiopian families, it is the custom that the young do not speak in the presence of their elders. They do not ask questions of their elders. This is simply out of respect. If a young Ethiopian meets a foreigner who is as old as his father, his natural tendency is to respect him and not to answer or speak to him unless directly questioned. Out of his ignorance of the Ethiopian psychology, a foreigner may make the silly generalization that "The Ethiopians have no initiative and are even unfriendly."

Ethiopians are very cautious people in every way, and in their speech they take great care not to use offending words. They have the belief that talking gently is the mark of politeness. They are friendly with anyone and, if well approached, a reasonable and adaptable people. The average Ethiopian has little home background; he is receptive, passive, and introverted; as the result of a home influence which is part of a feudal society, he is not objective in his judgment. He has had little opportunity to weigh and pass judgments for himself, for he has been strongly pressed to obey blindly. As a young Ethiopian assimilates more education, he sometimes tends to be reactionary and, as a result of a long suppressed personality, he has a strong impulse to assert himself, sometimes in a very aggressive manner.

While young, educated Ethiopians are liberal-minded, they do not have a taste for artificial behaviour. They like to be handled naturally. It has been said by many foreigners that Ethiopians are naturally lawyers. They are able to detect things, even when they are disguised. Ethiopians never fail to give the right honour to the right person. They sincerely respect any official and always address him by the title Mr. or by any other title he may have. They like to keep their dignity wherever they are; when any one talks to an Ethiopian, he must always say "Ato" (Mr.) plus his name.

259

A road in Raya after the rain.

A road becomes a bog in Keffa Province.

People should know something about the traditions of Ethiopia, such as the foods eaten by Ethiopians, and should not say their foods are of bad quality. They should try to understand, and not ridicule, differences in the way Ethiopians dress; for example, they will go with an umbrella but without shoes. And the Ethiopian way of salutation—bowing the head—should not be ignored. Because Ethiopians are very nervous, they must not be talked to angrily. Usually they are very shy; they don't want to speak with any stranger at first. Later on they begin to talk and become very friendly.

FRATERNIZING: Any foreigner in Ethiopia is generally accepted with the prejudice that he is an antagonist rather than a friend. This is probably because of the Italian and Ethiopian relations that existed in the past. No matter how sincere the foreigner may be, the tendency here is to think of him as a schemer, simply because he is a "ferenge." So there often is lacking heart-to-heart understanding between foreigners and Ethiopians. Foreigners are usually looked upon as completely different creatures, and they look upon Ethiopians as different from themselves. This is the result of not having had a common environment and background. Therefore, for a common understanding, it would be good to try constantly to make contacts.

Visitors should be patient with Ethiopians' slow tempo of doing things. And it would be wise if they were as polite and courteous as Ethiopians, even if they have to shake hands a hundred times a day. How can a foreigner understand Ethiopian psychology and philosophy of life? I think in the first place he must be willing and prepared to do so. Secondly, he must easily mix with Ethiopian families without showing his contempt for their traditions. The visitor should enter our country not with the idea of meeting cannibals, but with the idea of being intimate with our people.

GENERALIZATIONS: Often we hear persons from abroad giving sweeping generalizations about Ethiopia and its people. I think it would be wise to avoid drawing quick conclusions or making early generalizations. Foreigners usually make the mistake of having the idea that Ethiopia is one complete culture. From this error, they bring examples from a certain part of Ethiopia to apply to the whole of Ethiopia. For example, visiting only the southern part of Ethiopia may mislead a person to say that Ethiopians do not have well-constructed houses but only huts. It would be better for him to

261

say that among the Gallas there is one type of construction, among the Amharas there is a different form of construction, and among the Tigreans yet another way of constructing houses, etc. A foreigner should not make general statements on anything unless he is absolutely sure that there is more truth than nonsense to them; foolish general statements lessen the Ethiopian's confidence in a visitor.

GOVERNMENT AND TRADITION: We are proud of our traditions and the way we live. There are some people from abroad who would like us to adopt their ways, which we believe may be unnecessary. Any foreigner who wishes the respect of Ethiopians, or any Ethiopian, would not talk against the Ethiopian Government, whatever is done, or against government laws.

Few foreigners ever realize the extent to which the people love the monarch or realize that whatever the Emperor approves of cannot be criticized. The fact that a daring newspaper man criticized the first national beauty contest, in 1955, although His Majesty approved of it, was indeed a novelty if not a shock to the ordinary Ethiopian. Freedom of speech and press is only beginning to be used as an expression of true public opinion, but we must understand that in many fields it must remain quiet for many decades to come. A foreigner who studies Ethiopian customs and ways of life is considered to be sympathetic. Hence, the sensible approach for a sincere foreigner is to start by learning, by becoming acquainted with the proper titles of the Emperor, members of the royal family, dignitaries, the clergy, and civil servants. And he should use these titles when referring to these people.

Whenever a foreigner meets His Majesty on the way, he should bow; if he goes by car, he should stop the car, get out, and bow. This is our way of showing courtesy and respect. Visitors should be acquainted with the country's constitution and the political tendencies in world affairs. Foreigners usually refer to our system of government with contempt, without ever understanding the difficulties that it is faced with. For this reason, the foreigner would do well to try to understand in what stage Ethiopia was (after the Italian invasion) and the problems it faces today in trying to modernize its people; otherwise, he should merely keep quiet. No comparison or contrasts should be made between Ethiopia's system of government and any other systems of government. There should be no questions about, for, or against political affairs. Prudence is necessary in talking about the Ethiopian government, the nation, etc., especially about such subjects as national unity. Some Ethiopians may draw the newcomer into a political discussion on Ethiopia; he should answer the questions or say things prudently without creating any tensions or embarrassments for the Ethiopians. Many nations have passed through such phases as Ethiopia is now undergoing.

In Ethiopia there is one thing which is very common: An Ethiopian will say, "O.K., tomorrow." But really he does not mean tomorrow in the sense of the next day. It is simply a habit in this country to say. "O.K., tomorrow," if a man means sometime in the future. If a foreigner gets such an appointment, he should not take it for granted that tomorrow really means the next day; and he should not be critical of our culture if he fails to understand this simple cultural habit of speech we have.

OFFENSES: A thing which annoys me much is that foreigners I have met do not seem to fully understand our mentality, our psychology, and our traditions. We often times find the foreigners artificial rather than natural. The jokes they produce in most cases do not please us, or rather make us laugh to tears. Many times I have heard jokes which did not please me, but I have laughed just to please the person who told the joke. Most foreigners are annoyed because we do not respond to a stimulus as would their people in their own countries. They fail to recognize that we are Ethiopians with different culture and background. Many slang terms which are humorous to a foreigner might be quite rude here; they should avoid excessive use of colloquial expressions.

Foreigners often comment, in the face of Ethiopians, seeing our bread and sauces, "It is awful to me"; or they say, "You consume a staggering amount of food." The foreigner should not imply to Ethiopians that the "white" person is superior in any way. No one would like to be told about the defects found in his country. Most of the time we know what is wrong with us, how far backward we are, but it is intolerable to be told by others. Foreigners offend or embarrass Ethiopians when they use the second name to address them instead of the first name; the second name is his father's name, not his own name. The Ethiopian is very sensitive about his material inferiority to the other civilizations. The foreigner must be careful about asking an Ethiopian to do manual work.

In Ethiopia, somebody who talks loud is usually regarded as rude, especially if he is talking to his superiors. An Ethiopian must make considerable

Rural scene from highway.

effort to raise the pitch of his voice in a polite conversation. Foreigners should realize this. The visitor should know that the polite form of greeting is bowing. A greeting such as, "Hi!" or waving the hand makes an Ethiopian uneasy, however westernized or educated he may be. Foreigners, talking to or about Ethiopians, should not use such words as barbarians or savages. No country has come to its present standard without going through stages; it shows cruelty and it hinders others to use these words. The Ethiopian does not like to be told he is a Negro. Foreigners sometimes use such terms as "fat head," "ass," "woolhead," and similar terms without seriousness, sometimes even humorously. An explanation of the spirit in which these words are uttered might serve to avoid offense. The visitor should not mention beneficial effects of the Italian occupation even though the first thing he notices might be roads and buildings constructed by the Italians.

PHOTOGRAPHS: Most Ethiopians are traditionally suspicious of a European who is too inquisitive or curious about them or their country. If he asks questions, some will gladly enlighten him, and some will wonder why he asks too much. In this matter, the people in the rural areas are far more understanding than those in the cities who know some smatterings of English and think they know a lot about Europeans. The rural people are proud of the things they have, the clothes they wear, and the huts they live in. They don't think there is anything of which the Europeans can take pictures that would make a laughing stock of them.

The foreigner should avoid using a camera to take photos of a poor peasant, naked or partly naked, or of the slum areas of the countryside. Visitors should not take pictures of beggars. It is not good to take snaps of bad places and poor people in the presence of Ethiopians. No one should take a photo of a person without first asking his permission.

RELIGION AND THE CHURCH: The foreigner should not, under any circumstances, say anything that would harm the feelings of the Ethiopians. This strictly applies to such things as religion. Careless comments on the part of foreigners have led to unhappy results such as the expelling from the country of teachers who have remarked that the Ethiopian Orthodox religion is not a true religion and of teachers who have tried to convert students. Ethiopians are "tetchy" about their religion. One thing which sounds jarring to the Ethiopian ear is *"Abuna"*; the proper word is *Abune*, and it becomes *Abuna* only when it is connected with the name of the bishop. For example: The *Abune* at the time was *Abuna* Petros.

There are some religious fanatics who will not tolerate being told of the good of other religions outside their own. So it is better not to mention or argue about other religious institutions. Uneducated Ethiopians are very conservative about religious matters and are easily offended if they are informed about a strange religion. Criticism of the church is always unwelcome because of the hostilities that have been previously engendered by Catholic missionaries and other groups. Care should be taken not to criticize harshly the traditions and superstitions of some of the Ethiopian religions. When a person happens to visit a church, he should take off his shoes before entering.

A parade in progress in Addis Ababa. Note Chief's elaborate lion headdress.

Horsemen in parade.

266

UNDERSTANDING: It would be wise and profitable for the foreigner if he tried to understand the people. In Ethiopia many foreigners seem to have the idea that Ethiopians are simply among the relatively highly developed "savages" of Africa. Some foreigners forget how their country was some centuries back; we are trying our best to develop our people through education, and we don't like to be called uncivilized barbarians. Any Ethiopian who has had secondary-level schooling or above knows the shortcomings and handicaps of this country.

When a person is greeted warmly, he should reply warmly. Foreigners must understand that English is only a second language for us. A knowledge of the major tribes is necessary if a foreigner is to find harmony with Ethiopians from the various parts of the country. Some of the tribes, such as the Amharas or the Tigreans, have more historical background than the others, but the Gallas or Aderes do not like to hear comments which seem to suggest that they are inferior. This will be especially true when the visitor goes visiting outside Shoa Province.

Cultural beliefs and actions which have been practiced for centuries cannot be changed overnight. Beliefs and practices have been handed from generation to generation and are buried deep down in heads; you cannot get them out easily and put new things in.

Think of the individual and his dignity. A man will resist and become uncooperative—and may even hinder you from passing your ideas to other people by misinterpreting your ideas or by passing wrong information to the people—if you offend his dignity.

Ethiopian soldiers guarding Ministry of Education during protest of teachers demanding payment of salaries several months overdue.

X
Penal Code
of
Ethiopia

EXCERPTS FROM THE 1957 PENAL CODE OF THE EMPIRE OF ETHIOPIA

Article

248   *Outrages against the Emperor or the Imperial Family:*
Whosoever, in anyway, makes or attempts to make an attack on the liberty or security, or on the person or health, of the Emperor, of the Empress, or of their children, is punishable with rigorous imprisonment from five to twenty years.
Where the attack is against their life, the punishment is rigorous imprisonment from fifteen years to life, or death.

249   *Outrage against the Dynasty:*
Whosoever attepts to overthrow the Emperor or to break or modify the order of succession to the Throne, by violence, threats, conspiracy or other unlawful means, is punishable with rigorous imprisonment from five years to life, or in cases of exceptional gravity, with death.

771   *Blasphemous or Scandalous Utterances or Attitudes:*
Whosoever, in a public place or in a place open to the public or that can be viewed by the public, by gestures or words scoffs at religion or

expresses himself in a manner which is blasphemous, scandalous or grossly offensive to the feelings or convictions of others or towards the Divine Being or the religious symbols, rites or religious personages, is punishable with fine not exceeding one hundred dollars or arrest not exceeding eight days.

120 *Flogging:*

In the case of offences under Art. 635 (3) and 637 (1) in this Code, the Court may, in addition to the principal punishment, order that the convicted person be flogged at a place to be named in the judgment. Flogging may only be ordered in respect to male offenders between eighteen and fifty years of age and may not exceed forty lashes to be inflicted on the back. Flogging may only be ordered after a doctor has certified that the convicted person is physically fit to receive a flogging. It shall be carried out under medical control and may be stopped at any time if the doctor considers that for reasons of health it is necessary.

172 *Corporal Punishment:*

Where a young offender is contumacious the Court may, if it considers corporal punishment is likely to secure his reform, order corporal punishment. Corporal punishment shall be inflicted only with a cane and the number of strokes shall not exceed twelve to be administered on the buttocks. Only young offenders in good health shall be subjected to corporal punishment. The Court shall determine the degree of punishment taking into account the age, development, physical resistance and the good or bad nature of the young offender, as well as the gravity of the offence committed.

550 *Duels:*

Whosoever takes part in a duel, that is to say in an armed combat regulated in advance by tradition or custom, such as to endanger the life, person or health of the participants, is punishable with simple imprisonment or fine. The punishment is applicable whether or not wounds are inflicted. Where precautions have been taken to eliminate risk of death, simple imprisonment shall not exceed one year and the fine shall not exceed two thousand dollars. Where the combat was to last until the death of one of the combatants, the punishment shall be rigorous imprisonment which shall not exceed ten years where death actually ensued. An adversary who, knowingly, infringes the special rules or usages of combat and, by this deceit, wounds or kills the other combatant, shall be punished in accordance with the general provisions governing homicide and bodily injuries.

Duelling: Challenge, Incitement and Aiding:

Whosoever challenges another to a duel, transmits such challenge or accepts it, is punishable with fine. Where one of the adversaries withdraws from the contest, or prevents it, of his own accord the Court may exempt him, or both parties, from punishment. Whosoever incites another to fight a duel with a third person, whether by intimidation, by encouragement, by showing contempt or otherwise, is punishable with fine, or, where the duel is fought, with simple imprisonment not exceeding one year. The seconds, witnesses, members of the court of honour, helpers or doctors, appointed to ensure the regularity of the proceedings or to remedy their consequences, are liable to the same punishments only where they encourage or incite the adversaries to fight. The provisions relating to complicity do not apply to them.

565 Enslavement:

Whosoever: (a) enslaves another, sells, alienates, pledges or buys him, or trades or traffics in or exploits him; or (b) keeps or maintains another in a condition of slavery, even in a disguised form, is punishable with rigorous imprisonment from five to twenty years, and a fine not exceeding twenty thousand dollars. Those who knowingly carry off, transport or conduct, whether by land, by sea or by air, persons thus enslaved, in order to deliver them at their place of destination, or who aid and abet such traffic, whether within the territory of the Empire or abroad, are liable to the same punishments.

271

567 *Slave Trading: Bands or Associations:*

Where the injury to liberty, whether by intimidation, trickery, coercion, abduction, illegal restraint, enslavement, traffic or exploitation in one of the above forms, is the work of an association or band formed to engage in, or engaging in, the slave trade, no matter in what form, such band or association shall be punishable with a fine not exceeding fifty thousand dollars and its dissolution shall be ordered.

616 *Bigamy:*

Whosoever, being tied by the bond of a valid marriage, intentionally contracts another marriage before the first union has been dissolved or annulled, is punishable with simple imprisonment, or, in grave cases, and especially where the offender has knowingly misled his partner in the second union as to his true state, with rigorous imprisonment not exceeding five years. Any unmarried person who marries another he knows to be tied by the bond of an existing marriage, is punishable with simple imprisonment.

617 *Exception:*

The preceding Article shall not apply in cases where polygamy is recognized under civil law in conformity with tradition or moral usage.

661 *Fraudulent Exploitation of Public Credulity:*

Whosoever, for gain, knowingly deceives another by means such as invoking spirits, magic, or sorcery, consulting horoscope or astrology, by interpretation of dreams, soothsaying, chirography, divining or by any other means of exploiting human credulity, is punishable, upon complaint, with fine, and, in the event of repetition of the offence, with simple imprisonment, where the case does not fall under the provisions regarding petty offences (Art. 815).

815 *Quackery:*

Whosoever, apart from the cases punishable under the Penal Code (Art. 661): (a) obtains money by taking advantage of the credulity of others by soothsaying in any form whatsoever, by calling upon spirits, by indicating means for finding a treasure, or in any similar manner; or (b) publicly offers, by advertising or otherwise, to resort to such practices for gain, is punishable with fine or arrest not exceeding one month.

515 *Endangering by Mental Means or Practices:*
Whosoever knowingly endangers the health of another by inducing in him a state of hypnosis, trance or catalepsy, or any other change or suspension of his conscious faculties, is punishable under Art. 515 (i.e., with simple imprisonment not exceeeding three months, or fines, without prejudice to prohibition of professional practice, if necessary, where the offence is repeated.)

516 *Endangering by Philtres, Spells or Similar Means:*
Whosoever, knowing the danger which they imply, prepares, gives, sells, distributes, or administers to another a potion, powder, philtre or any other product or ingredient susceptible of impairing his health, is punishable under Art. 514.

555 *Deprivation of Powers of Decision:*
Whosoever deprives another against his will of his conscious faculties or of his freedom of decision or action, whether by hypnotic suggestion, by the administration of alcohol or narcotic substances, or by any other means, is punishable, upon complaint, with simple imprisonment not exceeding one year, or fine.

787 *Rendering another Person Unconscious or Stupefied:*
A person shall be liable to the same penalties when apart from the cases punishable under the Penal Code (Art. 515 and 516), first and second Article above-mentioned, he subjects another person to a treatment or practices of any kind whatsoever abolishing or altering the faculties of consciousness or free determination without being authorized so to do by his professional status and in conformity with generally accepted medical or pharmaceutical practice. Medical experiments or hypnotic passes or exercises in hypnotism or transmission of thoughts or conduct from a distance duly authorized and carried out by way of mere entertainment shall not be punishable.

Soemmerring's gazelle.

XI
Wild Life

East Africa is known throughout the world as one of the finest of all the "Big Game" areas, but Kenya, Tanganyika, and Uganda are usually the only countries thought of in this connection. Ethiopia is in East Africa, and borders on Kenya; so it should come as no surprise that vast quantities of game are to be found here as well. Surprisingly enough, however, few people are aware of this; one reason being that conditions in Ethiopia have not been publicized. Almost all of the animals to be found in the better known portions of East Africa are to be be found in Ethiopia, some in even larger numbers, and there are at least two animals native to Ethiopia that can be found nowhere else in the world—the Mountain Nyala and the Walia Ibex.

It is unfortunate that during the Italian occupation of Ethiopia, wild game was killed for food to an extent that all but eliminated wild life from some portions of the country. Large quantities of game also migrated to other areas during this period to escape. Only within the past few years have these previously occupied areas been regaining their wild life population. This return to normal, however, is taking place quite rapidly, and with the conservation and control measures being enforced by the government, it is

Reproduced with permission from *Land of the Lion of Judah*, by Ethiopian Air Lines.

275

A rare sight. The "Hyena Man" who lives near Harar in a compound frequented by wild hyenas feeding by hand one of his pets. He has given each of the most frequent visitors an Old Testament name, and they approach to eat when called by name.

believed that Ethiopia will soon take her rightful place in the East African big game picture.

Even at present, all of the well known big game animals are to be found in Ethiopia although some in limited extents. Elephant, buffalo, rhinoceros, giraffe, zebra, warthog, and most of the many varieties of antelope and gazelle, including the majestic greater African kudu and the graceful oryx, are plentiful in certain areas. There are large numbers of leopards, lions, cheetahs, and other members of the cat family which are scattered throughout the country. The mountain nyala and the Abyssinian ibex exist nowhere else in the world, and no larger herds of oryx than those roaming the Awash plains east of Addis Ababa can be seen.

Game birds are plentiful and varied. A number of varieties of ducks and geese, including the giant spurlock, are to be found almost anywhere there is water. Many other forms of water fowl can also be seen including marabou, egret, storks, pelicans, cranes, flamingoes, and the sacred ibis. Other wild fowl are partridge and guinea fowl, in abundance almost everywhere in the country, and the lesser birds such as quail, snipe, dove, pigeons, and grouse.

Many kinds of fish exist in large numbers in many of the lakes and rivers throughout Ethiopia. A very large variety of catfish, which is not only excellent to eat, but is also a surprising fighter, is found in some of the rivers. The largest of these will ruin almost anything but deep-sea fishing tackle. There are crocodiles in the majority of the rivers, but they are very wary and are difficult to kill.

XII
Vignettes

Ethiopian traditions, solidified by centuries, are in juxtaposition with the forces of 20th century technological changes and concomitant modernization of social institutions, including education and science. The visitor to Ethiopia is struck with the plight of children caught between the pressures of traditional elders or grandparents and progressive parents or peers. The following vignettes dramatize some of these pressures.

The Eye of the Beholder[1]

"Hold up your head," pleaded Miss Larson. "Don't look at the floor; the answer isn't down there. Look at my face when you answer a question. Are you ashamed of yourself? Ashamed of your answer? Please, my dear, why must you hang your head when you speak?"

Kebedetch cringed with shame as she forced reluctant steel into her neck-muscles. Her head jerked upright as if on a notched pully. "Ethiopia is composed of twelve provinces plus the federated state of Eritrea," she whispered.

"And speak up, talk out," begged Miss Larson in despair. "Your answer was right, Kebedetch, but I could hardly hear you. Why do you whisper as if you were telling a secret lie? You have a voice; I've heard you on the playground; you have a good, clear voice. Use it, please, please."

The school day ended. Tired Miss Larson took her classroom problems home with her and shared her concerns with friends at an informal cocktail party, shared her frustrations over teaching in the Ethiopian government school: "For three years I've tried to get those dear, little girls to behave like normal human beings, to have some pride, to hold up their heads, look me in

---

[1] This vignette is based on an actual occurrence.

277

the face, and answer a question in a voice I can hear without straining. They're so bright; they learn as fast as the children back home, but they're hopeless, absolutely hopeless. They just can't seem to learn to behave with human dignity. For all the good I've done here, I might as well have stayed home in Iowa and continued to teach there."

The school day ended. Kebedetch walked stiffly home. The strange steel she had forced into her neck-muscles seemed to have spread throughout her body. She felt rigid, brave, and frightened. Entering the *gojo* , Kebedetch was greeted warmly. Father asked the usual, daily question. "What did you learn in school today?"

Kebedetch threw back her head, looked her father in the eye, and proclaimed in a loud, clear voice, "Ethiopia is composed of twelve provinces plus the federated state of Eritrea." Crimson embarrassment flooded her brown cheeks to a rich chocolate. She stood stiff in the shocked silence. Mamma gave her only milk and an orange, and put her early to bed, but she could not sleep, and muffled voices drifted to her from the far corner of the hut.

Mamma and Pappa talked late that night. What had happened to Kebedetch? She was no longer behaving as a normal human being. "Did you notice how she threw back her head like a man?" asked Pappa; "what has happened to her shyness as a woman?" "And her voice," added Mamma, "how happy I am that our parents were not present to hear a daughter of ours speak with the voice of a foreigner."

"She showed no modesty; she seemed to feel no pride. If she were normal, she would be ashamed to raise her head like that, being a girl-child, and to speak so loud as that," Pappa added with a deep sigh.

"Kebedetch has learned so much," said Mamma; "she knows more than I, and this has given me great joy. But if her learnings are making of her a strange, un-gentle, beast-like person, I do not want her to learn more; she is my only daughter."

Pappa pondered. Finally he shook his head and spoke. "You are right, Mebrat, our daughter must not return to school. The new education is good, but only the strongest can survive. I had hoped Kebedetch could learn and remain normal and gentle, could become a woman of dignity. This frightening behavior of hers tonight has convinced me. She has lost her sense of pride, lost her sense of shame, lost her dignity. She must never return to the school. We shall try to help her find herself again."

[2] A *gojo* is a small house or hut. Foreigners frequently, erroneously, substitute the Sudanese word *tukul*.

The Coming of the Dawn[1]

The mission doctor studied the gasping infant. Probably pneumonia, but could be anything. Obviously dehydrated; injections for that. A shot of penicillin. Hospitalization. Maybe tomorrow a diagnosis; for now, keep the baby alive; treat the symptoms. The doctor penned orders. The Ethiopian nurse gently carried the dazed infant from the consulting room to the hospital nursery.

The young doctor hurriedly turned to the two women, the frightened, youthful mother, the grim, ancient grandmother. To the questions in their eyes, he answered. "Very sick baby, but don't you worry! We'll take good care of him. Go home now; come back tomorrow; he'll be better."

"What is his disease?" asked the grandmother.

"I don't know," the doctor admitted honestly; "could be a number of things. We'll see tomorrow." He glanced into the waiting room, crowded with sick and wailing children in the arms and about the long, white skirts of silent, anxious mothers. "Next," he called.

Reaching home, the two women prepared the noon meal. Neither spoke until the family had eaten and departed for work or for play. The old woman stood in the door of the hut, blocking most of the feeble light that might have entered the windowless *gojo*. There was a touch of scorn in her voice as she spoke to her daughter, prostrated and weeping on a mat in the far corner of the single room.

"You would not listen to me, your mother, when the child was heavy in your belly. You would not do the things a woman must do to protect her from the devil. Many times you ate fat and dared to stand in sunlight; do not deny it. And I watched you walk across the bridge, yes, I know that too; you crossed the bridge even though you knew, I've warned you often, that a devil lives in the waters under that bridge."

"Aheee, Aheee," moaned the anguished mother.

"Why do you cry now?" continued the grandmother. "You who so defiantly exposed your child, and yourself, to evil. Did you carry metal in your hand for forty days after the child's birth? No! You said this was old-

[1] This vignette is based on an actual occurrence.

279

fashioned. Did you put the weaving hook in your hair, after the birth of your child, to ward off evil? No! You called this a superstition. So now you see the consequences of your acts. Your baby is dying, and you are tormented. I told you that these things would happen."

"But my elder brother, Abebe," sobbed the mother, "he has studied long in the school; he reads and writes, not only Amarigna but even English. He laughs at me. He speaks of science."

The grandmother shook her head in pity. "Science is great," she conceded, "but my poor daughter, science only knows about things that can be seen. Science does not know the evil eye, does not study the devil as I, being a good Christian, have studied him. Did I not help you to take the infant, Bekele, to the hospital? If he had a disease, the mission doctor could cure the disease. This I know. I have seen this happen many times. But you heard what he said. He does not know the cause of the sufferings of the child.

"The mission doctor is a great and wise man, but the foreigners know only science, only medicine. They do not understand the evil eye; they cannot fight it; they do not even believe in this great power. Your child has been bewitched. He will die. You have seen how he grinds his jaws; is this not a sign of the evil eye? You saw, last night, how he was startled in his sleep and waked frightened. Is this not proof of the evil eye? Your child will die. It is not right that he should die in the foreigners' hospital. He should die here, in his home."

So the mother and the grandmother set about preparing the home for death and for the funeral. They boiled the grains, made the coffee, brought the *tula*, removed the bed from the room, and spread eucalyptus leaves on the earthen floor. Then they went to the mission hospital to bring the child back to the place where he belonged. The Ethiopian nurses on night duty were most reluctant to let the baby go; he had responded so well to the treatments, but he needed more, many more.

The mother stood still; the grandmother folded the child in her arms and sadly carried him away to die where a child should die, in his home.

And there, with the coming of the dawn, the infant Bekele died.

✿   ✿   ✿

THREE POEMS[1]

Death in the Jungle

Father went for the day,
Bravely walked his way
Down to the dark jungle straight,
With muscles manly, shoulders unbent.

Mother made our meal,
Father in the jungle still.
"I'm hungry now," I cried;
Told her to give me bread.

Merrily bread I ate,
To my bamboo bed I went.
After a long sleep I woke,
And saw my Mother weep.

"Mother, what troubles you?
Did you think I had died for ever?"
"No, Son. You are too young,
But Father does not come."

True, I remember now:
Dusk settled on the earth,
And I understood somehow,
He had left his land of birth:

His land of birth, his cabin home,
One that he loved, his only wife;
His son, myself, his only fruit.
Eternal liberty! Freedom sweet!

His spear of war, his shield,
His dagger and water gourd—
(These kept him from thirst and fear)
Hang now in his cabin here.

(Now that Father is gone,
Things are never the same;
Yet his memory will linger
Beyond time's scanty year.)

---

[1] These poems are not translations; they were written in English by a young Ethiopian who prefers to remain anonymous.

Conflict

I wandered far and wide,
Myriads of man's work I beheld,
And lo, man's vanity outweighed
All the good things to achieve he has managed.

In the West truth is robbed with words,
In the East it is disguised with lies,
In the middle nowhere it exists,
And no place has truth with deeds.

Our brothers are slaves in the West,
Our kinsfolk are hungry in the East,
Here we're threatened by wolves at night,
To rob us of our freedom sweet.

We die younger than our years,
We are deprived of our hopes,
And our motherland bemoans us,
For having left her in the wolves' mouths.

My Country, Ethiopia

I

My country, my country Ethiopia!
How sweet your name to speak!
Your hills and valleys, pastures green,
Your rivers—streams of pleasure
Which elevate one's mind to higher,
Brighter times to come.

Ethiopia! Beloved land!
Ethiopia! Name that I love,
Has shined through many ages,
Through times both high and low.
Ethiopia, my native country,
Hallowed be your name!

I love your august beauty,
Your hills greened by nature's bounty
Overshadowing your valleys
Yellowed with ripe fields of corn
All along the river banks—
Ethiopia—your rivers.

Far away, far, far away,
Yonder by the mountain's foot,
I see a vale of diverse beauty,
Of corn fields and green meadows.
Oh God! Your might and wisdom
Are seen in Ethiopia revealed.

Your mountains crowned with forests,
Your valleys rich with crops,
Your rivers watering the land
Are my delight by day
And fill my dreams by night.

II

Ethiopia! In the wake of my love
For you, my mother land, my home,
There shrieks the noise of wolves.
These would eat you, take you from me,
Take this dear land from your people,
Leave the people then in woe.

I dread the thought, abhor it;
A mother's breast turned sour
Against all: son and daughter,
A mother thus so grossly masked
Has neither love nor warmth to touch
The heart of warriors brave.

I must warn you well, my country,
Because I love you now.
One day we who care may be away,
Our flesh fed our Mother, fed you,
You, in ignorance, unconscious of yourself,
Dumb, mute, but yet alive.

While I have but one life, Mother,
Yours are millions.
Feed them, nourish them I say,
And let them die then poor but happy,
Naked yet warm, few but strong,
And God your life will prolong.

283

Move Mother; tarry not here.
Yonder your children need help,
Yours, who can plough the traitors
To death's silent embrace.
And here is my blood, my life,
Ready to flow; wipe away my grief.

III

Your rivers are fresh,
Your soil laden with riches.
Your mountains challenge
The peak of courage.
The sun's heat, rains and winds—
In defiance you stand age-old.

The meadows are green;
Shepherds laugh in the fields
While peacefully watching their flocks.
The calves bleat and dance
While the birds fly high
In the sweet, free air.

At the foot of that mountain,
Deep down in the valley,
A farmer toils; a sturdy fellow,
Tilling his ground apart,
As a man, having lost his diamond,
Everywhere looks for it.

There, that child, My Country,
That farmer is your son.
Witness he loves you blindly,
Dresses you wonderfully.
He asks of you nothing
But liberty, freedom sweet.

He loves you; love him.
He worships you; free him.
Consider the sweat of his brow,
The toil of his daily tasks,
The energy, life he expends—
All yours, yours, yours.

My Country, Ethiopia!

View in northern Ethiopia (Gerster).

Body of water near Addis Ababa.

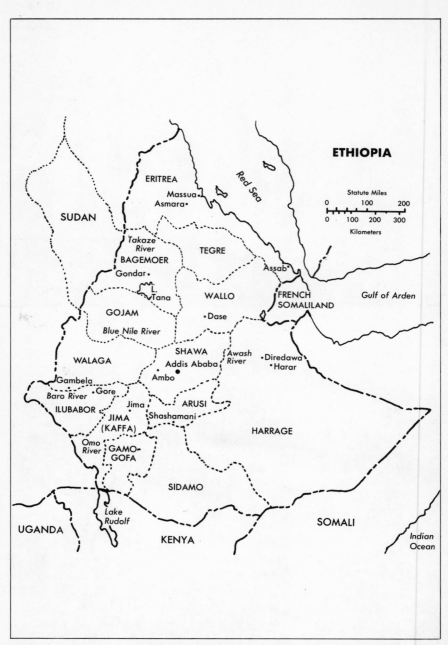

ETHIOPIA

ERITREA

Red Sea

SUDAN

Massua
Asmara

Statute Miles
0   100   200
0   100   200   300
Kilometers

Takaze
River
BAGEMOER

TEGRE

Gondar

Assab

L.
Tana

WALLO

FRENCH
SOMALILAND

Gulf of Arden

GOJAM

Dase

Blue Nile River

SHAWA

Awash
River

Diredawa
Harar

WALAGA

Addis Ababa

Gambela
Baro River   Gore
ILUBABOR

Ambo

ARUSI

Jima

JIMA
(KAFFA)   Shashamani

HARRAGE

Omo
River   GAMO-
GOFA

SIDAMO

UGANDA

Lake
Rudolf

KENYA

SOMALI

Indian
Ocean

Spelling of place names on this map follows that of the Imperial Highway Authority. Elsewhere in this book, spelling of place names follows that given by the Government of Ethiopia to the United Nations Economic Commission in 1959.

286

XIII
Facts
about
Ethiopia

Location—North of Kenya; south and west of the Red Sea and slightly to the north of the equator, east of the Sudan, north and west of Somalia, west of French Somaliland.

Composition—Eritrea and the twelve provinces of Ethiopia: Arussi, Beghmender, Gemu-Goffa, Gojjam, Harar, Illubabor, Sidamo, Kaffa, Tigre, Wollega, Wollo, and Shoa. Eritrea acquired near-provincial status in 1962, and subsequently became an integral part of Ethiopia.

Area—457,000 square miles.

Population—Estimates range from 15,000,000 to 30,000,000. Probably 22 million is a fair estimate. About 10 per cent urban. Annual growth is 1.5 per cent.

Topography—High and scenic plateau criss-crossed by mountain ranges, cut by deep canyons, and surrounded by deserts, except for Red Sea coastline of Eritrea. Altitudes range from 380 feet below sea level to over 15,000 feet above.

Temperature—Varies with altitude. Addis Ababa (8,000 to 9,000 feet), mean annual temperature of 62 degrees Fahrenheit. Nights and cloudy days are chilly. Coldest month, December, averages 59 degrees; warmest month, May, 66 degrees. Usual annual range, from 40 degrees to 80 degrees.

Rainfall—Varies with altitude and topography; generally adequate above 5,000 feet, heavy above 8,000 feet. Addis Ababa, annual average of 50 inches, 80 per cent of which falls from June through September.

Government—Empire, Haile Selassie I as Emperor. Constitutional Monarchy with bi-cameral parliament.

Currency—U.S. dollar equals $2.48 Ethiopian. Decimal system.

Economy—Agricultural: 60 per cent of land is arable (10 per cent cultivated; 50 per cent meadows and pastures); some industry: cement, salt, sugar processing, cotton goods.

Exports—Coffee, cattle and goat hides, leopard skins, cereals and grains, oil seeds, beeswax, civet, honey, livestock, butter, lard, eggs, spices, peppers, vegetables, cement, and lumber.

Race—Varied: Semitic about 35 per cent; Hamitic Gallas, about 40 per cent; other Hamitic groups, most of remainder; Arabs, about one per cent. Some Nilotic and Negro groups.

Peoples—Mixed: Amhara most dominant with Tigre a close second. Galla most numerous. Others are Somali, Sidamo, Danakil, Saho, Wollo, Wallamo, Arusi, Agau, Gurage, Falasha (Jewish), and a variety of others including Negro tribes around the borders to the south and west.

Languages—The Ethiopian Government recognizes three language families: Semitic, Cushitic, Nilotic. The official language is Amharic. The language of school instruction from approximately the fifth grade onward is English. Galligna, Tigrinya, Arabic, and many other languages are widely spoken.

Literacy—Estimates range from five per cent to 15 per cent; 10 per cent may be a fair estimate.

THE CALENDAR AND HOLIDAYS

The official Ethiopian year has thirteen months: twelve months of thirty days each, and a thirteenth month having five days during normal years, six days during leap years. Ethiopia conforms to the Julian calendar and the Ethiopian era, the Era of Mercy, which is seven years and eight months behind the Gregorian calendar. The first of the Ethiopian year falls on the eleventh of September in the Gregorian calendar, the twelfth of Sep-

ከመስከረም ግ. ም.   ጥቅምት   Oct. - Nov. 1956 **TEKEMT**

ዘመነ ማቴዎስ ወንጌላዊ ።

እሁድ : SUNDAY	ሰኞ : MONDAY	ማክሰኞ : TUESDAY	ረቡዕ : WEDNESDAY	ሐሙስ : THURSDAY	ዓርብ : FRIDAY	ቅዳሜ : SATURDAY
				፩ 1 / 11	፪ 2 / 12	፫ 3 / 13
፬ 4 / 14	፭ 5 / 15	፮ 6 / 16	፯ 7 / 17	፰ 8 / 18	፱ 9 / 19	፲ 10 / 20
፲፩ 11 / 21	፲፪ 12 / 22	፲፫ 13 / 23	፲፬ 14 / 24	፲፭ 15 / 25	፲፮ 16 / 26	፲፯ 17 / 27
፲፰ 18 / 28	፲፱ 19 / 29	፳ 20 / 30	፳፩ 21 / 31	፳፪ 22 / 1	፳፫ 23 / 2	፳፬ 24 / 3
፳፭ 25 / 4	፳፮ 26 / 5	፳፯ 27 / 6	፳፰ 28 / 7	፳፱ 29 / 8	፴ 30 / 9	

የዘውድ ፡ በዓል ።
ጥቅምት ፡ ፳፫ ፡ ቀን ።
CORONATION DAY
NOVEMBER 2

COMMERCIAL PRINTING PRESS

Page of Ethiopian Calendar for the month of Tekempt (spanning October and November of 1956 calendar used in the United States). The year is divided into twelve months of thirty days each, with the remaining five days considered as a special month at the end of the year (around the U.S. Labor Day in early September). Traditionally, no one is paid for services during this short month and no one is liable for charges, such as rent.

tember in leap year. Leap years are those which, when divided by four, leave a remainder of three.

For each month, there are six fixed religious holidays: the seventh, the twelfth, the sixteenth, the twenty-first, the twenty-seventh, and the twenty-ninth. There are three additional fixed holidays yearly, and eight movable ones. In addition to the religious holidays, there are national holidays of political origin.

Wednesdays and Fridays throughout the year are fast days for Christian Ethiopians; on these days, and during the fifty-six-days-long Lenten period, all forms of animal food, including meats, fats, milk and eggs, are forbidden, and no food of any kind can be taken before noon, or in areas of stricter observance, before 3:00 p.m.

New Year's Day (September 11) is an important festive holiday, but of even more importance is *Mascal,* which occurs on September 27-28. *Mascal* commemorates the finding of the True Cross by St. Helena. A feature of this day is the erection of huge bonfires of poles, which are set afire in the evening while the people dance and sing around them.

Christmas is celebrated on January 7 and 8. It is exclusively a religious celebration. The date of Easter varies from year to year; it is a day of great rejoicing and feasting, following a fifty-six-day fast. The Feast of the Assumption is celebrated on August 21st.

Timkat (January 19) is equivalent to Epiphany. On *Timkat* eve, processions of priests in elaborate robes carry the tabot to a pool. The tabot, a holy symbol kept in the churches, is covered by a rich cloth. The next day, the priests bless the waters and baptize the people. This ceremony is followed by singing and dancing. In Addis Ababa, the Emperor himself is baptized annually.

There are a number of other holy days of great importance, including a day in late January called *Astario Mariam* (the revelation of Mary), the Nativity of the Virgin in early May, the big festival of *Tekla Haimanot* (an Ethiopian saint) in late May, the Feast of the Transfiguration during the rainy season, and, two or three days before New Year's Day, the day of the Holy Water of Rafael.

Non-religious national public holidays include Commemoration Day of the Ethiopian Martyrs, February 19; Commemoration Day of the Battle of Adua, March 2; Liberation Day, May 5; the birthday of H.I.M. Haile Selassie I, July 23; and the Coronation Day of His Imperial Majesty, November 2.

In addition to these ceremonies of the calendar, the Ethiopian faith provides ceremonies commemorating birth, marriage, death., etc.

GOVERNMENT

The Ethiopian government is a constitutional monarchy patterned basically after that of a parliamentary form of government. A minister, at the head of each ministry, is in charge of each of the various branches of the government. A Council of Ministers, headed by a Prime Minister and appointed by His Imperial Majesty, sits with the Emperor in determining matters of policy and practice. This Council is also the executive branch of the government. There is in addition a Crown Council appointed by His Imperial Majesty. A parliament has been established to enact laws and legislation, which also functions in cooperation with the Emperor. It is bicameral, with an elected Chamber of Deputies and a nominated Senate. Parliament opens annually on November 5th, the anniversary of the coronation of Haile Selassie I, and is in session until June. As of 1969, there were sixteen Ministries in the Ethiopian Government; however, His Imperial Majesty retains an active and powerful place in all government affairs.

A system of courts has been established by law, ranging from Common Courts to the High Court, with His Imperial Majesty as the final court of appeal. The provinces are administered under the authority of the Ministry of the Interior. Governors-General of the provinces and district Governors are appointed by His Imperial Majesty.

A large and efficient police force, under the Ministry of Interior, effectively controls the internal security of the country. Eritrea has its own police force. A well equipped and well trained army has been the outgrowth of what was formerly the Imperial Body Guard. Contingents of these troops thoroughly proved themselves in the Korean war.

The moving power behind the government and all major policy is His Imperial Majesty, Haile Selassie I, Emperor of Ethiopia, King of Kings, Elect of God, and Conquering Lion of Judah. He is a man of extremely high character and wide knowledge, and enjoys the devoted respect and admiration of a large majority of his people. He has consistently upheld the policies and practices of the United Nations. His Imperial Majesty has, without question, done more to further Ethiopia's interests than any other man in Ethiopia's long and interesting history.

291

MODERNIZING AND PROGRESS[1]

The most important single factor in the modernization of Ethiopia has been the education of the Ethiopian people. There are three media through which this education is taking place.

The first of these has been an intensive expansion and modernization of the school system throughout the country. Children are being educated on a scale that was undreamed of in Ethiopia a few years ago. The results of this educational program are not yet greatly evident, but they will undoubtedly soon be felt. A knowledge of the rest of the world is being given the present generation. They are learning of ways of life other than their own, and change in their outlook has already started to take place.

A second form of education presently in full swing is through the influence of foreign technicians and advisers working for both the government and private enterprise within Ethiopia. Many people are being trained in this manner, and being given an insight into modern ways, means, and methods that would otherwise be impossible. In a comparatively short space of time, many Ethiopians have been trained to satisfactorily fill jobs which have already greatly improved their living standards and hopes for the future.

The third educational medium has been through sending Ethiopian students abroad for training in a wide variety of fields. Many of these students have distinguished themselves in the schools they are attending, and have returned to Ethiopia either to teach or to apply their newly gained knowledge in other endeavours. The entire educational program is based on a long-range result and is sound in its application. A change for the better is already apparent, and there is no question but that with the next generation the greatest stride forward in Ethiopia's history will take place.

A number of other factors are of equal importance in the present progress in Ethiopia, among which are a government-owned airline, welding the country together and bringing it within reach of the rest of the world; an extensive program to improve and expand the almost unlimited export potentialities of the country; the control exercised by the State Bank of Ethiopia; and the union of Eritrea with Ethiopia which offers many possibilities for expansion of trade and commerce, as well as giving Ethiopia her own seaports.

[1] Reproduced with permission from *Land of the Lion of Judah*, by Ethiopian Air Lines.

An Ethiopian girl, en route to Awash for a weekend camp out, dressed in modern attire bought in Addis Ababa, is admired by rural residents.

Young girls admire man from Addis Ababa.

Ethiopian Airlines has made Ethiopia readily accessible to the rest of the world, has expanded and assisted in the development of many of the natural resources of the country, and has been a major factor in Ethiopia's rapid progress.

An intensive program is under way to improve Ethiopia's roads, and this much-needed modernization will do much toward furthering the development of the country's vast resources.

The trend toward industrialization in Ethiopia is slow but is definitely expanding. As an outgrowth of the natural desire to make the most of the resources available to the country, this industrialization will in time make the necessity for certain presently expensive imports appreciably lower.

The results of the economic development, modernization, and progress taking place in Ethiopia today are already bearing fruit. Living conditions have improved, health conditions have improved, better utilization is being obtained from Ethiopia's greatest asset, her land, and the potentiality for future development and progress is bright.

The modernization of Ethiopia has been a persistent goal of H.I.M. Haile Selassie since, as Ras Tafari Makonnen, he first rose to imperial power as Regent and Heir Apparent in 1917, thirteen years before he became Emperor. As an Absolute Monarch, he practically forced a Constitutional Monarchy on the people of Ethiopia. His faith in God, education, and international relations as media for modernization are exemplified in the following excerpts from one of his speeches to the Parliament.

Major Accomplishment in the Past Years

Today We can look back with pardonable pride—and you with Us—at Our country's achievements, both domestically and in the field of foreign relations, since We first opened the Parliament We created, out of Our free will. . . . (in 1931).

At home, our development programme has, in all areas of life, resulted in a striking improvement in the living conditions of Our peoples. . . .

Advances in the Field of Education

We are convinced that education is a vital and proven means for securing the well-being and prosperity of Our beloved people. As a vital step in the implementation of a wide and extensive educational programme, We have established, with the assistance of United States technical aid, a Teacher Training Center at Debre Berhan. This Center will assist Us to provide education for civilians, education for Our Military forces and, ultimately, education for the whole population. . . . If We had not provided Our people with the opportunity for developing their knowledge, who could have then commended or criticized Our activities? We have provided Our beloved people with institutions wherein to develop their knowledge, convinced as We are that nothing can constitute a more enduring and imperishable heritage for posterity, or contribute more to the country, than education.

On the whole, Our efforts in the field of education are now bearing fruit. When we consider the increasing number of graduates from the University College which We established and the growing number of new educational institutions, when We think of the large numbers of young men whom We have been able to send abroad from time to time to pursue courses of higher education, among them many who have already returned to Our country to devote their specialised training to their country's service, Our happiness knows no bounds.

In addition to those students sent abroad to be trained in various specialised fields, We have caused to be established, with assistance obtained from friendly nations, various professional schools such as agricultural and technical colleges which will contribute to the rapid development and exploitation of Our natural resources. . . .

Public Health

The increasing of Our country's standards of public health occupies an important and prominent place in the plans We have prepared for the peaceful growth and development of Our nation. Life is obtained by the aiding of life—especially for the coming generation—and however high the cost of successfully carrying on this work, it must be accomplished. Agreements have been executed with the United States for the furnishing of aid to assist Our efforts in this direction. We long ago determined that, with the help of Our people, no one in Ethiopia would lack adequate medical treatment because of his inability to pay for it, and a plan to implement this goal has already been prepared. . . .

*   *   *

Our Country Ethiopia, whose faith in God is the basis of Her wisdom, desires only to live in peace, with enmity toward none and goodwill towards all. Our faith in the essential goodwill of mankind is deep enough to assure Us that the love of peace on the part of the rest of the world is equally strong and abiding.

Finally, We would remind you that Our accomplishments in the past and Our hopes for the future have but a single end: the sharing by Our nation in the wisdom and knowledge of the outside world. Only in this fashion can Ethiopia develop fully the manifold wealth which Our country possesses. And only by exploiting Her wealth can Ethiopia ensure that coming generations will be self-supporting and free from suffering and oppressive debt, and, as We would hope, fully able to extend the hand of assistance to their neighbours.

The labour of man is in vain without divine aid. We hope and pray that God will assist and prosper every future undertaking of Ours for the development of Our country and the welfare of Our peoples.

የኢትዮጵያና የአሜሪካ መንግሥት የትምህርት ተራድኦ ድርጅት መሥሪያ ቤት አማካሪ የሆኑት ዶክተር ኢዲት ሎርድ ፤ ለአሥር የኢትዮጵያ ድሆች ል ጆች ስለአደረጉት የርኅራኄና የደግነት መልካም ሥራቸው የምሥጋና ድርሰት በአጭሩ ።

የአሜሪካ ተወላጅ የሆኑት ዶክተር ስማቸው ኢዲት ሎርድ በፖይንት ፎር የሕፃናት ወዳጅ የሕፃናት ፍቅር የተመሰገኑ በመልካም ምግባር ሥራቸውን ልጣለጽ ሳይበዛ በአጭሩ በጥቂቱም ቢሆን ይኸ ነው ዝርዝሩ ልጅ ከመውደዳቸው ማስተማራቸው እናትነታቸው ርኅራኄአቸው ልብሱ በያይነቱ ጌጡ ጫማው ነው በህብት ላይ ህብትን እግዜር ይስጣቸው ። ልግለጸው እንግዲህ ውለታቸውን ልብስና ምግብ ስጥተው የረዷቸውን ለየተማሪ ቤት የሚከፍሉትን በኔ ስም ሲጀምር በቃል ኃይሉን ፤ ጌታቸው መንግሥቱ ደግሞ ዘር ይሁን አስካለ መንግሥቱ እዚያው ታሪኸን መኮንን ነገሬ አሰፋ ወርቁን እሸቱ ማተቤ ደግሞ መኮንን አሥረኛ አበራ እነዚህ የዘረዘርኍቸው ድሆችም ቢሆኑ ችግር ሳይነካቸው

መልካም ለብሰው በልተው የሚማሩት ናቸው ።

ዶክተር ኢዲት ሎርድ የድሆች ወዳጅ ሰብስበው ይዘዋል የድሆችን ልጅ እኔ ልብስና ምግብ ሳያስቸግሩኝ ትምህርቴን በደስታ እየቀጠልኩኝ ከኔኛ ክፍል ይኸው ደረስኩኝ ተዘርዝሮም አያልቅ የደግሰው ዋጋ በከንቱ እንዳይቀር ነው ይኸንም ሳወጋ አምላክ ይክፈላቸው አያስቀረው እን ዲያው

ዶክተር ኢዲት ሎርድ የዶህ እናት ናቸው በሥጋ በነፍስ አምላክ ያክብራቸው የመልካም ሰው ዋጋው አይቀርም በከንቱ የወህ ጠብታ የሰጠ ከህብቱ እጥፍ ድርብ ሆኖ በዳግም ምጽአቱ ኃላ ያገኘዋል ከሰማይ አባቱ ዶክተር ኢዲት ሎርድ ክብራቸው ከፍ ያለ

ሐሳብ ገንዘባቸው ከድህ ጋር ዋለ ዶክተር ኢዲት ሎርድ ያምላክ ወዳጅ ናቸው ድህን ይረዳሉ እርሱ እንዳዘዛቸው እኔ ብድርዖን ልመልስ አልችልም አምላክ ይክፈላዎ በላይኛው ዓለም ሲረዱን ከኖሩት ሁነው እንደናት በቃለ ኃይሉ ነኝ ይኸን የጻፍኩት ።

XIV
Introduction to Spoken Amharic

Edith Lord and Wolde Christos Bekele

Amharic is the official language of Ethiopia. It is the medium of instruction in the schools in grades one through four. Amharic is a Semitic language, a modern derivation of ancient Ge'ez, which is still the ritual language of the Ethiopian Orthodox Christian Church.

There are five explosive sounds in Amharic which do not exist in English, each with its non-explosive equivalent: k, t, p, ch, and ts. In this brief introduction to the Amharic language, no attempt is made to indicate explosive sounds; words requiring explosives for discrimination have been omitted from the text. Nevertheless, the student who wishes to speak Amharic correctly must learn to produce the explosive sounds.

The formation of explosive sounds is dependent on control of the glottal closure, which can be developed by practicing "oh-oh" with glottal tension between the "oh's." Next, practice inserting the explosive sounds at the point of tension: oh-t-oh, oh-k-oh, etc. Finally, omit the "oh," tense the glottis, and explode the speech sound. Simple!

As an exercise to develop the explosive sounds essential in spoken Amharic, it is suggested that the student repeat the following sentence, exploding every italicized consonant: *P*eter *P*iper *p*ic*k*ed a *p*eck of *p*ic*k*led *p*eppers and *ch*op*p*ed them *t*o bi*t*s.

The Amharic language contains seven vowel sounds, only four of which can be said closely to approximate English vowel sounds: a, e, o, u. The remaining three are only loose approximations: a, e, i. Following is a key for the approximate English equivalents of Amharic vowel sounds:

A, wait; a, father; E, beet; e, bet; i, bit; o, go; u, rude

297

ENGLISH	AMHARIC
Greetings, Daily Phrases, and Useful Words	*Yelet Nigigirochna Silamtaoch*
Hello	tenastiling
Goodbye	tenastiling
How do-you-you-do?	endemin allu?
Very well	dehina neng
Please	ibakwon (ibako)
Thank you	igziabhar istiling
Thanks	igzArstiling
You are welcome	abro istiling
It doesn't matter	gid yeɲlem
Excuse me	yikirrta
Yes	ao
No	yellem
O.K.	ishE
How much?	sint no?
It is expensive	wid no
It is cheap	rikash no
I do not understand	algibayim
I understand	gebang
Stop	akum
Wait	koi (coy)
Let's go	inhEa
Hurry	tolo belu
Slowly	Kes belu
It is . . .	. . . no (neu)
good	tiru
bad	metfo
right	lik
wrong	sihitet
big	tilik
small	tinish
hot	muk
cold	kezkaza
here	izE
there	izEa
To the right	wede keng
To the left	wede gra
Straight ahead	wede fEt
Opposite	fEt lefet
Enough	baka
Today	zarA
Tomorrow	nege
Yesterday	tilant
Morning	twat
Afternoon	kesaat behwala
Evening	mata
Who?	man
What?	mindin (min)
When?	mechay
Where?	yet (wedat)

298

ENGLISH	AMHARIC
Greetings, Daily Phrases, and Useful Words	*Yelet Nigigirochna Sïlamtaoch*
It is not	aideḷem
New	adɛs
Old (thing)	arogA
Old woman	arogEt
Old man	shimagilA
(my) Mother	inat (A)
(our) Father	abat (achen)
(his) Sister	ihit (u)
(her) Brother	wendem (wa)
(their Child)	lij (acheu)
Where is the . . . ?	. . . yet no?
hotel	hotelu
office	bɛRo
airport	awirplan marefɛya
station	tabeya
post office	posta bAt
palace	bAte mengist (gïbE)
restaurant	migib bAt
movie	sɛnɛma
toilet	sagara bAt
wash room	metatebɛya bAt
doctor	hakEm
hospital	hakEm bAt
door	mazgEya
window	maskot
house	bat
hut (small house)	goȷo
book	metsahaf
wood	inchet
fire	isat
candle	shama
Girl	lijagered
Maid servant	gered
Boy (or man servant)	mamo
Servant	asker
Woman	sAt
Man	wend
Person	seu
Friend	wedaj
Relative (clan, tribe)	zemed
Dog	wisha
Cat	demit
Room	kifil
Sleep	tenya
Bedroom	menyeta bAt
Guest	ingida
Living room	ingida bAt
Sauce (or stew)	wet

ENGLISH	AMHARIC
Greetings, Daily Phrases, and Useful Words	*Yelet Nigigirochna Silamtaoch*
Kitchen	*wet* bAt
Food	me*bil*
Dining room	me*bil* bAt
At the Hotel	*Be*hotel Wust
I want a room	ki*fil* ifelig*a*leu
with one bed	bale*and alga*
with two beds	balehu*lt al*ga
with bath	me*ra*tEbeya bAt gara
How much does it cost?	sint no?
O.K., I'll take it	*ish*E, iwesi*da*leu
I'm checking out	me*h*Ada no
My bill please	sint no, i*ba*kwon?
I want	ifeleg*a*leu
porter	teste*ka*mE
baggage (thing)	i*ka*
key (button)	kulf
newspaper	ga*zA*ta
stamp	tembir
post card	*post ka*rd
letter	debi*dab*A
envelope	*an*volep
paper	*we*reket
(this) pen	(*yih*i) bi'*ir*
(that) pencil	(ya) ir*sas*
At the Restaurant	*Be*buna BAt Wust
I want a table for . . .	and terepaze le . . .
(numbers are on page 303)	ifelig*a*leu
The bill, please	sint no, i*ba*kwon
Waiter (hear me)	*ma*mo (si*ma*)
Please give me . . .	ibakwon, . . . ifelig*a*leu
breakfast	kurs
lunch	mi*sa*
dinner (supper)	i*rat*
bread	*dab*bo
butter	*ki*bE
fried eggs	tibs i*n*kulal
scrambled eggs	yeteme*ta* i*n*kulal
boiled eggs	ki*kil* i*n*kulal
FRUIT	FI*RA*
orange	*bir*tukan
banana	m*uz*
grapes	*wA*n
lemon	lo*mE*
DRINKS	META*TOCH*
water	wi*ha*

ENGLISH	AMHARIC
At the Restaurant	*Bebuna Bat Wust*
DRINKS	METATOCH
coffee	*bun*na
black (only)	ti*kur* (*bi*che)
cream	sil*ba*bot
sugar	su*quar*
milk	wetet
tea	shy (*sha*i)
beer	*be*ra (*te*la)
wine	wAn tej
ice	*be*redo
FISH	*A*SA
POULTRY	*DO*RO *MAR*BEA
chicken	*do*ro
duck	da*k*Eyi
MEAT	SI*GA*
beef	yeber*A* si*ga* (lam)
pork	a*sa*ma
lamb	ti*bot* (*beg*)
mutton	yi*beg* si*ga*
VEGETABLES	*A*TAKILT
potatoes	di*nich*
fried	tibs
boiled	yi*fe*la
peas	*a*ter
beans	ba*k*Ala
green beans	fosilEa
artichokes	*sir*Ata
onions	*shin*kurt
garlic (white onion)	nech *Shin*kurt
corn	i*hil*
carrots	*ka*rot
spinach	*k*osta *g*omen
cauliflower	abe*ba g*omen
tomatoes	to*ma*tim
lettuce	sa*la*ta
cucumber	*du*ba
MISCELLANEOUS	*LA*LA
soup	*sho*rba
dessert	mata*fe*cha
cheese	*a*ib
salt	*cheu*
mustard	sina*fich*
glass	*bir*chako
cup	*se*nE (*fin*jal)
knife	be*la*wa
fork	*shu*ka
spoon	*man*kya *(man*ka)
plate	se*han*
napkin (towel)	yia*ffo*ta (*fo*ta)
cigarette	SE*ja*ra
match	ki*br*Et

ENGLISH	AMHARIC
Days of the Week	*Yesamint Kinoch*
Sunday	*ihud*
Monday	*senyo*
Tuesday	mak *senyo*
Wednesday	rob
Thursday	*hamus*
Friday	arb
Saturday	ki*dam*ᴀ
*Imperatives**	*Tizazoch*
Answer	mels
Begin	*jemmir*
Boil	*af*la
Bring	*am*ta
Buy	G*iza*
Close (shut)	z*iga*
Come	na (nu)
Come in	g*iba*
Cook	ab*sil*
Do	a*dirg*
Drive	n*ida*
Eat	b*ila*
Fill	m*ula*
Fry	t*ibes*
Give	*sit*
Go	hᴇd
Go (come) out	w*ita*
Help	*ir*da
Hold	yaz
Listen	*sima*
Open	k*ifet*
Pick up	*ar*sa
Push	g*ifa*
Put	a*skemt*
Run	rut
Say (tell)	n*iger*
See (look)	*i*ᴇ
Send	lak
Try	*mok*kir
Wait (stay)	*koi* (coy)
Wake	n*ika*
Wash	i*teb*
Work	s*ira*
Write	tsaf

*Only masculine, informal forms are given in Amharic; add a final *u* for formal address, both masculine and feminine, singular and plural.

ENGLISH	AMHARIC
Numbers	*Ku*troch
One	*and*
Two	hu*let*
Three	sost
Four	a*rat*
Five	a*mist*
Six	si*dist*
Seven	sa*bat*
Eight	si*mint*
Nine	ze*teng*
Ten	a*sir*
Eleven	*as*ra *and*
Twelve	*as*ra hu*lt*
Thirteen	*as*ra sost
Fourteen	*as*ra a*rat*
Fifteen	*as*ra a*mist*
Sixteen	*as*ra si*dist*
Seventeen	*as*ra sa*bat*
Eighteen	*as*ra si*mint*
Nineteen	*as*ra ze*teng*
Twenty	ha*y*a
Twenty-one	ha*y*a *and*
Thirty	sal*sa*
Forty	a*r*ba
Fifty	a*m*sa
Sixty	s*i*lsa
Seventy	sa*b*a
Eighty	se*man*ya
Ninety	ze*ten*a
One hundred	ma*t*o
Two hundred	hu*let* ma*t*o
One thousand	sh*E*
Currency ($1.00 Ethiopian = U. S. 40¢)	
Cent, penny	*san*tEm
Five cents, nickel	a*mist* san*tE*m, hu*let* *frank*
Ten cents, dime	a*sir* san*tE*m, a*rat* frank
25 cents, quarter	ha*y*amist san*tE*m, a*n*d si*mun*E
50 cents, half dollar	a*m*sa san*tE*m, a*n*d shil*l*ing
Dollar	birr
One dollar and a half	a*n*d birr ti*kul*, sost shi*l*ling

BETTY	በቲ	GERTRUDE	ገርትሩድ
DOROTHY	ዶሮቲ	LOUISE	ሉኢዝ
EDITH	ኤድት	NAOMI	ኔአሚ
ETHEL	ኤትል	JUDITH	ጁድት
CAROLYN	ካሮልን	·PATRICIA	ፓትርሻ
MARY	ሜሪ	KAREN	ኬረን
HELEN	ኸለን	DIANA	ዳይአና
RUTH	ሩት	BRENDA	ብረንዳ
DORIS	ዶርስ	FLORENCE	ፍሎረንስ
MARGARET	ማርጋሬት	JANE	ጄን
ANN	አን	KATE	ኬቲ
JOHN	ጆን	JACK	ጃክ
BILL	ብል	SAM	ሳም
JOE	ጆ	MIKE	ማይክ
CARL	ካርል	BOB	ባብ
GEORGE	ጆርጅ	ALBERT	አልበርት
ARTHUR	አርተር	DICK	ድክ
FRANK	ፍራንክ	FRED	ፍረድ
DANIEL	ደንየል	FRANCIS	ፍራንሰስ
PAUL	ፓል	CHARLES	ቻርልዝ
HERBERT	ኸርበርት	JIM	ጅም
HAROLD	ኸሮልድ	PETER	ፒተር

Approximate Amharic spelling of some common American names.

XV
Some
Ethopian Names
and
Their Meanings

Throughout the Ethiopian Empire, persons are named in such a way that there is no way of identifying a family group through surnames beyond one generation. A child receives a given name from his parents or grandparents and, at the same time, adopts the first name of his father as a second or last name. This is the case for both boys and girls. That is, girls take as their last name the first name of their father and not the first name of their mother.

When a woman marries she does not change her name in any respect. Recently (20th Century) women have introduced a new custom: When a girl marries, she changes her title from Weizerit to Weizero. She does not adopt the name of her husband. This is quite logical when one considers that there is no family name to perpetuate.

Furthermore, persons are universally addressed by first name rather than by last name. In formal address, the name is always preceded by a title. For a man the common title, comparable to Mister, is Ato. For a woman the common title is Weizero (Weizerit, if the lady is unmarried). However, there are a great many titles other than the simple ones. Some of these titles are of nobility. Others indicate special high functions in the military or civil service. When a person possesses one of these special titles, he is always addressed by

Adapted, in part, from "Ethiopian Names," by Beiene Gebresellassie.

it. Some of the more common titles and their meanings are as follows:
Ras, Chief or Head; Grazmatch, Leader (military) of the left; Kagnaz-
match, Leader (military) of the right; Fitaurari, Leader (military) of the
front and center.

Many names in Ethiopia are taken directly from the Bible, and most
other names have some religious connotation or an implied hope concerning
the character and life of the person named. It is a very common practice to
combine two names into one. Some common Biblical names are the following: Solomon, Samson, Yesus, Hohannes, Immanuel, Issac, Paulos, Mariam (Mary), Petros, Aster, Marta, Yosef, Christos, etc.

The masculine form of names frequently ends in *e*, the feminine in *a* or
tch. For example: Ato Abebe and Weizerit Abebetch; Ato Zelleke and Weizero Zelleka. Following is a list of common names, their gender, and their
meaning in English.

Name	Gender	English Meaning
Abebe	m.	Flourished, blossomed
Aberra	m.	He caused the light to shine
Abbay	m.	Great
Alemayehu	m.	I saw the world
Almaz	f.	Diamond
Ambaye	m.	My shelter or fortress
Amde-Mariam	m.	The Pillar of St. Mary
Aimut	m.	May he not die
Aradom	m.	He made them tremble
Araya	m.	Exemplary
Assefa	m.	He expanded
Asegedetch	f.	She made them bow
Alemmasha	f.	You caused prosperity
Afework	m.	Golden mouth
Admassu	m.	Extremity
Akalework	m.	Golden body
Aklilu	m.	His crown, the crown
Alemu	f.	The world
Amare	m.	It became good, handsome
Bahre Selassie	m.	The nature of Trinity
Bariau	m.	His slave
Beidemariam	m. f.	By the hand of St. Mary
Beienetch	f.	She gave justice
Belaineh	m.	You are far above
Bekele	m.	He avenged, grew, increased
Berhane	m.	The light
Berhane Meskel	m.	The light of the Cross
Belachew	m.	Tell them or beat them

Name	Gender	English Meaning
Buzuneh	m.	You are sufficient
Belletetch	f.	She excelled
Befekadu	m.	By His (God's) Will
Debri	f.	Convent
Desta	m. f.	Happiness
Endalkatchew	m.	As you tell them
Fessaha	m.	Happiness
Firay-Haimanot	m.	The fruit of faith
Fantaye	m.	My share
Gashaw	m.	His shield
Gebre-Egziabiher	m.	The servant of God
Gebre-Medhin	m.	The servant of the Savior
Gebre-Meskel	m.	The servant of the Cross
Gebre-Negus	m.	The servant of the King
Gebre-Selassie	m.	The servant of the Trinity
Gebre Tensae	m.	The servant of the Resurrection
Gennet	f.	Paradise
Getachew	m.	Their master
Getahun	m.	Be a master
Girmay	m.	My Majesty
Girma	m.	Majesty
Gobezie	m.	My young
Habte	m.	Wealth
Haile-Ab	m.	The power of the Father (God)
Haile Selassie	m.	The power of the Trinity
Hailu	m.	His power (God's)
Hagos	m.	Joy
Haregot	m.	Gift
Hiwet	f.	Life
Kasa	m.	Compensation
Kebre-Ab	m.	The honor of God
Kibret	f.	Honor
Kebbedetch	f.	Become heavy, burdensome
Ketema	m.	City or town
Kiflom	m.	Their share
Kidane	m.	Covenant
Kifelew	m.	Pay it, pay him, divide
Lakkew	m.	He excelled
Lemma	m.	He prospered
Leul	m.	The High (God), Highness, Prince
Mahari	m.	Merciful
Manna	m. f.	Manna
Makonnen	m.	Officer or Dignitary
Mebratu	m.	His light
Mehret	f.	Mercy
Melake	m.	Angel

Name	Gender	English Meaning
Maaza	f.	Sweetness, aroma
Menelik	m.	Son of King
Mengistu	m.	His Kingdom
Mengesha	m.	Of the Kingdom
Mesfin	m.	Prince
Mesgenna	m.	Thanks
Merid	m.	He who makes others tremble
Mulugeta	m.	A perfect master
Mulunesh	m. f.	You are perfect
Meskelua	f.	Her Cross
Negash	m.	The ruler, one who sought to rule
Neguse	m.	The King
Retta	m.	He won a cause
Sahle	m.	Mercy
Sebhat	m.	Praise
Seifu	m.	His sword, the sword
Seyoum	m.	The elect
Shiferaw	m.	Feared by one thousand
Shimelles	m.	One who can withstand one thousand (One who can withstand)
Taddesse	m.	He is renewed
Taffese	m.	He was gathered
Tedla	m.	Joy
Taye	m.	He was seen
Tefferra	m.	Feared
Tekle	m.	Plant
Telahun	m.	Be a shade
Tesfaye	m.	My hope
Tesemma	m.	He was heard
Turunesh	f.	You are pure
Tsegaye	m. f.	My grace
Tsehaye	m. f.	The sun
Ugbai	m.	My protege
Wolde-Ab	m.	Son of God
Welette-Zion	f.	Servant of Zion
Worku	m. f.	His Gold, the gold
Werede-Mahret	m.	Mercy has descended
Wubishet	m.	Beautiful, young grain
Yemane	m.	Right
Yilma	m.	May he prosper
Yigezaw	m.	May he rule over . . .
Zelleke	m.	He excelled
Zennebe-Werk	f.	It has rained gold
Zerihun	m.	The seed
Zauditu	f.	The Coronet
Zewde	m.	My Crown

Bibliography

Allen, W.E.D., *Guerrilla War in Abyssinia*, Penguin Books, Harmondsworth, 1943.

Alvares, F., *Narrative of the Portuguese Embassy to Abyssinia during the years 1520-1527*, English translation by Lord Stanley of Alderley, Hakluyt Society, London, 1881.

Armbruster, C.H., *Initia Amharica*, an introduction to spoken Amharic (in three parts), Cambridge University Press, 1908-1920.

Badoglio, Pietro, The *War in Abyssinia*, Putnam's, New York, 1937.

Bohannan, Paul, *African Outline*, Middlesex, England: Penguin Books Ltd., Harmondsworth, 1966.

Bauer, Peter T. and Basil S. Yamey, *The Economics of Under-developed Countries*, University of Chicago Press, Chicago, 1957.

Bent, J. T., *The Sacred City of the Ethiopians*, Longmans, Green, London, 1898.

Berkeley, G. F. H., *The Campaign of Adowa and the Rise of Menelik*, Constable, London, 1902 (re-printed in 1935).

Bidder, Irmgard, *Lalibela, The Monolithic Churches of Ethiopia*,* Thames and Hudson, London, 1959.

Bruce, J., *Travels to Discover the Source of the Nile in the Years 1768-1773*, (5 volumes), Edinburgh, 1790.

Buchholzer, John, *The Land of Burnt Faces*, McBride, New York, 1956.

* Highly recommended.

Budge, Sir E. A. Wallis, *The Queen of Sheba and her only Son Menyelek*, A complete translation of the Kebra Negast, Medici Society, London, 1922, Second Edition, 1932.

XXXXX, *A History of Ethiopia (Nubia and Abyssinia)*, (Two Volumes), Methuen, London, 1928.

Burton, R. F., *First Footsteps in East Africa, or An Exploration of Harar*, London, 1856, (New edition 1894, London, Tylson & Edwards; reprinted in Everyman's Library, London, Dent.).

Busk, Donald, *The Fountain of the Sun*, Parrish, London, 1957.

Buxton, David, *Travels in Ethiopia*, Drummond, London, 1949.

Chamber of Commerce of Addis Ababa, *Guide Book of Ethiopia*, Addis Ababa, 1954.

XXXXX, Economic Handbook, Addis Ababa, 1958.

XXXXX, "Ministry of Commerce, Industry, and Planning," *Ethiopian Economic Review*, No. 1, December, 1959.

Cheesman, Robert Ernest, *Lake Tana and the Blue Nile*, Macmillan, New York, 1936.

Cole, Sonia, *The Prehistory of Africa*, D.C. Heath & Co., Boston, 1954.

Courlander, Harold and Wolf Leslaw, *The Fire on the Mountain*,* Henry Holt and Company, New York, 1950.

Curtin, Philip D., *The Image of Africa*, New York: Macmillan, 1965.

Davies, T. D., and Esther Fancher Lister, *A Beginner's Amharic Grammar*, North Washington Press, Washington, D.C., Revised Edition, 1952.

Davidson, Basil, *The Lost Cities of Africa*, Little, Brown, Boston, 1959.

Davis, Russel and Brent Ashabranner, *The Lion's Whiskers*, Little, Brown, and Company, Boston, 1959.

Doresse, Jean, *Ethiopia*, Elek Books, London, 1959.

Dunckley, F. C., *Eight Years in Abyssinia*, Hutchinson, London, 1935.

Farago, Ladislas, *Abyssinia on the Eve*, G. P. Putnam's Sons, New York, 1935.

Findlay, L., *The Monolithic Churches of Lalibela in Ethiopia*, Cairo, 1943.

Fitzgerald, Walter, *Africa: A Social, Economic and Political Geography of Its Major Regions*, (8th ed.) Dutton, New York, 1955.

Foster, George M., *Traditional Cultures: and the Impact of Technological Change* * Harper & Brothers, New York, 1962.

Fortes, M. (ed.), *Marriage in Tribal Societies*, London: Cambridge University Press, 1962.

Fuertes, L. Agissiz & Osgood W. Hudson, *Artist and Naturalist in Ethiopia*, Doubleday, Doran, Garden City, New York, 1939.

Geiger, Theodor, *TWA's Service to Ethiopia*, National Planning Association, Washington, 1959.

Gloe, James A., *Audio-Visual Amharic*, Commercial Printing Press, Addis Ababa, August, 1958.

* Highly recommended.

310

Greenfield, Richard, *Ethiopia: A New Political History,* New York, Frederick A. Praeger, 1965.

Guarage Exhibition Committee, *The Guarages and Their Social Life,* Commercial Printing Press, Addis Ababa, 1955.

Gunther, John, *Inside Africa,* Harper & Brothers, New York, 1953. (Chapters 15-16.)

Hartlmaier, Paul, *The Golden Lion,* Bles, London, 1956.

Hempstone, Smith, *Africa—Angry Young Giant,* Frederick A. Praeger, New York, 1961.

Herskovits, M. J., *The Human Factor in Changing Africa,* London: Reutledge & Kegan Paul, 1963.

Hodson, Sir Arnold, *Seven Years in Southern Abyssina,* Fisher Unwin, London, 1927.

Howard, W. E. H., *Public Administration in Ethiopia,* Wolters, Gronigen, 1956.

Huntingford, G. W. B., *The Galla of Ethiopia,** International African Institute, London, 1955.

Jesman, Czeslaw, *The Russians in Ethiopia: An Essay in Futility,* Chatts & Windus, London, 1958.

Jones, A. H. M. and E. Monroe, *A History of Ethiopia,* Oxford University Press, London, 1935

Kimble, George H. T., Vol. I, *Tropical Africa,* New York, 1960.

Kitchen, Helen (ed.), *The Press in Africa,* Ruth Sloan Associates, Washington, 1956.

Leighton, Alexander H., *Human Relations in a Changing World,** E. P. Dutton & Company, Inc., New York, 1949.

Leslau, Wolf, *Bibliography of the Semitic Languages of Ethiopia,* New York Public Library, New York, 1946.

XXXXX, *Falasha Anthology,* translated from Ethiopic sources, Yale University Press, New Haven, 1951.

Levine, Donald N., *Wax & Gold,* University of Chicago Press, Chicago, 1965.

Linton, Ralph, *The Study of Man,* Appleton-Century-Crofts, Inc., New York.

Lipsky, George A., *Ethiopia—Its People, Its Society, Its Culture,** HRAF Press, New Haven, Conn., 1962.

Longrigg, *A Short History of Eritrea,* Clarendon Press, Oxford, 1945.

Luther, Ernest, W., *Ethiopia Today,** Stanford University Press and London Oxford University Press, 1958.

Marein, Nathan, *The Ethiopian Empire: Federation and Laws,* Royal Netherlands, Rotterdam, 1955.

The Judicial System and the Laws of Ethiopia, Royal Netherlands Print and Lithographing Co., 1951.

---

* Highly recommended.

Mead, Margaret and Rhoda Metraux, Editors, *The Study of Culture at a Distance*, University of Chicago Press, Chicago, 1953.

Mead, Margaret, Editor, *Cultural Patterns and Technical Change*, The American Library of World Literature, Inc., New York, 1955.

Mead, Margaret, and Martha Wolfenstein, *Childhood in Contemporary Cultures*, University of Chicago Press, Chicago, 1955.

Mathew, David, *Ethiopia, The Study of a Polity*, 1540-1935, Eyre and Spottiswoods, 1947.

Murdock, George Peter, *Africa: Its People and Their Cultural History*, Mc-Graw-Hill, New York, 1959.

Myorowitz, Eva L. R., *At the Court of an African King*,   London: Saber & Saber, 1962.

Nesbit, L. M., *Desert and Forest, the Exploration of Abyssinian Danakil*, Penguin Books, London, 1935.

Negarit Gazeta, *Penal Code of the Empire of Ethiopia*,*   Extraordinary Issue, Addis Ababa, 1957.

Obukar, Charles and John Williams, *The Modern African*,   London: Macdonald & Evans Ltd., 1965.

O'Hanlon, Douglas, *Features of the Abyssinian Church*, Society for Promoting Christian Knowledge, London, 1946.

Pankhurst, E. Sylvia, *A Cultural History of Ethiopia*, Lalibela House, Woodford Green, Essex, 1955.

XXXXX, 'Eritrea on the Eve, The Walthamstow Press Ltd., Great Britain, 1952.

Pankhurst, E. Sylvia, and Richard Pankhurst, *Ethiopia and Eritrea*, Lalibela House, Woodford Green, Essex, 1953.

Perham, Margery, *the Government of Ethiopia*,*   Faber & Faber, London, 1947.

Playne, Beatrice, *St. George for Ethiopia*, Constable, London, 1954.

Plowden, Walter C., *Travels in Abyssinia and the Galla Country*, Longmans Green, London, 1868.

Rennell of Rodd, Lord, *British Military Administration in Africa, 1941-1947*, His Majesty's Stationery Office, London, 1948.

Rosen, Bjorn von, *Game Animals of Ethiopia*, Swedish-Ethiopian Co., Addis Ababa, 1953.

Rossini, Carlo Conti, *Ethiopia e Genti di Ethiopia*, Bemporad, Florence, 1937.

Sanceau, Elaine, *Portugal in Quest of Prester John*, Hutchinson, London, 1943.

Sanford, Christine, *The Lion of Judah Hath Prevailed*, (1946 edition), *Ethiopia Under Haile Selassie*, Dent, London, 1955.

Seligman, C. G., *Races of Africa* (3rd ed.), Oxford University Press, London, 1957.

* Highly recommended.

Simoons, Frederick J., *Eat Not This Flesh*, University of Wisconsin Press, Madison, 1961.

XXXXX, *Northwest Ethiopia: Peoples and Economy*, University of Wisconsin Press, Madison.

Skinner, R. P., *Abbyssinia of Today*. An account of the first mission sent by the American Government to the court of the King of Kings (1903-4), Arnold, London, 1906.

Stern, H. A., *Wandering Among the Falashas in Abyssinia*, Wertheim, London, 1862.

Spicer, Edward H., *Human Problems in Technological Change*, Russell Sage Foundation, New York, 1952.

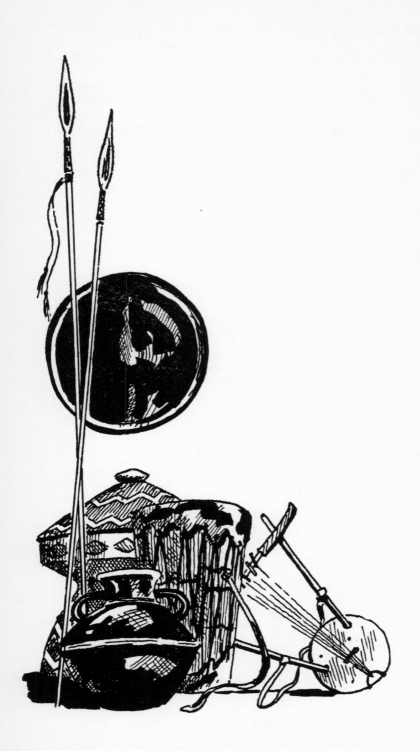

Index

315

317

Italy, 17, 238, 239, 240, 241, 242, 243, 244, 248, 249

Muslims, 17, 39, 230, 234, 235, 236, 237, 238; birth customs in Jimma, 96; in Harrar, 78; marriage among Kotus, 124; polygyny among, 65; proportion of, 163; in Raya-Azabo, 73
Murad, 237
Mussolini, 17, 232, 243

— N —

Nagar Abat, 114, 115
Names, 305-308
Napier, Sir Robert, 238, 241
Navy, 19
Naval College, 248, 249
Negro, 37
Negarit Gazeta, 244
Netherlands, 249
New Zealand, 243
Newspaper, Ethiopian, 296
Nile, 22, 85, 232, 233, 234, 236, 240, 247, 248, 250
Nixon, Richard, 7, 21, 249
Norway, 249
Nubians, 233, 235
Nursing, 213, 247, 248

— O —

Obedience, 91
Offenses, 263 ff.
Old Testament, 15, 16, 33
Organization of African Unity, 20, 251
Oromo, 258
Outrages, 269
Oviedo, 236

— P —

Pagan: 39, 258; *atete*, 177-178; beliefs and rites, 172-178; marriage among, 126-128; mountain, 173; population, 163; river, 173; road, 174; snake, 174; tree "God," 171, 173, 175-177
Panacea, 193
Paris Peace Conference, 245
Penal Code, 39, 242, 246, 269-273
Peoples, 288
Peru, 258
Police, secret, 19
Polyandry, 65
Polygamy, 39, 128, 234
Polygyny, 65
Pope, 235, 236
Population, 287
Portugal, 230, 235, 236

Poverty, 68
Preservation, 91
Priests, 164-169, 181
Primogeniture, 129
Property, 81
Proverbs, 45
Ptolemy, 233
Public Health College, 247, 249
Public Safety Program, 247

— Q —

Qezanas, King, 234
Quackery, 272
Queen of Sheba. See Sheba
Queen of the South, 25
Quiz, Cross-Cultural, 30 ff.

— R —

Race, 37, 288
Railroad, 239, 240, 241, 242, 244, 245
Rainfall, 288
Rama, 75
Ramadan, 117
Ras Imru Haile Selassie, 250
Raya-Azabo, 71-77
Recreation, 51-59
Red Sea, 25, 230, 233, 238
Religion: 163-185, 265; *atete*, 177-178; Coptic beliefs, 170; mountain, 173; river, 173; road, 174; snake, 174; tree "God," 171, 173, 175-177
Respect, 47 ff.
Roman Catholics, 17, 235, 236
Russia, 18, 20, 239, 250

— S —

Sabaean, 234
Sabres, 81
Sahla Selassie, 237
Saladin, 234
Scabies, 198
Secret Police, 19
Semites, 37, 229, 233
Senate, 17
Septuagint, 16, 233
Sertsa Dengel, 236
Sesla Kristos, 236
Seventh Day Adventists, 242
Sex: child training, 91; satisfaction, 68
Shankillas, 37
Sheba, 15, 16, 25-27, 40, 104, 206, 233, 235, 251

Shields, 81
Shoa, 238
Sidama, 22, 80
Sinclair Petroleum Company, 245, 248
Sisinnius (Sosneyos or Susenyos), 236
Slavery, 39, 241, 242, 271-272
Smallpox, 195, 240
Solomon, 15, 16. 25-27, 40, 233, 234, 235, 237, 239, 241, 242, 251
Somaliland, 239, 240, 242, 245, 249
Somalis, 18, 78, 245, 250
Sore throat, 196
Soviet Union, 249
Spain, 236
Spears, 81
Spells, 273
Sterility, 98-99, 193
Story themes, 227
Sudan, 18, 21, 242, 248, 249, 250
Suez Canal, 238
Suggestions for foreigners, 255-267
Sultan el Nasir, 235
Superstitions: 193-202; research on impact of education on, 205-226
Sweden, 245, 247, 249
Switzerland, 243, 249
Symbolic objects, 81-82
Syphilis, 185, 193, 196
Syria, 234

— T —

Tafari Makonnen, Ras, 16, 240, 241, 242
Taitu, Empress, 240
Takla Haymanot II, 237
Taywofilos, 237
Tattooing, 90
Teacher training school, 76
Tekla Haymanot I, 234, 237
Tekle George (Giorgis), 238
Temperature, 287
Tesemma, Ras, 240, 241
Theodore (Teywodros), 238
Tigers, 81
Tigre, 75, 233, 234, 237, 238, 239, 246
Tigreans, 40, 47-51, 72
Timkat, 290
Topography, 287
Tradition, 262
Treaty of Friendship, 241, 242
Treaty of Ucciali, 239
Trans-World Airlines, 245
Truth, 91
Turkey, 230, 236, 238, 239, 241
Tunisia, 25

— U —

Understanding, 267
UNESCO, 249
Uganda, 21
Ulcer, 193
UNICEF, 249
United Arab Republic, 248
United Kingdom. See England
United Nations, 17, 246, 248, 249, 250, 251
Urinating, 246
United States, 17, 71, 243, 244, 246, 247, 248, 249, 250, 251

— V —

Vignettes: Coming of the Dawn, 279; Eye of the Beholder, 277

— W —

Wal Wal, 242
Wardair, 242
Warts, treatment of, 192
Weizerit, 34
Weizero, 34
West Germany, 249
Wett (Wet), 78
World Health Organization, 249
Wibeet, 237
Widow, status among Wollomos, 128
Wild Life, 275-276
Witch doctors, 187-202
Wollos, 18, 246
Women of Jara, 69-71
Women's Vocational Education School, 247
World Security Charter, 246

— Y —

Yemen, 230, 233
Yekuno Amlak, Emperor, 234
Yohannes, 75
Yugoslavia, 17, 18, 19, 248, 249, 250

— Z —

Za Dengel, 236
Zague, 16, 234
Zauditu, 16, 240, 241, 242
Zobel, 75
Zoscales, King, 233
Zuquala, 164-169